"Will Rogers is an American [...] to read this book is to conju[...] eye. Imagine him slouching [...] rope in his hand, a stick of gu[...] simple words of common s[...] common sense to the level of genius.

—Alex Ayres, editor of
The Wit and Wisdom of Will Rogers

"No nation in the history of the world was ever sitting as pretty. If we want anything, all we have to do is go and buy it on credit. So that leaves us without any economic problems at all, except perhaps some day to have to pay for them."

"I am not a member of any organized political party. I am a Democrat."

"It won't be no time till some woman will become so desperate politically and just lose all prospectus of right and wrong and maybe go from bad to worse and finally wind up in the Senate."

"Live your life so that whatever you lose, you are ahead."

ALEX AYRES is the editor of *The Wit and Wisdom of Mark Twain, the Wit and Wisdom of Abraham Lincoln,* and most recently, *The Wisdom of Martin Luther King, Jr.* (all in Meridian). He lives in Valencia, California.

The Wit and Wisdom

—— *of* ——

WILL
ROGERS

EDITED BY
ALEX AYRES

A MERIDIAN BOOK

To the roping spirit
whose aim is true

MERIDIAN
Published by the Penguin Group
Penguin Books USA Inc., 375 Hudson Street,
New York, New York 10014, U.S.A.
Penguin Books Ltd, 27 Wrights Lane, London W8 5TZ, England
Penguin Books Australia Ltd, Ringwood, Victoria, Australia
Penguin Books Canada Ltd, 10 Alcorn Avenue,
Toronto, Ontario, Canada M4V 3B2
Penguin Books (N.Z.) Ltd, 182–190 Wairau Road,
Auckland 10, New Zealand

Penguin Books Ltd, Registered Offices:
Harmondsworth, Middlesex, England

First published by Meridian, an imprint of Dutton Signet,
a division of Penguin Books USA Inc.

First Printing, December, 1993
10 9 8

 REGISTERED TRADEMARK—MARCA REGISTRADA

Library of Congress Cataloging-in-Publication Data

Rogers, Will, 1879–1935.
  [Selections. 1993]
  The wit & wisdom of Will Rogers / edited by Alex Ayres.
    p. cm.
  ISBN 0-452-01115-9
  I. Ayres, Alex. II. Title. III. Title: Wit and wisdom of Will Rogers.
PN6161.R664425 1993
792.7'028'092—dc20   93-4249
                                                              CIP

Printed in the United States of America
Set in Palatino
Designed by Eve L. Kirch

Acknowledgments

Thanks to Will Rogers for adding light to darkness and levity to gravity. Thanks to Joseph Carter, Director of the Will Rogers Memorial Commission; to Greg Malak, Curator, and Pat Lowe, Librarian, of the Will Rogers Memorial and Birthplace in Claremore, Oklahoma. Thanks to Hugh Rawson, Jennifer Moore and Paula Smith for help with the manuscript; thanks to the publisher for publishing it; thanks to you for looking at it.

Why Read This Book?

Will Rogers is an American original—and a link to the original Americans. Born in Indian territory in Oklahoma, the "Cherokee Kid" grew up to become one of the most versatile performers of all time. He was a rope-trick artist, a vaudeville showman, a stand-up comedian, a cowboy philosopher, a political humorist, a syndicated columnist, an author, a radio commentator, and a movie star. At the peak of his career in 1934 he held the unique distinction of being America's top box-office film attraction *and* most popular newspaper columnist at the same time. He was the best-known and best-loved American in the world. Perhaps no private citizen has ever represented the United States more effectively abroad, for he was the unofficial American ambassador-at-large.

Will Rogers defies all categories. We trust him intuitively because he is not partisan; he has no enemies; he takes sides against no one; he impartially gives a piece of his mind to one and all. "I think I am as independent as any one writing," he declared proudly. "I have as many Republican as Democratic papers, as many readers that can't read as can."

The cowboy philosopher's philosophy is ultimately

one of tolerance, for he teaches us to see more than one point of view. Look up a controversial topic such as gun control, for example, and you will encounter statements that will delight and dismay both sides of the issue. "Everybody is so heated up over it till they can't see the other fellow's side, or any other side but theirs," he said. The same is true of nations as well as individuals. He teaches us to consider the point of view of other nations so that we are not blinded by patriotism or provincialism to the larger concerns of humanity.

Will Rogers is a great American as well as a great American humorist. He pricks the national conscience in the self-appointed—or divinely appointed—role of a national jester. While his character is uniquely American, his values are ultimately human rather than American; thus he is both profoundly funny and eminently lovable.

He had the common touch, yet he was more uncommon than all the kings and queens and presidents in the world, for there will never be another quite like him. He showed us what we can do if we are true to ourselves, for he was always true to himself. He lived out the American dream of success, and he did it without resorting to violence, hatred, or exploitation.

His method, he said, was simply to "try to keep to the truth." He told the simple truth, and it was so rare and refreshing it came as a revelation, provoking the laughter of recognition. He expressed the folk wisdom of the American people through his own individuality.

Our greatest heroes are often those who embody qualities that we fear are passing away. Will Rogers was an authentic American hero, for he embodied qualities of native American wit, common sense, cowboy independence, small-town simplicity, honesty, moral courage, friendliness, and irrepressible good humor—qualities we cannot afford to lose. We can rediscover in Will Rogers some of the best in ourselves.

The best way to read him is to conjure him in your mind's eye. Imagine him slouching on a stage before you, a rope in his hand, a stick of gum in his mouth, speaking simple words of common sense. Will Rogers raised common sense to the level of genius. "I don't know opera," he said, "but I know common sense when I see it, and the commoner the better I know it."

Don't be fooled by his act. Will Rogers plays the fool. He's not a fool pretending to be wise, which is all too common. He's wise, pretending to be a fool, which is an art.

The wit and wisdom of Will Rogers is a part of our American national heritage. I hope you will pick a topic and look it up to see what Will Rogers had to say—and what he is saying to us today.

—A.A.

ON WILL ROGERS

The impact upon the people of America at the death of Will Rogers was similar to that produced by the death of Abraham Lincoln.

—Robert Sherwood, author and playwright

There is a curious parallel between Will Rogers and Abraham Lincoln. They were rare figures whom we could call beloved with ease and without embarrassment. A great tradition is that of Will Rogers. He ought to be taught in the schools because of what he embodied of the best of the Constitution and the Declaration of Independence. He was as homely as a mud fence and yet as beautiful as a sunrise over an Oklahoma field of alfalfa.

—Carl Sandburg, poet and biographer of Lincoln

Will Rogers, to begin with, is an American. Equipped as he is with a generous supply of genuine Indian blood, he's a lot closer to 100% American than are most of the people who brag about it. In the second place, Will Rogers is a humorist. If elected, he would be the first president in sixty-two years who was funny intentionally.

—*Life* editorial, 1928, "Will Rogers for President"

Probably the most widely known citizen of the United States, and certainly the best beloved.

—Senate Majority Leader Joseph Robinson

Nowhere in the memory of the oldest newspaperman is there a record of the passing of a private citizen rating an eight-day "follow-up" series in the national press. Few presidents who died in office held general interest so long.... And yet of the amazing matters I have covered—crimes, war, disaster—never has any account I have written elicited such a flood of communications from the entire country.... Only intense worship of an individual could cause people to so cherish little anecdotes, to so crave answers to little questions of fact.

—Jack Lait, newspaperman

He enjoyed a position never before attained by anyone of whom I ever heard. He could go any place, see anything, talk or write about it afterward, and in such a way that the humble and the great accepted it.

—Gene Buck, entertainer

Will Rogers was America's most complete human document. He reflected in many ways the heartbeat of America. In thought and manner of appearance and in his daily life he was probably our most typical native born, the closest living approach to what we like to call the true American.

—Damon Runyon, short story writer

He had a unique career, which we all like to think could have been run only in America. He came to hold such a place in the public mind that, of his passing from the

stage it might be said, as it was by Dr. Johnson of Gar-
rick's, that it will "eclipse the gayety of nations." For Mr.
Rogers had an inimitable and genial wit which endeared
him to all sorts and conditions of men. His rise to fame
was much like the slow emerging of a star above our ho-
rizon. . . . It is certain that we shall not look upon Will
Rogers' like again.

—from *New York Times* editorial on Rogers' death

Will Rogers' analysis of affairs abroad was not only more
interesting but proved to be more accurate than anything
I had heard . . . I doubt if there is among us a more useful citizen than the one who holds the secret of banishing
gloom, of making tears give way to laughter, of sup-
planting desolation and despair with hope and courage,
for hope and courage always go with a light heart. There
was something infectious about his humor. His appeal
went straight to the heart of the nation. . . . When he
wanted to make a point for the good of all mankind, he
used the kind of gentle irony that left no scars behind
it. . . . The American nation, to whose heart he brought
gladness, will hold him in everlasting remembrance.

—President Franklin Delano Roosevelt
Radio broadcast on day of Rogers' funeral

A superior power had seen fit to fling into the world, for
once, a truly fine specimen—fine in body, fine in soul,
fine in intellect.

—James Agate, English critic

He was far ahead of his time. Not only as a human being, but as an actor, too.

—Lew Ayres, actor

One of the best-known, and one of the least-known, men
in the world.

—Spencer Tracy, actor

There has rarely been an American humorist whose words produced less empty laughter and more sober thought. Perhaps Will Rogers has done more to educate the American public in world affairs than all the professors.

—from *New York Times* review of *Letters of a Self-Made Diplomat to His President,* 1926

Because in his comedy he breathes the essential spirit of America; because he has brought the lariat and the lasso into the highest society in America; because he is a well-loved figure in movies; because the Ziegfeld Follies have long successfully revolved around him; but chiefly because as an author and political observer he is as shrewd, satirical, and clever as they make them.

—From nomination to *Vanity Fair*'s "Hall of Fame," 1924

No man in the history of time reached the pulse of the majority like Will Rogers. He had that fine composite something of reaching the hearts of all of us, little and great alike.

—Tom Mix, Western hero

I like to think of Will Rogers as flying on ... Freed of the cloddish body, he must be ascending new heights, scaling new peaks. If Will Rogers were not one of the most talented men of his time, he could have achieved greatness for this simple statement in a world swollen and angry red with hate: "I never met a man I didn't like."

—O. O. McIntyre

It wouldn't be right to give Will Rogers to just one world and cheat some other world out of all the kindness and fun, all that sweetness and humility and ripe philosophy and precious wit.

—Irvin Cobb

Nothing could be written about America during the 1918–1935 period without including Will Rogers, because he spoke on the events as they happened, day to day. Reading Will Rogers gives one the best history of America during this crucial period, told in that inimitable Rogers manner, sparked with spontaneous wit and wisdom, and set down in a style that all can understand and enjoy.

—Paula McSpadden Love
Curator, Will Rogers Memorial, 1938–73

THE WIT AND WISDOM
OF WILL ROGERS

ACADEMY AWARDS

Will Rogers was Master of Ceremonies at the 1934 Oscar presentations of the Academy of Motion Picture Arts and Sciences.

"This is the highest sounding named organization I ever attended," said the country-mannered man whose boyish face, shock of uncombed brown hair and impish smile made him appear an eternal outsider among the well-groomed, well-heeled insiders. "If I didn't know so many of the people who belonged to it personally I would have taken that name serious. But everything that gives pleasure and makes money is not an art or a science. If it were, bootlegging would have been the highest form of artistic endeavor."

Will Rogers, even at the height of his fortune in Hollywood, preserved the homespun rural innocence that made him look like an underdog among top dogs. He appeared to be no match for the rich, the powerful, or the educated into whose circles he came as a nonthreatening country jester. There was always something surprising about the shrewdness and sharpness of the words that came from the lips of this humble rural character.

Scanning the audience, Rogers noticed many familiar faces in the glittering gallery. "I see many of you are still friends. I would have sent Christmas cards to more of you folks, but in this business you just don't know in early December who your friends are going to be three weeks later."

Rogers remarked upon current events, as was his custom. He commented on the latest sex scandal, involving shocking revelations of the existence of what was called a "sex cult" along the Riviera. "On the Riviera in France they found a bunch of people wearing no clothes and not particularly caring who they were married to, and they called it a cult. Over here we call it *society*."

Eventually he turned to the topic of the evening, paying homage to the achievements of great actors. "There is great acting in this room tonight," Rogers said in tribute to the Academy Award nominees, "greater than you will see on the screen. We all cheer when somebody gets a prize that every one of us in the house knows should be ours. Yet we smile and take it. Boy, that's acting!"

ACTORS

"An actor is a fellow that just has a little more monkey in him than the fellow that can't act," explained Will Rogers, who was the movie industry's leading box office draw in 1934, the last full year of his life.

"If you have ever been an actor ... why it just about ruins you for any useful employment for the rest of your life," said Will, who confessed he was not a very good actor.

"About the only thing an actor can start is a fad, or a divorce."

(see BANKING CRISIS, MOVIES, MOVIE STAR)

ADAPTERS

Presenting an award for a screen adaptation, Will Rogers had this to say about adapters:

"Adapters are commonly known among authors as 'book murderers.' They are the people that show you how the book should have been written in the first place. If given the Bible to adapt, they would claim that it started too slow, that the love interest should start in Genesis, and not Leviticus, and that the real kick of the story was Noah trying to have each animal find its mate. They would play that for suspense."

(see MOVIE ADS, MOVIE TITLES)

ADVERSITY

Nothing makes a man broad-minded like adversity.

—*Daily Telegrams:* May 5, 1933

ADVERTISING

"Let advertisers spend the same amount of money improving their product that they do on advertising," said Will Rogers, "and they wouldn't have to advertise it.

"If I wanted to put an object on market today I would advertise, 'It will last until it is paid for.' Nothing could be better than that."

(see FIRST PAYMENTS)

ADVICE ON GAMBLING

Don't gamble; take all your savings and buy some good stock, and hold it till it goes up, then sell it.

If it don't go up, don't buy it.

—*Daily Telegrams:* October 31, 1929
(see STOCK, WALL STREET)

ADVICE ON LIFE

Live your life so that whenever you lose, you are ahead.

—Weekly Articles: July 5, 1931
(see PHILOSOPHY)

ADVISING CANDIDATES

"I have learned that you must never advise a man in politics to do anything but run," explained Will Rogers, who was known for his political wisdom. "If you advise him not to, you just lose his friendship. So it's always best to advise him the way he wants to be advised.

"So from now on I am advising everybody to run. In that way I will be friends to the world."

(see PRESIDENTIAL CANDIDATES)

ADVISORS

Never underestimate the power of the president's advisors. The president tells the nation what he is going to do while the advisors tell the president what he is going to do.

It is easier to replace the president's advisors than to replace the president. The quickest way to improve the government is to replace the president's advisors, according to Will Rogers. "Sometimes we don't need a different man as bad as we need different advisors for the same man."

AFTERLIFE

"Believe in something for another world," Will Rogers advised us, "but don't be too set on what it is, and then you won't start out that life with a disappointment."

ALASKA

This Alaska is a great country. If they can just keep from being taken over by the U.S. they got a great future.

—*Daily Telegrams:* August 13, 1935

AMERICA, UNITED STATES OF

"It's a great country, but you can't live in it for nothing," Will Rogers telegrammed from Beverly Hills on February 5, 1934.

Will was a proud American, but he felt that Americans were too arrogant in their dealings with other nations. When the Depression hit he felt it was our comeuppance for riding too high too long.

"We had enjoyed special blessings over other nations, and we couldn't see why they shouldn't be permanent. We was a mighty cocky nation, we originated mass production, and mass produced everybody out of a job with our boasted laborsaving machinery. It saved labor, the very thing we are now appropriating money to get a job for. They forgot that machinery don't eat, rent houses, or buy clothes. We had begun to believe that the height of civilization was a good road, bath tub, radio, and automobile.

"I don't think Hoover, the Republicans, or even Russia, is responsible for this. I think the Lord just looked us over, and decided to set us back where we belonged.

"We might be the wealthiest nation that ever existed, we might dominate the world in lots of things, but as nations are individuals, why, we are just an individual, and because we are richer than all our neighbors or than anybody else, that don't necessarily mean that we are happier or really better off.

"We are going through a unique experience. We are the first nation to starve to death in a storehouse that's overfilled with everything we want."

* * *

7

Two hundred years from now history will record: America, a nation, which flourished from 1900 to 1942, conceived many odd inventions for getting somewhere, but could think of nothing to do when they got there.

—*Daily Telegrams:* April 28, 1930

That's what makes us a great nation. We take the little things serious, and the big ones as a joke.

—*Daily Telegrams:* September 15, 1933

We are are so big, and move along with such momentum, that we are able to live through everything. As cockeyed as we are, we are better than all the rest put together.

—*Weekly Articles:* June 19, 1934
(see HIGH STANDARD, NATURAL RESOURCES, PESSIMISTS, UNITED, WORK)

AMERICAN CITIZENS

There are two things that tickle the fancy of our citizens: one is to let him act on a committee, and the other is promise to let him walk in a parade.

What America needs is to get more mileage out of our parades.

—*Daily Telegrams:* September 1, 1929
(see PARADES)

AMERICAN FOREIGN POLICY

It always will seem funny to us United Staters that we are about the only ones that really know how to do everything right. I don't know how a lot of these other nations have existed as long as they have till we could get some of our people around and show 'em really how to be pure and good like us.

—*More Letters:* February 27, 1932

You can take a sob story and a stick of candy and lead America right off into the Dead Sea.

—*Weekly Articles:* December 2, 1933

Here we go again! America is running true to form, fixing some other country's business for 'em just as we always do. We mean well, but will wind up in the wrong as usual.

—*Daily Telegrams:* June 22, 1931

No nation ever had two better friends than we have. You know who they are. The Atlantic and the Pacific Ocean.

—*Weekly Articles:* April 9, 1933
(see EUROPE, FOREIGN RELATIONS, INTERNATIONAL RELATIONS)

AMERICAN HEROES

This is a great country. You never know where our heroes will come from.

—*Daily Telegrams:* June 6, 1933

AMERICAN INTERESTS

America has a great habit of always talking about protecting American interests in some foreign country. *Protect 'em here at home!* There is more American interests right here than anywhere.

—*Weekly Articles:* June 28, 1925

AMERICANS

Will Rogers saw the American people as he saw himself—basically good-hearted, simple and unpretentious, when not confused. "Give Americans a one-piece bathing suit, a hamburger, and five gallons of gasoline, and they are just as tickled as a movie star with a new divorce."

9

Another characteristic of Americans was big spending. "I don't know where any of all this money is coming from we are spending now, any more than a congressman does," said Will, "but if Americans are going to start worrying about whether they can afford a thing or not, you are going to ruin the whole characteristic of our people."

Both individually and nationally, we are just living in a time when none of us are in any shape to be telling somebody else what to do.

—*Weekly Articles:* July 17, 1935

The American people are a very generous people and will forgive almost any weakness, with the possible exception of stupidity.

—*Weekly Articles:* February 24, 1924

We are a great people to get tired of anything awful quick. We just jump from one extreme to another.

—"How To Be Funny," March 30, 1929

We live fast and move slow.

—*Daily Telegrams:* September 11, 1929
(see HAMBURGERS, SAPS)

AMERICAN WEALTH

"So here we are in a country with more wheat and more corn and more money in the bank, more cotton, more everything in the world," said Will Rogers in a radio broadcast for Unemployment Relief in 1931. "There's not a product that you can name that we haven't got more of than any other country ever had on the face of the earth—and yet we've got people starving. We'll hold the distinction of being the only nation in the history of the world that ever went to the poor house in an auto-mobile."

ANARCHIST

If one wants to do right, our political system is so arranged that he can't do it. The minute one wants to do what no one else has been accustomed to do, why, they call him an anarchist.

—*Weekly Articles:* March 15, 1931

ANCESTORS

Will Rogers was an American hybrid original. He described himself as an Irish-American-Indian.

"There is a fine breed for you, Irish-Indian. Ziegfeld says I have a touch of Hebraic in me, too. Which would make me an Irish, Jewish, Indian.

"My family crest would in that case be, a shillelagh with a tomahawk on one end, and a percent sign on the other."

(see FAMILY TREE)

ANTIQUES

"Us middle class never have to worry about having old furniture to point out to our friends," asserted Will Rogers. "We buy it on payments and before it's paid for it's plenty antique."

ARGUMENTS

"The human animal is endowed with mighty powers of mind," according to the gospel of Will Rogers. Thus the human animal is able to come up with good arguments for or against anything, right or wrong.

"You give us long enough to argue over something,"

said Will, "and we'll bring you in proofs to show that the Ten Commandments should never have been ratified.

"If you can start arguing over something, and get enough publicity, and keep the argument going, you can divide our nation over night as to whether spinach or broccoli is the most nutritious."

ARKANSAS

Will Rogers was captivated by the Arkansas mystique. "There is pretty strong characters down there," he said of the state of Arkansas. "You can't redeem 'em, you just join 'em. That's what I had to do about twenty-seven years ago with one of 'em."

His wife, Betty Blake, was an Arkansan. She hailed from a town with the unpromising name of Rogers, Arkansas.

"Anytime you tangle with an Arkansaw hillbilly or hillbillyess," said Will, "you are going to run second."

(see ROGERS, BETTY)

ARMED FORCES

Will's advice on what to do with our armed forces is not to use them:

"Get 'em all home, add to their number, add to their training, then just sit tight with a great feeling of security and just read about foreign wars. That's the best thing in the world to do with them."

ARMS TRADING

"We want to be in the position where we can sell to both sides."

This was Will Rogers' way of explaining the U.S. foreign policy of providing weapons to both sides of strategic conflicts around the world.

"Then they wonder why Europe thinks we are always out for the dough. Let's don't kid ourselves, we are out for it a lot of the time.

"All our highly civilized nations are great humanitarians, but if two countries are going to kill each other off, neutrals at least would like the privilege of furnishing the ammunition. When Judgment Day comes, civilization will have an alibi, 'I never took a human life, I only sold the fellow the gun to take it with.'

"No nation will buy anything to eat or anything to wear from you, but if you got a gun they will buy it and more than likely shoot it back at you."

(see DISARMAMENT)

ART

When the history of an age is done, when the kings and queens have gone and the wars are over, it is the art that lasts. The art is the soul of a society that lives on after the body is dead. Art is what lasts. In fact, whatever lasts is apt to be defined as art.

"No matter how you built anything or painted anything," said Will Rogers, "if it accidentally through lack of wars or rain happened to live a few hundred years, why, it's art now."

ART DEFINITION

Art is when you do something just cockeyed from what is the right way to do it, then it's art.

—*Weekly Articles:* October 2, 1932

ATHLETICS

Athletics came of age in the twentieth century. Initially there were concerns about the possibly harmful effects of athletics and exercise. Some of these fears were allayed by scientific research findings, such as laboratory experiments with rats.

Laboratory rat experiments were the rage in the Roaring Twenties. "There is an awful lot in the papers the last few days about these experiments these college professors are making with rats," Will observed. "One professor had to turn his out, for the rats knew enough not to try any of the experiments.

"Another one wanted to find out what effect athletics had on any one's intelligence. They wanted to see if he was dumber, or keener, after running back punts, and tackling another rat for a while.

"The experiment showed that the rat was keener with athletics by him demanding tuition and board for nothing and 10 percent of the gate on all big games. The rat with no exercise wound up as a bond salesman."

This athletic racket is a pretty tough thing at that. There is about as many disappointments as successes. I think us fellows that can't do anything are just as well off. We are never disappointed.

—*Weekly Articles:* August 7, 1932

AUDIENCES

Will Rogers' routine was generally a crowd-pleasing performance. But there was one audience with which he could not cope. They didn't get his jokes because they didn't read the papers.

Rogers recalled one night he flopped at a high-society function. "I will never forget one time I went over to Sherry's, a fashionable restaurant, after the Follies show, to play a charity affair for some New York society ladies. I thought I had some good material at the time. The League of Nations was in the height of its argument, Ireland and England was fussing, disarmament was the

14

headline topic. I breezed out there rather cocky, thinking I had some surefire material.

"Well, you never saw jokes hit a ballroom floor and slide off like those did. Those old dowagers and those young debutantes had no more read a paper than I had Shakespeare."

Soon after his high-society flop Will Rogers put on a charity show at a prison.

"Then two nights later after that fiasco, I went to Sing Sing and did a show for them and I never had so well-read an audience in my life. They didn't miss a thing. Ever since then I have always felt we had the wrong bunch in there."

Ah, folks, you can act, and talk, and do stunts, all over the world, but the applause of a home audience is sweeter to your ears than anything in the world.

—*Daily Telegrams:* April 22, 1930
(see CRIMINALS, GERMAN HUMOR)

AUTOMATIC PISTOL

The automatic pistol has taken all the class out of crime. Now anybody can be a criminal, even the lowest elements of society.

"In the old Wild West days," Will recalled, "the bandit had to back out shooting and make his horse by the blaze of his guns."

Nowadays any young punk can pull a holdup. "Well, the young man simply walks up with no mask, no western hat, no big forty-five, just a little automatic, which a baby can shoot as well as Billy the Kid could, for all you do is point and keep the trigger pulled and you hit everything in the place, there is no possible way you can miss any part of anyone in the building. The more nervous you are the more you hit.

"If there is one thing that has increased crime, it's been the automatic pistol. It's made no practice necessary to

15

be an outlaw. Give any young egotist two shots of dope and an automatic and he will hold up the government mint. He goes in, gets his money quicker than you can get it with a bona-fide check. Out he comes. His partner has his car running, and away they go perhaps to their country home, or their golf club. The toughest part of robbing nowadays is to find somebody that has something. The minute a robber gets a clue, why, the rest is easy. Now that's about the routine of the modern robbery, and the murder is about along the same routine, course it's a little more expensive on account of having to use a little ammunition."

(see CRIMINALS, HUSBAND KILLING, KILLERS, MURDERS)

AUTOMOBILE

We'll hold the distinction of being the only nation in the history of the world that ever went to the poor house in an automobile.

—*Radio Broadcasts*, October 18, 1931

AUTOMOBILE AGE

This is the Automobile Age, as Will Rogers described it:
"There is more money invested in garages than in schools and churches.

"98½ percent of the building permits in small towns are for filling stations. Over two-thirds of the unemployed in this country are working in filling stations.

"If people slept in filling stations instead of just driving by them, it would solve the housing problem of this country.

"There is 300,000 men just pumping gas into cars every minute of the day in America alone.

"193,000 just fixing punctures.

"800,000 just looking on; 750,000 of 'em offering advice, .009 successfully.

16

"187,000 people every minute of the day just cranking the old ones; 81 with results.

"There is 43,000 just holding up the hoods of Fords looking at them, 42,598 with the same expression."

We owe it all to Henry Ford, stated Will Rogers. "Ford made a car that runs with your feet instead of your head and hands. He was smart enough to know more people knew how to use their feet than they did their head or hands.

"Why, there is 23,078 Ford radiators boiling over on the hills of this country every day of every month, and think what that means in February, when leap year comes and brings it to 29.

"He has made more business for an undertaker than any other one thing, with the exception of Prohibition. Monday morning after a beautiful sunshiny Sunday finds the undertaker singing at his work.

"He has caused more people to go into debt than for rent or food.

"He has drove more states, counties, towns, and federal governments in debt than the World War. We owe more for roads than we did to persuade the Germans to 'please leave Belgium.' Had we no good roads we would miss all the scandal in the Highway Department; no state worries about who will be governor. It's 'Who will be on the Highway Commission?' I care not who writes a nation's songs; give me the highway contracts to deal out, and I will show you what hard work, perseverance, and taking advantage of your opportunities will do.

"He has given us the biggest problem we have in America today, and that is, 'Where am I going to park it?'

"He has given us our second biggest problem we have today, namely, 'After it's parked (and you come back and get it), how am I going to get home in it through the traffic?' That's why so many people just leave 'em parked."

(see FORD)

BANKERS

"If you think banking ain't a sucker game, why is your banker the richest man in town?" Will Rogers asked. "Bank failures break banks but bankers don't go broke, do they?"

The bankers just got four years of good cussing by everybody for loaning too much money. Well, they got some awful nice buildings. So when a banker fails, he fails in splendor.

—*Daily Telegrams:* February 7, 1934
(see BANKING CRISIS)

BANKING CRISIS

In the early days of the Great Depression, Will Rogers aroused the wrath of the financial gods of the banking industry with his remarks on the banking crisis.

"I said the bankers were the first to go on the dole. The wrath of the mighty ascended on me. Even the *Wall*

Street Journal said I should confine my jokes to some semblance of truth."

Will expressed sympathy for the bankers, saying he understood how much the truth hurts.

"Now I want to be fair, even with the bankers, for they are pretty touchy now. I have had some critics come out and say 'As an actor old Will is not so hot.' Well, I just wanted to come out and call him a liar, but in my heart and conscience I knew he was right. So I know how you boys feel."

Will's final advice to the bankers: "Now if you will take this money and loan it out to a lot of the little fellows that need it you bankers got a chance to redeem yourselves."

(see TRUTH HURTS, WELFARE)

BASEBALL

From politics to baseball is quite a jump upwards. Not only financially, but morally.

—Weekly Articles: April 26, 1925
(see HOME RUN, POLITICS)

BEANS

Will Rogers knew beans. He was a connoisseur of beans. He was a bean man all the way. There was nothing he would rather eat than beans. He was perfectly content with a sufficiency of beans.

"Going to have beans for supper tonight," he said with anticipation, "navy cooked in Oklahoma ham, raised on the Dog Iron ranch at Oologah. Cooked plenty soupy like. Got to eat 'em with a spoon, raw onions, and corn bread, nothing else. Anybody that would want anything else ought to be shot."

(see CHILI, FOOD)

BEER

"Somebody figured out that now we can have two and three quarter percent beer," said Will, who was skeptical of what was called Progress. "But who wants to drink thirty-seven and-a-half bottles to be 100 percent drunk?"

(see PROGRESS)

BELIEFS

It seems the more learned a man is the less consideration he has for another man's belief.

—*Weekly Articles:* January 20, 1924
(see AFTERLIFE, KNOWLEDGE, LEARNING)

BEVERLY HILLS

Will Rogers could boast of a nearly perfect political record—he never lost an election. On the other hand, he never won an election, so he could not be accused of selling out to political interests.

So great was the popularity of Will Rogers in his prime, he might have won almost any office for which he had run. But he never ran for one. The only office he ever held was bestowed upon him without his knowledge or consent, in his absence—honorary mayor of Beverly Hills.

The august title was conferred upon him while he was away on a nationwide lecture tour. Returning home on December 21, 1926, he was met by an imposing delegation. Local residents, movie actors, motorcycle policemen, and two brass bands greeted him, presenting him with a five-foot scroll honoring him as mayor.

Will Rogers made a graceful acceptance speech. "They say I'll be a comedy mayor. Well, I won't be the only one," he confided to the crowd. "I never saw a mayor yet that wasn't comical. As to my administration, I won't say I'll be exactly honest, but I'll agree to split fifty-fifty with you and give the town an even break."

In his hour of triumph the honorary mayor did not forget his debt to the common people. "I'm for the common people," he claimed, "and as Beverly Hills has no common people I won't have to pass out any favors."

Actually Mayor Rogers did do a few favors for the common people. With his own money he paid for the construction of a new gymnasium and a handball court. His term as mayor was short-lived, however. The California legislature, perhaps threatened by the prospect of sweeping reforms initiated by a wisecracking Cherokee Indian with no loyalty to the existing power structure, passed a bill declaring that in a town of the sixth class the president of the board of trustees was constitutionally considered mayor. This put Will Rogers unceremoniously out of office.

Stepping down from the seat of power August 28, 1927, Rogers said with chagrin, "If I had known that Beverly Hills was a town of the sixth class, I would'a never taken the job."

(see MAYORS)

BIG BUSINESS

"When your business is not doing good you combine with something and sell more stock," Will Rogers observed.

"The poor little fellow, he can't combine with anything but the sheriff in case he is going broke, which he generally is. But big business merges with another that's not going good and both do nothing together.

"Big business sure got big, but it got big by selling its stocks and not by selling its products."

(see MERGERS, REPUBLICANS)

BIG CITY

I believe a big city changes less than any other place.

—*Weekly Articles:* September 23, 1928

BIG IDEAS

"I have a lot of big ideas," Will Rogers admitted, "they just don't seem to work out. There must be a bit of college professor in me somewhere."

(see IDEALS, THEORIES)

BIG WORDS

"I never try to fog the issue by using any big words in any of my sermons or speeches, no matter what type the audience is," explained Will Rogers. He also preferred to avoid big words, he said, because he didn't know many.

"Course with a speech you can use some big words, and it comes in handy sometimes. Your audience will be confused over it and that will give you a chance to think of something. Big words in speeches, you see, are just used for about the same reason as a speaker stopping and taking a drink. He ain't thirsty."

(see SPEECHES)

BIOGRAPHERS

Trouble with a lot of these biographers is, they go and lower the moral of character with a lot of facts. Nothing will spoil a big man's life like too much truth.

—*Weekly Articles:* October 29, 1933
(see BIOGRAPHY 1935)

BIRTH CERTIFICATE

When Will Rogers applied for a passport to go abroad in 1926 he stumbled into an unexpected bureaucratic barrier: he had no birth certificate.

"You see, in the early days of the Indian Territory where I was born," the Native American wrote to President Coolidge, "there was no such thing as birth certificates. You being there was certificate enough. We generally took for granted if you were there you must have at some time been born. Having a certificate of being born was like wearing a raincoat in the water over a bathing suit."

The requirement was waived. The passport was granted.

BORROWING

Borrowing is the American way. How else did the national debt get so big?

"Our only solution of relief," said Will, "seems to be to fix it so people who are in a hole through borrowing can borrow some more."

(see DEBT)

BOULDER DAM

Don't miss seeing the building of Boulder Dam. It's the biggest thing that's ever been done with water since Noah made the flood look foolish.

You know how big the Grand Canyon is. Well, they just stop up one end of it and make the water come out through a drinking fountain.

—*Daily Telegrams:* September 6, 1932

BRAVERY

Cowardice or bravery is never racial. You find both in every country. No country has a monopoly on bravery; great deeds of heroism are liable to break out in the most unexpected places.

—*More Letters:* March 12, 1932
(see WOMEN'S BRAVERY)

BREVITY

Whoever wrote the Ten Commandments made 'em short. They may not always be kept but they can be understood. They are the same for all.

—*Weekly Articles:* March 17, 1935
(see MOSES)

BRITISH

We dislike their tea, we kid their poor English dialect and we think they are snobbish, but by golly, we know that their honor all over the world is recognized.

—*Daily Telegrams:* October 9, 1933

BROTHERLY LOVE

Brotherly love has never crossed a boundary line yet. Geography has more to do with brotherly love than civilization and Christianity combined.

—*Weekly Articles:* July 7, 1935

BUDGET

Congress is eternally debating the national debt, arguing over whether to allocate a few billion here or a few billion there or to spread out a few fewer billion everywhere. Will Rogers felt there was an air of unreality about the whole process of deciding the national budget:

"The budget is a mythical beanbag. Congress votes mythical beans into it, and then tries to reach in and pull real beans out."

Rogers offered a common-sense solution to the nation's never-ending budgetary crisis:

"We will never get anywhere with our finances till we pass a law saying that every time we appropriate something we got to pass another bill along with it stating where the money is coming from."

Political leaders have not been inclined to take Will Rogers' advice, regarding it as impractical.

(see GOVERNMENT SPENDING, TAXES)

BUENOS AIRES

Say, you talk about a city, this Buenos Aires is as big as Chicago, as live as Paris, beautiful as Beverly Hills, and as substantial as Claremore, Oklahoma.

—*Daily Telegrams:* October 18, 1932
(see CHICAGO, CLAREMORE)

BUSINESS

Will Rogers was raised in a simple frontier economy based on the exchange of goods and services. He was baffled by the more speculative business practices of sophisticated city slickers who preferred manipulating paper assets, credit, and futures. Here is how he summed up these modern business practices:

"We are continually buying something that we never get, from a man that never had it."

If you want to know how a man stands, go among the people who are in his same business.

—*Weekly Articles:* September 28, 1924

There is two things that can disrupt business in this country. One is war, and the other is a meeting of the Federal Reserve Bank.

—*Daily Telegrams:* April 2, 1929
(see BIG BUSINESS, MOSES, WALL STREET)

BUSYBODIES

The prize two old "Busybodys" of the world is England and America. If Dempsey and Tunney exercised their physical superiority as much as England and America do their naval superiority, why they would be walking around punching guys in the nose every five minutes, or at least telling them what to do.

—*Weekly Articles:* February 6, 1927

C

CABINET MEETING

"Say, can't you just see a cabinet meeting?" Will asked.

The secretary of war reports: "Sir, wars—none; peace—none; average: 50 percent."

The postmaster general reports: "Sir, so many letters sent, so many letters received, so many letters lost."

The secretary of agriculture reports: "Sir, farms in the United States—eleven million; farms mortgaged—eleven million; farms carrying second mortgages—10, 998, 634. The department reports progress."

The secretary of labor reports: "Sir, number of people laboring—ten million; people living off people laboring—ninety-eight million, including twenty-three million government employees."

CALIFORNIA

California is called the Golden State. It used to belong to Mexico.

"We took it away from Mexico the next year after we found it had gold," explained Will Rogers.

"It's a great old state; we furnish the amusement to the world; sometimes conscientious; sometimes unconscientious; sometimes by our films; sometimes by our orators.

"Everything is in California, all the great sights of nature, and along with all these wonders what we have out here is the world's greatest collection of freak humans on earth. We maintain more freak religions and cults than all the rest of the world combined. Just start anything out here and if it's cuckoo enough you will get followers.

"California acts a good deal like a dog pound does in any town. It gets the undesirable strays off the streets. We are the human pound of America. Some of their own communities even go so far as to catch 'em and send 'em out here. But being good humanitarians we just take 'em right in, and in a week they are as big liars as the natives, which shows they are not without some genius at that."

"You know, if you have lost anyone, look out here, because sooner or later they will come here to visit relatives, for anybody that has relatives comes here."

—*Weekly Articles:* September 16, 1923
(see DROUGHT, RANCH)

CALIFORNIA CHRISTMAS

"This has been the hottest day we have had in California for years," reported Will on Christmas Day 1929. "Everybody that is not at the beaches bathing is huddled under the thousands of outdoor Christmas trees to get in the shade. Even the imitation snow is melting. All Santa Clauses are in bathing suits and wearing a palm-leaf fan for whiskers. There will be two heat prostrations to every Christmas present."

CAMPAIGNS

Will Rogers was dismayed at the rising cost of political campaigns. It cost almost as much to elect an honest candidate as to elect a dishonest one, he observed. At the approach of the 1928 presidential election, he expressed reservations:

"The promising season ends next Tuesday, and at about eight o'clock that same night, the alibi season opens, and lasts for the next four years.

"So much money is being spent on the campaigns that I doubt if either man, as good as they are, are worth what it will cost to elect them."

Will's recommendation: "Take your campaign contribution, and send it to the Red Cross, and let the election be decided on its merit."

CANADA

"Canada is a mighty good neighbor and a mighty good customer. That's a combination that is hard to beat," declared unofficial American goodwill ambassador Will Rogers.

"Canada. They have truly been a good companion; I won't call 'em neighbors, for they haven't borrowed enough from us to be called neighbors; I would prefer to still call 'em friends. They are a fine tribe of people. They are hardy—they got to be to live next to us and exist."

CANDIDATE

"History has proven that there is nothing in the world as alike as two candidates. They look different till they get in, and then they all act the same," Will observed.

"You know it don't take near as good a man to be a candidate as it does to hold the office, that's why we wisely defeat more than we elect."

(see ELECTIONS, VOTERS)

CAPITAL LETTERS

Never was a country in the throes of more capital letters than the old U.S.A. But we still haven't sent out the S.O.S.

—*Daily Telegrams:* September 22, 1933

CAPONE, AL

Everybody you talk to would rather hear about Capone than anybody you ever met. What's the matter with an age when our biggest gangster is our greatest national interest?

—*Daily Telegrams:* March 11, 1932
(see CRIMINALS)

CARNEGIE HALL

"Carnegie Hall is where they have all the big concerts," Will Rogers explained New York highbrow culture to out-of-towners. "If a foreign fiddler comes here, as soon as he is fumigated they throw him down and get a musician's dress suit on him, and put him in Carnegie Hall for a recital."

CAR ACCESSORIES

A new car has two prices: with and without optional accessories.

"The big thing is still accessories," Will Rogers noted in 1929 when the Age of the Automobile was yet young. "You price a car nowadays, and he gives you a figure. It sounds pretty reasonable. Then you say: 'That includes everything?'

" 'Well, no. If you want wheels on it, that will come extra; you can get either wheels or runners. Most people prefer wheels. But on account of us not knowing just what they might like, why, we make 'em extra. Then the bumpers, front, rear, and side, and the lights. Of course, you will want lights, in case you might want to use the car at night. And the mirrors are extra, in case you want to see what's going on in the back seat.'

" 'Well, just what does go with the car at the original price you quoted me?'

" 'The name and the goodwill.' "

(see FORD, NEW CARS)

CHAMBER OF COMMERCE

The minute a fellow gets into the Chamber of Commerce he quits mowing his own lawn.

—*Weekly Articles:* May 20, 1923

CHAPLIN, CHARLIE

When Charles Chaplin married a sixteen-year-old woman on November 25, 1924, it made headlines all over the world. Will came to the defense of the Chaplins: "The big thing headlined is CHARLIE CHAPLIN'S WIFE ONLY 16 YEARS OLD, and, if so, what to do with her.

"If she is sixteen and said at her wedding ceremony that she was nineteen she is the only female of the species that ever increased her age voluntarily. She is a novelty already and if those odd traits keep up she will show as much originality as Charlie.

"Now Los Angeles, to be sure and get its share of the publicity out of the wedding, has said she would be compelled to go to school. I am glad they put an age limit on knowledge instead of a test limit out there, because if a lot of us (me particularly) had to stand an educational test before marriage we would have all been bachelors.

"This girl don't need to go to school. Any girl smart enough to marry Charlie Chaplin should be lecturing at Vassar College on 'Taking Advantage of Your Opportunities.' I consider Charlie Chaplin not only the funniest man in the world, but I consider him to be (and this comes not from hearsay but from personal observation and contact with him) to be one of the smartest minds in America. Any man that can stay at the absolute head of his profession as long as he has, can't do it on a pinhead. He is the only man, actor, statesman, writer, painter that has ever been able to please the entire world.

"He is the greatest economist in the world. Every nation has lost its export trade. Yet stop and think of it, Chaplin manufactures the only article in the world that hasn't depreciated. While all the world's big industrialists were greedy, Charlie never went in for mass production. Seems odd that a comedian can do what governments are not smart enough to do."

CHARITY

That's one trouble with our charities, we are always saving somebody away off, when the fellow next to us ain't eating.

—*Daily Telegrams:* March 22, 1932
(see MISSIONARIES)

CHARITY DEDUCTIONS

Will Rogers argued that a donation to a Democratic campaign should count as a charitable deduction.

"By the way, did you charge off money given to the Democratic campaign?" he asked. "You could, it's a legitimate charity, not organized but a charity nevertheless."

(see DEMOCRATS)

CHEROKEES

"My ancestors didn't come on the *Mayflower* but they met the boat," joked the nation's most famous Native American.

Rogers was proud of his Indian heritage. He was born in Indian Territory in Oologah, Oklahoma, on November 4, 1879. "My father was one-eighth Cherokee Indian and my mother was a quarter-blood." Although he was a hybrid—part-Indian, part-white—Will Rogers' sympathies lay wholly with the Cherokees. The only tribe with their own written language, the Cherokees were among the most civilized of the Native American Indians, but with the advent of the white man in the nineteenth century they suffered a long, sad history of oppression.

The U. S. government forced the Cherokee Indians into twenty-four treaties involving land cessions between 1794 and 1819. Cherokee losses then increased during the subsequent Indian Wars. The tragic conflict culminated in the episode of American history sometimes called "the great removal." In his first message to Congress, President Andrew Jackson announced a plan to remove all the southeast Indians and relocate them on lands west of the Mississippi. The Cherokees referred to their forced emigration as "the trail of tears"—a hegira in which the Choctaw, Chickasaw, Creek, Seminole, and Cherokee tribes were evicted from their ancestral lands. Pushed back beyond the Mississippi, many of the Cherokees wound up on reservations in Oklahoma. Many thousands more died during the journey.

One of the U.S. Army regulars who accompanied the Cherokees on their exodus wrote in his memoirs: "I fought through the Civil War and have seen men shot to pieces and slaughtered by thousands, but the Cherokee removal was the cruelest work I ever knew." He described how many of the Indians were dragged from their homes by Georgia volunteers. "Well-furnished houses were left a prey to plunderers, who, like hungry wolves, follow in the train of the captors. These wretches rifle the houses and strip the helpless, unoffending owners of all they have."

"They sent the Indians to Oklahoma," recounted Rog-

33

ers with sadness. "They had a treaty that said, 'You shall have this land as long as grass grows and water flows.' It was not only a good rhyme but looked like a good treaty, and it *was* until they struck oil. Then the government took it away from us again. They said the treaty refers to 'water and grass; it don't say anything about oil.'

"So the Indians lost another bet—the first one to Andrew Jackson, and the second to the oil companies."

I think the government only give us about a dollar an acre for it. We had it for hunting grounds, but we never knew enough to hunt oil on it.

—*Weekly Articles:* May 4, 1930
(see INDIANS, NAVAJOS, NATIVE AMERICANS)

CHEWING GUM

Chewing gum was a patented part of Will Rogers' standup act. He never appeared on stage without a rope in his hand and chewing gum in his mouth. When he was forty-nine years old he confessed he had "never in my life made a single dollar without having to chew some gum to get it."

Here is a Will Rogers homily on the virtues of chewing gum:

"If it wasn't for chewing gum, Americans would wear their teeth off just hitting them against each other. Every scientist has been figuring out who the different races descend from. I don't know about the other tribes, but I do know that the American race descended from the cow. And Wrigley was smart enough to furnish the cud. He has made the whole world chew for democracy.

"That's why this subject touches me so deeply. I have chewed more gum than any living man. My act on the stage depended on the grade of gum I chewed. Lots of my readers have seen me and perhaps noted the poor quality of my jokes on that particular night. Now I was

34

not personally responsible for that. I just happened to hit on a poor piece of gum."

CHEWING GUM INGREDIENTS

"Chewing gum is the only ingredient of our national life of which no one knows of what it is made," Rogers acknowledged. "We know that sawdust makes our breakfast food, we know that tomato cans constitute automobile bodies, we know that old secondhand newspapers make our fifteen-dollar shoes, we know that cotton makes our all-wool suits, but no one knows yet what constitutes a mouthful of chewing gum."

He added: "Maybe it's better that way."

CHICAGO

Will Rogers was not quite as sentimental about Chicago as Carl Sandburg, the poet who described the windy city in his poem *Chicago* as:

> Stormy, husky, brawling,
> City of the Big Shoulders.

Rogers wrote this tribute to Chicago in his national column during a midwestern sojourn:

> Just passed thru Chicago. The snow was so deep
> the crooks could only hit a tall man.
> To try to diminish crime they laid off six
> hundred cops.

"Even out in Chicago, why, there is just an awful lot of fine things about the old town besides bullet holes. It's one of the most progressive cities in the world. Shooting is only a sideline."

—*Weekly Articles:* June 22, 1930

I don't see how it is that people can afford to live in Chicago and afford to change with the times. Now they switched from pistols to machine guns, and now from machine guns to bombs. I can't see how a poor man can afford it.

—*Weekly Articles:* March 11, 1928

Chicago has no more cussedness than any other city but it's been better advertised.

—*Weekly Articles:* July 6, 1930

It's a great old city and they are doing the best they can, and time has proven that they haven't got the sole and exclusive right to organize crime.

—*Weekly Articles:* May 28, 1933

There was a few murders while I was there, but not enough to keep up the town's reputation.

—*Weekly Articles:* May 6, 1928
(see DETROIT)

CHILDREN'S VOTE

"Everybody is always asking if women voting has made any real change in our political system," remarked Will Rogers. "It has. It has just about doubled the amount of candidates. The only way we can possibly have more people seeking public pensions is to give the children the vote.

"Children have the same qualification for office the grown-ups have," professed Will, "they are out of work."

CHILI

Will Rogers was able to survive several years on the banquet circuit without succumbing to stomach trouble. His secret was chili.

"There is only one way a person can survive a year of banquets and not wind up with a burlesque stomach—that is not to eat there at all.

"Now I tell you how I did. There is a little chili joint on Broadway and 47th Street, where there is just a counter and a few stools, but what chili! Well, on any night I had to go to a banquet, I would go in there and play about two rounds of enchiladas, and a few encores on the chili, and I want to tell you that I was fortified. Not only to refuse anything that might be offered to me at the dinner, but I could just set through almost any kind of a speech.

"That is why I recommend chili. It's the only thing I have ever found that will strengthen a man up to listen to all he hears."

(see BEANS, FOOD)

CHINA

Don't waste too much pity on poor old China; she will be here when some strange race of people will be excavating some of our skyscrapers and wondering what tombs they were. There is none of us that don't feel that China will be here five thousand years from now, and none of us are sure that other nations will be here.

—*More Letters:* April 12, 1932

CHINA MYTHS

Whenever Will Rogers went abroad, the roving ambassador-at-large would foster international understanding by exploding cultural myths and stereotypes. One such myth was "that a Chinaman's word was as good as his bond. That might have been in the old days, but not since the missionaries and business men come in. Chinese are just as human as anybody now."

Will also disputed the myth that China's greatness lay in her numbers. The truth was quite the contrary, he said.

"Nothing in the world's smarter than one Chinaman and nothing dumber than two."

CHINESE MISSIONARIES

What we ought to do is import some Chinese missionaries from over there to come and show us. We just got the missionary business turned around. We are the ones that need converting more than they do.

—*Weekly Articles:* April 10, 1927

CHINESE SAGE

"Gentlemen," said Will Rogers coming to the microphone after a longwinded speaker, "you have just been listening to that Chinese sage, On Tu Long."

(see BREVITY, SPEECHES)

CHRIST

In the age of mass media, heroes are defined by publicity. It was not always so, Will said. "Our Savior performed some pretty handy feats in the early days and his exploits have been handed down through the ages and made him our greatest hero, all accomplished without the aid of a newspaper."

CHRISTMAS

Everybody faces it with, "Oh my goodness, Xmas is coming, and how I dread it!" Then you decide "The whole thing is the bunk, I will just send cards." Then about three days before Christmas you commence to get a few little boxes and remembrances from alleged friends, and you say, "I can't do this. I have to return something." Then out you go at the last minute to round up some tokens for friends who in your heart you curse for sending you anything. So the whole thing is an uproar from about Thanksgiving on.

It would be all right if we could again believe in Santa Claus.

—*Weekly Articles:* January 5, 1930

CHURCH

If they are going to argue religion in the church instead of teaching it no wonder you see more people at a circus than at a church.

—*Weekly Articles:* January 20, 1924

CIGARETTES

"Everywhere I go down here somebody invariably asks me for a cigarette," remarked Will during a trip to Mexico, "so if you ask me what this country needs it's more cigarettes."

(see MEXICO)

CIVILIZATION

"Any man that thinks that civilization has advanced is an egotist. Fords and bathtubs have moved you and cleaned you, but you was just as ignorant when you got there," Will shrugged. "We know lots of things we used to didn't know but we don't know any way to prevent 'em happening. Confucius perspired out more knowledge than the U.S. Senate has vocalized out in the last fifty years.

"We have got more toothpaste on the market, and more misery in our courts than at any time in our existence. There ain't nothing to life but satisfaction.

"Indians and primitive races were the highest civilized, because they were more satisfied, and they depended less on each other, and took less from each other. We couldn't live a day without depending on everybody. So our civilization has given us no liberty or independence.

"Civilization has taught us to eat with a fork, but even now if nobody is around we use our fingers."

You can't say civilization don't advance, however, for in every war they kill you in a new way.

—*Daily Telegrams:* December 22, 1929

We will never have true civilization until we have learned to recognize the rights of others.

—*Weekly Articles:* November 18, 1923

I must get back from these political parties and get back to civilization, for there's nothing in common between politics and civilization.

—*Radio Broadcasts,* April 14, 1935

They talk about civilization. Say there ain't no civilization where there ain't no satisfaction, and that's what the trouble is now, nobody is satisfied.

—*Weekly Articles:* January 5, 1930
(see PROGRESS, SUCCESS)

CLEVELAND

The 1924 Republican convention was held in Cleveland. Employed as a newspaper correspondent, Will Rogers endured it for a few days and then left town before it was over. He tried to put his hasty departure from Cleveland in a good light by comparing it to the acts of immortal heroes.

"I have just done something that, when the facts are known, will make me one of the immortals and when I die my headpiece will read, 'Here lies the body of the first man that left the Cleveland convention.'

40

"It's just an intuition that comes to every man to do something now and then that every other man wants to do but he just can't rake up the courage. That's why some of us will go down as heroes, while the others will always be with the mob."

Will compared leaving Cleveland to the feats of George Washington, Abraham Lincoln, and General Pershing.

"Pershing said: 'Lafayette, I am here.'

"I said: 'Cleveland, I am gone.'

"These others stand on something they said. I rest my case on what I did. I claim a man should be known by his deeds and not by mere words. I didn't stay and talk. I acted. I saw my duty and I done it.

"Now I want this distinctly understood, that I have nothing against Cleveland. I love Cleveland because I knew them before this catastrophe struck them. She will arise from her badges and some day be greater than ever. But I simply couldn't stand the incessant sweeping by of bands, the din, the roar, the popping of corks, and the newness and brightness of the speeches."

Will went back to work with the Ziegfeld Follies in New York. "I just had to have a rest and return to the solitude and quiet of a Ziegfeld rehearsal, where everything is still and orderly as a prayer meeting."

There was some speculation at the convention about the reason for Will Rogers' abrupt departure from Cleveland. Will set the record straight. "It has been rumored around town today that I left to prevent my being nominated as vice president. I wish to state that this was exactly the case."

(see PARTY, ZIEGFELD FOLLIES)

CLOSE CALLS

Big cars were prestigious in the 1920s. Each year the cars grew bigger and bigger as car companies competed for dominance of the roads by occupying more and more road space. Rogers was troubled by this trend:

"I see where one automobile manufacturer announced that his car was going to be four inches wider. Now how many times have you missed someone by less than four inches? Well, from now on you will hit him."

(see AUTOMOBILE, FORD, PROGRESS)

COFFEE

"Your coffee is so bad," said Will Rogers between sips, "I hate to get up in the morning."

COLLEGE

Will Rogers did not have the disadvantages of a college education. Due to his lack of education and simple-mindedness, he never learned that the world was all wrong.

"It's funny how quick a college boy can find out that the world is wrong," said Will. "He might go out in the world from high school and live in it, and make a living in it for years and think it wasn't such a bad place, but let him go to college and he will be the first one down on the square on May Day to shout down the government. But as soon as they grow up and go out and if they happen to make anything, why, they backslide."

(see HIGHER EDUCATION)

COLLEGE ATHLETES

"When should a college athlete turn pro?" It was one of the moral dilemmas of the time. Will Rogers' answer: "Not until he has earned all he can in college as an amateur."

COLLEGE DEGREES

Villains are getting as thick as college degrees and some-times on the same fellow.

—*Weekly Articles:* September 11, 1932

COLLEGE FOOTBALL

What defines a successful college? A successful football team.

"Successful colleges will start laying plans for a new stadium," said Will. "Unsuccessful ones will start hunting a new coach.

"It's better to turn out one good coach than ten college presidents."

COLORADO

Colorado is our grand seat to see the world from.

—*Weekly Articles:* January 1, 1933

COMEDIAN

A comedian can only last till he either takes himself serious or his audience takes him serious, and I don't want either one of those to happen to me till I am dead (if then).

—*Daily Telegrams:* June 28, 1932

COMEDY

Will Rogers was a great comedian but he did not claim the crown of comedy. There were other comedians far greater, he said, to whom he paid homage:

"The way to judge a good comedy is by how long it will last and have people talk about it. Now Congress has turned out some that have lived for years and people are still laughing about them."

(see LAWS)

43

COMMISSIONS

Like a prophet Will Rogers spoke out against the evils of the twentieth century, such as the appointment of too many commissions.

"While everybody is off on some sort of vacation today," Will observed on Independence Day, 1929, the president was still at work in the White House. This may appear to be a praiseworthy act on the president's part, but actually it was a national tragedy, for Hoover was busy appointing more commissions.

"Hoover, our hardest worked man, is at the White House appointing commissions. He is going to have to appoint a commission to keep track of the commissions that he has appointed. It just looks like there won't be enough people in the country to go on all these commissions; I know there won't be enough good ones."

(see INVESTIGATIONS, SENATE)

COMMON PEOPLE

Nobody wants to be called "common people," especially common people.

—*Weekly Articles:* June 21, 1925

COMMON SENSE

I don't know opera, but I know common sense when I see it, and the commoner the better I know it.

—*Weekly Articles:* October 24, 1926

COMMUNISM

"Communism is like Prohibition," said Will Rogers, "it's a good idea but it won't work.

"When you get everybody alike, that should be the height of communism.

"Communists have some ideas, of course, but they got a lot more that sound better than they work.

"Communism to me is one-third practice and two-thirds explanation.

"I have found that this communism stuff is more for outsiders than anybody else. I didn't see any of them splitting with each other or anybody else.

"It just looks to me like communism is such a happy family affair that not a communist wants to stay where it is practiced. It's the only thing they want you to have but keep none for themselves.

"The old communist preaches his doctrines, but he wants to do it where he is enjoying the blessings of capitalistic surroundings. He preaches against the pie, but he sure eats it."

(see RUSSIAN COMMUNISM, THEORIES)

CONDEMNATION

Let's be honest with ourselves, and not take ourselves too serious, and never condemn the other fellow for doing what we are doing every day, only in a different way.

—*Self-Made Diplomat to His President*, p. 146

CONFERENCE

"America has a unique record. We never lost a war and we never won a conference in our lives," said Will Rogers, unofficial ambassador-at-large, who was skeptical of the value of the twentieth century political orgies called "conferences."

"We could, without any degree of egotism, single-handed lick any nation in the world, but we can't even confer with Costa Rica and come home with our shirts on.

"I have always said that a conference was held for one reason only, to give everybody a chance to get sore at everyone else. Sometimes it takes two or three conferences to scare up a war, but generally one will do it.

"I bet you that history don't record any two nations ever having war with each other unless they had had a conference first."

Will was especially wary of secret conferences, which were excuses for politicians to gang up on the people and hatch secret plots against them. "We won't really hear what was done at this conference till we read one of the delegates' memoirs after the next war," he predicted.

"If America worked as much as they conferred we would be so wealthy that we wouldn't know which style car to buy.

"So, we hereby plead with all nations, let's quit holding conferences, stop conferring and just be friends again.

"But we are a nation of conferrers.

"Congress ought to pass a law prohibiting us conferring with anybody on anything—till we learn how."

(see PEACE CONFERENCE, WAR)

CONFIDENCE

After the stock market collapse in 1929 President Hoover tried to restore confidence to America and called on other leaders, including Will Rogers, to help do the same.

"Now we have a new one," Will commented. "It's called 'restoring confidence.' Rich men who never had a mission in life outside of watching a stock ticker are working day and night 'restoring confidence.'

"Railroad officials met today with Mr. Hoover and agreed to lower the fares on prominent delegates rushing to conferences to 'restore confidence.'

46

"Writers are working night shifts, speakers' tables are littered up, and ministers are preaching statistics, all on 'restoring confidence.'

"Confidence will beat predictions every time," Will affirmed.

"Now I am not unpatriotic, and I want to do my bit in this great movement. But you will have to give me some idea of where 'confidence' is. And just who you want it restored to.

"I discovered confidence hasn't left this country. Confidence just got wise and the guys it got wise to are wondering where it has gone."

(see AMERICA, DEPRESSION)

CONFUSION

Worry and confusion are often confused, Will Rogers said. "When you are worried you know what you are worried about, but when you are 'confused' it's when you don't know enough about a thing to be worried."

(see WORRY)

CONTACT MAN

"Contact man" is one of the twentieth century's most insidious developments. The term refers to a person who holds a job that is undefined and therefore can be performed indefinitely without success or failure.

Will Rogers called this the joke job.

"There is one joke job. I think it started with the movie magnates in Hollywood. It's when nobody really knows what your work is around an executive office. You call yourself a 'contact man.' "

Will observed with dismay that the president of the United States, Calvin Coolidge, was calling himself a contact man.

"I wish he had taken up some steady work. Work that could have been explained clearly as what he was doing.

"Just think, our most industrious citizen being nothing but a 'contact man.' But that's what makes you a 'contact man' when nobody knows what you are supposed to do."

(see COMMISSIONS, GOVERNMENTESE)

COOLIDGE, CALVIN

President Calvin Coolidge had a reputation as a humorless man who never laughed and rarely even showed his teeth.

A senator once bet Will Rogers that the humorist couldn't make the poker-faced president laugh. Rogers accepted the bet.

Upon being formally introduced by the senator to President Coolidge at a White House reception, Will Rogers extended his hand and then leaned aside as if he had missed a few words. "Beg pardon," he said, "I didn't catch the name."

Will Rogers won the bet.

COOLIDGE LEGACY

Calvin Coolidge was the business-oriented thirtieth president of the United States, who served from the death of Harding in 1923 to the succession of Hoover in 1929. Will Rogers, unofficial American historian, sums up the Coolidge legacy:

"Here comes Coolidge and does nothing and retires a hero, not only because he hadn't done anything, but because he had done it better than anyone.

"Coolidge was the only president nobody ever knew when he was acting, and when he wasn't. He was like a ukulele. You know, you can't ever tell when somebody is playing one, or just monkeying with it.

"Coolidge is the first president to discover that what the American people want is to be let alone."

COOLIDGE IMITATION

Will Rogers was criticized for an incident that occurred on January 4, 1928. In a national radio broadcast on the "Dodge Victory Hour," Will Rogers imitated President Calvin Coolidge, who had just delivered his state of the union message.

Mimicking the president's familiar Vermont twang, Will Rogers told his radio listeners:

"Ladies and Gentlemen: It's the duty of the president to deliver a message to the people on the condition of the country. I am proud to report that the condition of the country as a whole is prosperous. I don't mean by that the whole country is prosperous. But as a hole it's prosperous. That is it is prosperous for a hole. There is not a 'hole' lot of doubt about that."

Some listeners were fooled by the imitation. Receiving complaints, Rogers wrote a note to the president explaining that his talk was merely done in good fun. The president wrote back: "I hope it will cheer you up to know that I thought the matter of rather small consequence myself though the office was informed from several sources that I had been on the air. I hope you will not give the matter another troubled thought."

In his newspaper column Will Rogers publicly thanked President Coolidge for being big enough to take a joke. "I knew my man before I joked about him," wrote Will. "It's as I have often said: You can always joke goodnaturedly a big man, but be sure he is a big man before you joke about him."

(see HUMOR)

CONGRESS

"The national joke factory," as Will Rogers dubbed Congress, was the target of much of his sharp-pointed humor. "People ask me where I get my jokes," he shrugged. "Why, I just watch Congress and report the facts."

Congress is inherently comical. When in session it works like this, Will explained. "Somebody gets up to speak and says nothing. Nobody listens. And then everybody disagrees."

Despite all his barbs, Will Rogers was beloved in Congress—recognized as a kind of national jester—and warmly welcomed whenever he visited the galleries. Some of his jokes were even entered into the congressional record. When he heard about this honor, Will Rogers could not help but be pleased.

"I feel pretty good about that. That's the biggest praise a humorist can have, is to get your stuff into the congressional record. Just think, my name will be right along side all those other big humorists.

"They are the professional joke makers. I could study all my life and not think up half the amount of funny things they can think of in one session of Congress.

"Compared to them I'm an amateur. My jokes don't hurt anyone. You can take 'em or leave 'em. They don't do any harm. But Congress, every time they make a joke, it's a law. And every time they make a law, it's a joke."

But our Congress is still the best in the world. In fact, boasted Will Rogers, "we have the best Congress money can buy."

This country has come to feel the same when Congress is in session as we do when the baby gets hold of a hammer. It's just a question of how much damage he can do with it before you can take it away from him.

—*Daily Telegrams:* July 4, 1930
(see GOVERNMENT, POLITICIANS)

CONGRESSMAN-AT-LARGE

Will Rogers was elected congressman-at-large by the National Press Club in 1927. He was invited to a formal dinner at the Press Club in Washington, D.C., on August 27, where Senator Ashurst presented his official commission as congressman-at-large.

"Be it resolved," the senator read the official document, "that the National Press Club, recognizing superlative statesmanship when it sees it and believing that the country's greatest need is not a good 'five cent cigar' but a congressman, Will Rogers, hereby appoints the said Hon. Will Rogers congressman-at-large for the United States of America, effective immediately, his tenure to continue during good behavior."

Accepting the award, Will Rogers said, "I certainly regret the disgrace that's been thrust on me tonight. I certainly have lived, or tried to live, my life so that I would never become a congressman, and I am just as ashamed of the fact I have failed as you are. And to have the commission presented by a senator is adding insult to injury."

Will Rogers did his best to live down to his responsibilities as congressman-at-large.

CONSERVATIVE

"A conservative is a man who has plenty of money and doesn't see any reason why he shouldn't always have plenty of money," said Will Rogers. Republicans are generally conservatives, he explained, while Democrats generally can't afford it. "A Democrat is a fellow who never had any money but doesn't see why he shouldn't have some."

(see DEMOCRATS, REPUBLICANS, REVOLUTIONARY)

CONSTITUTION

If ever an industry was having a field day, it's the industry of paid leaders in every line, who are explaining to their followers "what the government owes them."

"If I remember right we owed more to the Constitution than it did to us.

(see TEETH)

COOKING

"When you have helped to raise the standard of cooking, you have helped to raise the only thing in the world that really matters anyhow," wrote Will Rogers in the foreword of *Fashions in Beverly Hills Foods,* a glorified cookbook published in 1931. "We only have one or two wars in a lifetime but we have three meals a day. There is nothing in the world that we do as much as we do eating."

CORRESPONDENCE

Like most celebrities, Will Rogers had difficulty keeping up with all his correspondence. It was in danger of becoming a burden to him until, through a combination of experimentation and meditation, he arrived at a method for dealing with it in an efficient and timely manner:

"Once a month I answer telegrams marked URGENT. Once a year I answer letters marked IMPORTANT."

CORRUPTION

It's awful hard to get people interested in corruption unless they can get some of it.

—*Weekly Articles,* April 22, 1928

CORSETS

In 1922 Will Rogers toured the banquet circuit. Instead of delivering the usual after-dinner speech, he startled his audiences by insulting them in the modern tradition of the comic "roast."

There was one professional group, however, about whom he could not find anything unkind to say: the corset manufacturers. Addressing the weighty leaders of the women's undergarment industry Will Rogers told them how essential their work was. "Just imagine, if you can, if the flesh of this country were allowed to wander around promiscuously! Why, there ain't no telling where it would wind up.

"The same problem confronts you that does the people that run the subways in New York City. You both have to get so many pounds of flesh into a given radius. The subway does it by having strong men to push and shove until they can just close the door with only the last man's foot out. But you corset manufacturers arrive at the same thing by a series of strings."

Will confessed that he did not fully understand the technical workings of the strings, or how to operate them unassisted. However, he did understand that the front lace "can be operated without a confederate," while the others require "accomplices."

(see FASHIONS, NUDE)

COST

It's not what you pay a man but what he costs you that counts.

—Weekly Articles: March 22, 1925

COST OF LIVING

Will Rogers was excited to learn from newspapers that a government committee appointed to investigate the high cost of living had released its anxiously awaited findings.

"I see a committee that was investigating the high cost of living turned in their report: 'We find the cost of living very high and we recommend more funds to carry on the investigation.'"

COUNTRY

A country is known by its strength, and a man by his check book.

—*Weekly Articles:* April 7, 1929

COUNTRY BOY

"I'm just an old country boy in a big town trying to get along." That's how Will Rogers described himself in a 1924 article.

A key to his success was staying true to his country boy instincts without falling into the trap of city sophistication. "I have been eating pretty regular," said Will Rogers with satisfaction, "and the reason I have been is because I have stayed an old country boy."

(see NATURAL)

COURAGE

Ain't it funny how many hundreds of thousands of soldiers we can recruit with nerve. But we just can't find one politician in a million with backbone.

—*Daily Telegrams:* February 18, 1929

COVERUP

"You can't believe a thing you read in regards to official statements," Will commented on a government statement that was very economical with the truth.

"The minute anything happens connected with official life, why, it's just like a cold night, everybody is trying to cover up. But the truth will gradually come out, though."

(see GOVERNMENT, TRUTH)

COWBOY

Cities are overcrowded and overpriced while ranch land sits idle. "So buy a ranch somewhere in the West," was Will's recommendation to the warriors of Wall Street. "All your life every man has wanted to be a cowboy. Why play Wall Street and die young when you can play cowboy and never die?"

(see WALL STREET)

CREDIT

No nation in the history of the world was ever sitting as pretty. If we want anything, all we have to do is go and buy it on credit. So that leaves us without any economic problems whatsoever, except perhaps some day to have to pay for them.

—*Daily Telegrams:* September 6, 1928

CRICKET

Will Rogers attended a cricket match during a visit to England, but he did not fully grasp the nature of the game and behaved inappropriately.

"That cricket game that I told you about, well, I have been thrown out of the grounds twice for applauding. They contend I was a boisterous element."

(see POLO SPILLS, PRINCE OF WALES)

55

CRIME

Crime does pay but not very well, according to Will Rogers. It's a fair living, but not a good living.

"Statistics have proved," he said, "that very few of the present-day criminals ever wind up with much. Then the late hours, and with the present price of ammunition and the inconvenience of getting it, and pistols—sometimes you have to walk a block—it just in the end figures out a fair living.

"As for crime and robberies, that is carrying just as heavy a burden now as it possibly can. It looks like it was making a lot of money, but it's not. The business is overcrowded."

(see ROBBERIES, TAX ON MURDERS)

CRIME AND PUNISHMENT

We are forgiving of the guilty, but not so forgiving of the innocent. We forgive the guilty, especially if they confess, but not the innocent, especially if they don't confess.

"It looks like after a person's guilt in this country is established," Will Rogers observed, "why then the battle as to whether he should be punished is the real test of the court. Of course if a fellow is never convicted and never confesses, why then they will hang him. But if he is lucky enough to get convicted or confess why he has a great chance of coming clear."

CRIME TAX

"We don't seem to be able to even check crime, so why not legalize it and put a heavy tax on it?"

Will Rogers' solution to the crime problem in the United States was to legalize it and tax it out of existence.

"We have taxed other industries out of business; it might work here."

(see ROBBERY, TAX ON MURDERS)

CRIMINALS

"We don't give our criminals much punishment, but we sure give 'em plenty of publicity." That was Will Rogers' caustic comment on the American criminal system in 1934 when organized crime was in its golden age.

On one occasion Rogers was allowed to interview the notorious Al Capone in jail. It was a journalistic coup. Rogers spent hours with Capone and took notes. Newspapers all over the country were clamoring for Rogers' report. But ultimately, after wrestling with his conscience, he decided not to publish a story. He felt criminals were already receiving too much publicity as it was. "There was absolutely no way I could write it and not make a hero out of him," Rogers reflected sadly. "What's the matter with an age when our biggest gangster is our greatest national interest?"

The gentle, humanitarian humorist surprised many social reformers by advocating stricter punishments for criminals:

"Of course, the surest way out of this crime wave would be to punish the criminals, but, of course, that is out of the question! That's barbarous, and takes us back, as the hysterics say, to the days before civilization."

Will Rogers felt courts were too lenient; he was in favor of stiffer sentences: "Nowadays the sentence reads: 'You are sentenced to prison as long as it's made comfortable for you and you desire to remain. In checking out kindly let the warden know, so he will know how many there will be for dinner.'

"Of all the cockeyed things we got in this country at the present time, it's some of our judges, and courts, and justices. We got more bandits out on bond than we got people for 'em to rob.

"It must be awful monotonous, belonging to one of these state parole boards. There is days and days when they just have to sit around, waiting for new criminals to be caught, so they can parole them."

The salvation of American murderers was the insanity plea, a cherished institution.

"American murder procedure is about as follows: foul enough to commit a crime, dumb enough to get caught, smart enough to prove you was crazy when you committed it, and fortunate enough not to hang for it."

No class of criminals have benefitted more from progress in our democracy than robbers.

"Robberies where they used to take your horse, and if they was caught, they got hung for it; now they take your car, and if they are caught it's a miracle, and they will perhaps have the inconvenience of having to go to court and explain."

Robbers have improved their standard of living greatly through the use of automatic weapons.

"Oh, we are living in progress," said Will Rogers. "All of our boasted inventions, like the auto and the automatic, and our increased 'dope' output, terrible liquor, lost confidence in our justice, graft from top to bottom, all these have made it possible to commit anything you can think of and in about 80 percent of the cases get away with it. We can get away quick in a car. He can't miss with the gun he's got. If he is caught he knows it will be accidental. Then if he is caught, his connections with his gang will get him out, so it's not a dangerous business after all, from the looks of it."

All they have to do to find out who the criminal is nowadays is just to find the one that's been pardoned the most times.

—*Daily Telegrams:* June 10, 1935

We go to great lengths to keep track of what a robber did, but none to find out where he went.

—*Daily Telegrams:* December 1, 1930
(see AUTOMATIC, MURDERERS, ROBBERS, WOMEN MURDERERS)

CRITICISM

I have found out that when newspapers knock a man a lot, there is sure to be a lot of good in him.

—*Weekly Articles:* April 15, 1923

CULTURE

Culture, after all, is nothing but studied indifference.

More Letters: May 19, 1928

D

DARK HORSE

Will Rogers received one vote at the 1924 Democratic convention. It came from the Arizona delegation where, according to some strange procedure which scarcely bears repeating in public, two half votes had been cast for Will Rogers, adding up to one vote total.

"These two half portion delegates from Arizona were by far the most intelligent men I have met during the entire convention," observed Will with considerable candor. "I had never met or heard of the men before. I had, by the way, heard of Arizona, and I want to here compliment the state on the men they produce."

Will admitted that with only one vote his chances of nomination were slim. "I am the dark horse. I am so dark that a black cat looks illuminated to me. I am such a dark candidate that they can't vote for me in the daytime."

(see NOMINATION, RESIGNATION, WITHDRAWAL)

DEATH

"Why is it the good ones are the ones that go?" asked Will Rogers. "That's one thing about an ornery guy, you never hear of him dying. He is into everything else but a coffin."

It is human nature to be fascinated with death. "Deaths get twice the notice that births do in papers. Nobody wants to know who was born, but everybody is anxious to know who dies, and the better known they are the more anxious they are to read about their death.

"It's only the inspiration of those who die that makes those who live realize what constitutes a useful life."

Will Rogers, who died too soon in a 1935 plane crash, advised against dying too soon. "We are living in great times. A fellow can't afford to die now with all this excitement going on."

If you live right, death is a joke to you as far as fear is concerned.

—*Weekly Articles:* May 24, 1925

DEBT

Will Rogers proposed a radical solution to the problem of debt.

"Every nation and every individual, their principal worry is debt.

"What would be the matter with this for relieving practically everybody's depression: just call all debts off.

"There can't be over a dozen men in the world that are owed more than they owe, so you wouldn't be hurting very many and besides if you give them some worry, that's what they had everybody else doing for years.

"This would give great temporary relief to 99 percent and would not hurt the others long," concluded Will Rogers, knowing the wealthy, "for they would soon have it back again."

There never was a debt that wasn't at some time or another misunderstood. Every debt, be it personal, or any other kind always winds up in one side feeling they got the worst of it.

—*Weekly Articles:* January 15, 1933

A debt is just as hard for a government to pay as it is for an individual. No debt ever comes due at a good time. Borrowing is the only thing that is handy all the time.

—*Daily Telegrams:* March 1, 1931
(see POOR, NATIONAL DEBT, UNEQUAL DISTRIBUTION)

DEMOCRACY

One of the evils of democracy is you have to put up with the man you elect whether you want him or not. That's why we call it democracy.

—*Daily Telegrams:* November 7, 1932

On account of us being a democracy, and run by the people, we are the only nation in the world that has to keep a government for four years, no matter what it does.

—*Daily Telegrams:* February 21, 1930

If the people had anything to do with the nominations, personally, instead of it being done by a half dozen men in the back rooms of some hotel, why America would be a democracy.

—*Weekly Articles:* November 2, 1924
(see VOTE)

DEMOCRAT

"I am not a member of any organized political party," declared Will Rogers, "I am a Democrat."

Will was broadminded politically. In other words, he was opposed to the policies of *both* the Democratic and

Republican parties. But he leaned a little more toward the Democrats' side. He understood the democratic character: part politician, part dreamer. "A Democrat never adjourns," Will observed. "He is born, becomes of age, and starts right in arguing over something, and his political adjournment is his date with the undertaker. Politics is business with the Democrat. He don't work at it, but he tells what he would do if he was working at it.

"These Democrats are a great bunch. Just as happy as if they were working."

Most Democratic voters were not loyal Democrats, they were aspiring Republicans who hadn't yet struck it rich. "They only vote for our gang when they are starved out," explained Will. "We fatten 'em up and then they turn Republican again."

You got to be funny to be a Democrat. It takes more humor to be a Democrat than it does a Republican anyhow.

—*Radio Broadcasts:* April 27, 1930

There is always excitement at a Democratic anything.

—*Weekly Articles:* June 14, 1928

The Republicans want a man that can lend dignity to the office, and the Democrats want a man that will lend some money.

—*Daily Telegrams:* July 11, 1930
(see REPUBLICANS)

DEMOCRATIC PARTY CORRUPTIONS

Will poked fun at the traditional corruption of each party. One of the corruptions Democrats were famous for was voting more than once. In Chicago there were not only many repeaters but many of them were dead. However, stricter voting procedures had forced the Democrats to abandon their traditional corruptions. According to Will Rogers, this was a reason for the decline of the party.

"What's wrong with the Democratic party?" Will asked. "The law killed it. It won't let a man vote but once, and there just ain't enough voters at one vote each to get it anywhere."

(see JACKSON, REPUBLICANS)

DEMOCRATIC POLITICS

Any two years away always looks like a Democratic year. In fact any two years away is a Democratic year. Democratic politics is what you might call future politics.

—*Letters of a Self-Made Diplomat,* p. 117
(see REPUBLICAN)

DEPRESSION

When the nation plunged into the Great Depression in late 1929, President Hoover swiftly took bold action. He appointed a commission to investigate.

"I could have told him before sundown what's changed our lives," said Will Rogers. "Buying on credit, waiting for relief, Ford cars, too many Republicans, Notre Dame coaching methods, and two-thirds of America, both old and young, thinking they possessed 'it.'

"It's really not depression, it's just a return to normalcy. It's just getting back to two-bit meals and cotton underwear, and off those one-fifty steaks and silk rompers. America has been just muscle bound from holding a steering wheel. The only callous place we got on our body is the bottom of the driving toe.

"We are getting back to earth and it don't look good to us after being away so long.

"We have watched the parade but we got no money to go to the show on, and we can't make up our minds to go home and start saving till next year."

Although the Republicans were in power, Will Rogers refused to blame them. "I don't want to lay the blame on the Republicans for the Depression. They're not smart enough to think up all those things that have happened."

Rogers placed some of the blame for the Depression on the gambling fever of speculation. The American dream of wealth through work had been replaced by the dream of wealth without work. "Half our people starving and the other half standing around a roulette wheel. They going to get some easy money if they have to go broke to do it."

Depression ain't nothing but old man interest just gnawing away at us.

—*Daily Telegrams:* February 7, 1933
(see CREDIT, NATIONAL DEBT, TAXES, WALL STREET)

DETROIT

Detroit has long suffered in the shadow of Chicago. "Chicago has been receiving tremendous amounts of advertising on their crime waves," noted Will, "while Detroit was having just as many casualties and not getting one tenth the publicity out of it. They were becoming discouraged.

"They said to me, 'What's the use of having all these robberies and killings? No one ever reads about them. Chicago seems to be the only place most people think that can put on a murder. They get more national recognition out of one retail shooting than we can out of the same thing done wholesale.'"

(see CHICAGO)

DILLINGER, JOHN

In 1934 the FBI's most wanted criminal, the gangster John Dillinger, was gunned down by government agents while leaving a movie theater one July evening.

"This is what comes of not following advice," remarked Will Rogers when he heard the news of Dillinger's death. Dillinger, he said, like all of America's young people, had been warned to stay away from the movies' bad influence.

"I wonder what picture it was that got him," Rogers added. "Hope it was mine."

(see MOVIES)

DINNER SPEECHES

Will Rogers sat through many long dinner speeches in his day, and he had great sympathy for those who had to sit through dinner speeches, including his own. He recommended chili.

"You know a man with a message is a whole lot harder to listen to than any other species of speaker," he said. "That is why I recommend chili."

(see CHILI)

DIPLOMACY

Diplomacy: doing just what you said you wouldn't.

—*Weekly Articles:* June 30, 1929

DIPLOMAT

"A diplomat is a man who tells you what he don't believe himself," explained Will Rogers. Not that he is believed. "The man he is telling it to doesn't believe it any more than he does. So diplomacy is always equal. It's like good bookkeeping. He don't believe you and you don't believe him, so it always balances.

"A diplomat is one that says something that is equally misunderstood by both sides and never clear to either."

Diplomats don't usually accomplish much, but they have always been indispensable in starting wars. "Diplomats are just as essential to starting a war as soldiers are for finishing it," stated Will Rogers.

"Diplomats don't mind starting a war because it's a custom that they are to be brought safely home before the trouble starts. There should be a new rule saying: 'If you start a war while you are your country's official handicap to some other country, you have to stay with any war you start.' "

(see FOREIGN RELATIONS, INTERNATIONAL RELATIONS, PEACE, WAR)

DIPLOMATIC SELECTION

Will Rogers' recommendation for selecting diplomats in the future is to get people that "love to travel and don't take international affairs too serious. Just go for the trip and the laughs."

DISARMAMENT

There is nothing to prevent their succeeding except human nature.

—Daily Telegrams: February 3, 1932
(see WAR)

DISTRIBUTION OF WEALTH

"We are known as the wealthiest nation of all time," said Will Rogers. "The difference between our rich and poor grows greater every year. Our distribution of wealth is getting more uneven all the time.

"Everybody knows that one of our great ills today is the unequal distribution of wealth. You are either at a banquet in this country, or you are at a hot dog stand."

(see UNEQUAL DISTRIBUTION)

DIVORCE

A rising divorce rate is a symptom of affluence, according to Rogers. "Somebody is always quoting figures to prove the country is prosperous, but the only real bona fide indication of it was in the paper today: 'Divorces in Reno have increased over 105 percent in the last year.' Now, that's prosperity, for you can't be broke and get a divorce. That's why the poor have to live with each other."

Rogers offered this suggestion to prevent a decline in the institution of marriage: "I maintain that it should cost as much to get married as to get divorced. Make it look like marriage is worth as much as divorce, even if it ain't. That would make the preachers financially independent, like it has the lawyers."

(see HOLLYWOOD WEDDINGS, MARRIAGE PREDICTION)

DOCTORS

In the age of specialization, Will Rogers feared doctors were becoming overspecialized. "This is a day of specializing, especially with the doctors. Say, for instance, there is something the matter with your right eye. You go to a doctor and he tells you, 'I am sorry, but I am a left-eye doctor; I make a specialty of left eyes.' "

Rogers gave another medical example. "Take the throat business. A doctor that doctors on the upper part of your throat doesn't even know where the lower part goes to."

A human being should be treated as a whole being, not a part. "The old-fashioned doctor didn't pick out a big toe or a left ear to make a life's living on. He picked out the whole human frame. Personally, I have always felt that the best doctor in the world is the veterinarian. He can't ask his patients what is the matter—he's got to just know."

(see GALLSTONES, TEETH)

DOG

"I love a dog," said Will in tribute to man's best friend. "He does nothing for political reasons."

DOLLAR

Our problem is not what is the dollar worth in London, Rome, or Paris, or what even it is worth at home. It's how to get hold of it, whatever it's worth!

—*Weekly Articles:* July 23, 1933

There is not a country in the world that can change our outlook as quick as we can. Just a dollar in our pocket makes a different man out of us.

—*Weekly Articles:* April 21, 1935

DOPEY

Will's favorite old horse was named Dopey. "But Dopey belonged to the family," he reminisced. "Our children learned to ride at two, and during his lifetime he never did a wrong thing to throw one off, or do a wrong thing after they had fallen off. He couldn't pick 'em up, but he would stand there and look at 'em with a disgusted look for being so clumsy."

(see HORSES)

DRESS SUITS

Will Rogers was reluctant to wear full dress suits, even on very formal occasions. It went against his code of naturalness. He claimed to be the only man to do a concert at Carnegie Hall without wearing a dress suit.

"I have seen a lot of artists' dress suits and I knew I couldn't compete with them, so I didn't rent one. I just stuck to the old blue serge with the mirror effect in the seat and knees."

(see CARNEGIE HALL)

DRIVING

When an Englishman, Malcolm Campbell, set a world automobile speed record of 276 miles per hour in March, 1935, Will commented: "It does seem strange that we don't hold the automobile speed record, for we have millions trying to break it every day."

(see SPEED, PROGRESS)

DROUGHT

Sunny Southern California weather is oversold. It's not ideal weather. "We need rain," wrote Will Rogers, surveying the scene from his Santa Monica ranch.

"It hasn't rained here since Noah took two of every kind of moving picture actor and actress into the ark with him. Moths have lived on raincoats for years. They revived the great stage play of *Rain* and had a footnote telling the audience what it was.

"This is mighty dry humor, but, friends, we would welcome the Johnstown flood right now."

"P.S." Will added, "California paper, go ahead and print this, and show 'em we can take it on the chin and still grin."

(see CALIFORNIA)

E

EATEN

"No thanks, I've already et," Will Rogers patted his stomach as he declined a dinner invitation.

"You should say 'have eaten,'" he was kindly corrected by a friend who possessed greater mastery of English.

"Well," drawled Rogers, who was proud of having achieved success without benefit of formal education, "I know a lot of fellers who say 'have eaten' who ain't et!"

(see HIGHER EDUCATION)

ECLIPSE

There was a lot of excitement over the "100 percent eclipse" in Mexico in September of 1926. An inveterate trend-observer, Will Rogers followed a brigade of scientists and other interested persons to Tia Juana, Mexico, to see the eclipse.

Afterward he wrote about the experience with mixed

feelings. "I have just this minute returned from Tia Juana, Mexico, where I, along with some thousands of other scientists, went to observe the total eclipse."

Will frankly admitted he was somewhat disappointed by the eclipse. "It didn't do anything. You see from the amount of press stuff written about it most people kinder thought it would do some tricks, maybe juggle or shimmy or something like that. It just passed—that's all. I personally, along with all the others, couldn't see anything so wonderful about its doing that.

"If the two planets hadn't passed but had hit, that would have been something to see.

"Of course, I will admit in this day of congested traffic, for any two given objects to meet and pass without hitting is considered wonderful."

ECONOMIC CRISIS

Why don't somebody print the truth about our present economic situation? We spent six years of wild buying on credit (everything under the sun, whether we needed it or not) and now we are having to pay for 'em under Mr. Hoover, and we are howling like a pet coon.

P.S. This would be a great world to dance in if we didn't have to pay the fiddler.

—*Daily Telegrams:* June 27, 1930
(see DEBT, DEPRESSION, NATIONAL DEBT, WORK)

ECONOMIC JARGON

As economic problems get worse, economic jargon gets more complicated. In a 1933 radio broadcast Will Rogers tried to explain President Roosevelt's New Deal legislation during the Depression:

"What we are trying to do is elevate the commodity prices, plus the cost of production, and increase the purchasing power within the means of the purchaser, or plus the cost of production and thereby enhance the buying power plus liquidation and receiving fees, etcetera, etcetera."

Here his voice began to break under the weight of the jargon, and he hastened to a conclusion. "*E pluribus unum* ... which about covers the whole situation as Mr. Einstein laid it out to us."

ECONOMICS

The one way to detect a feebleminded man is to get one arguing on economics.

—*Daily Telegrams:* October 6, 1933

ECONOMIST

An economist is a man that can tell you anything—he'll tell you what can happen under any given conditions, and his guess is liable to be just as good as anybody else's, too.

—*Radio Broadcasts,* May 26, 1935

ECONOMIST COMPANION

When Will was introduced to a senator, he noticed the senator had a peculiar companion. The companion turned out to be an economist.

"This fellow had an economist with him. Pretty near everbody's got one, either that or a police dog, and the more wealthy have got both."

EDUCATED MAN

There is nothing as stupid as an educated man if you get him off the thing he was educated in.

—*Weekly Articles:* July 5, 1931

EDUCATION

"Education never helped morals. The most savage people we have are the most moral. The smarter the guy the bigger the rascal," said Will Rogers.

"Education is just like everything else. You got to judge it by its results. Here we are better educated (according to educational methods) than we ever were. And we are worse off than we ever were, so it's not living up to its billing. It's over rated. It's not worth the price.

"It's costing us more than it's worth. They got to devise some way of giving more for the money. All he is getting out with now is credit and nobody on the outside is cashing 'em.

"For our own educational system is to teach our youth to learn something so that he will feel assured he won't have to do any manual labor through life."

According to Will Rogers, Americans lost respect for education once the state took it over and made it compulsory. Free education in the public schools was common. Common things in a democratic society are held in contempt. The only education Americans respect is high-priced education or higher education.

"The minute a thing is high-priced, you immediately create a desire for it. You give liquor away tomorrow like water and the novelty of being drunk would be over in a week, and nobody would touch the stuff. It's like golf, you let the poor all get to playing it and you watch the rich give it up. So make the government make it, and give it away, and we will all be disgusted with it. Americans don't like common things."

(see PROHIBITION, SCHOOLS)

EDUCATIONAL REFORM

There is nothing new about the crisis in the American educational system. In Will Rogers' day, as today, people were very concerned about the decline in American education. Based on the national experience with Prohibition, Rogers offered this prescription for educational reform: "Why don't they pass a constitutional amendment prohibiting anybody from learning anything? And if it works as good as the Prohibition one did, in five years we would have the smartest race of people on earth."

ELECTIONS

"Wouldn't it be great" if other countries "started electing by the ballot instead of the bullet," asked Will Rogers, "and us electing by the ballot instead of by the bullion?"

While Rogers believed religiously in democracy for Americans, he did not want to see America forcibly impose elective government on other nations. "When we start trying to make everybody have 'moral' elections, why, it just don't look like we are going to have enough Marines to go around."

American elections were more peaceful and regular than other countries, perhaps, but no less ridiculous.

"Well, the election will be breaking out pretty soon," said Will in 1930, "and a flock of Democrats will replace a mess of Republicans in quite a few districts. It won't mean a thing, they will go in like all the rest of 'em, go in on promises and come out on alibis."

"Elections are a good deal like marriages, there's no accounting for anyone's taste. Every time we see a bridegroom we wonder why she ever picked him, and it's the same with the public."

Elections are invaluable, however, for providing the people with a peaceful way of throwing politicians out of office. Without elections there would be no getting rid of them. "That's the trouble with a politician's life," said Will, "somebody is always interrupting it with an election."

75

When there is money in an election, it's always doubtful.

—*Weekly Articles:* September 23, 1928

It's really more of an endorsement to be defeated than to be elected.

—*Daily Telegrams:* January 30, 1927
(see MUNICIPAL ELECTIONS, POLITICIANS)

ENDORSEMENT

A piano manufacturer once asked Will Rogers to write a brief testimonial for one of their pianos. Unable to play the piano, Rogers was unwilling to endorse anything he could not personally put to the test. "Dear Sirs," he wrote politely, "I guess your pianos are the best I ever leaned against. Yours truly, Will Rogers."

(see HEALING WATERS)

ENGLAND

"Always remember she never looks good till it looks bad, then she comes through." That was Will Rogers' description of the English national character. "A nation is built on character the same as a person is and no matter what their financial difficulties are that old character shows up."

ENGLISH GENTLEMAN

In England it's easy to tell who is a gentleman and who is not, said Will. "A gentleman in England is a man that disagrees with whatever the laboring party wants."

(see GENTLEMEN, GOLF)

ENGLISH INSULTS

Will Rogers liked the Englishmen he met, but he couldn't tell if they were for him or against him.

"That's one thing about an Englishman, he can insult you, but he can do it so slick and polite, that he will have you guessing until away after he leaves you just whether he was friend or foe."

ENGLISH STRIKERS

There was a strike going on in England during a Will Rogers visit. Although he expressed democratic solidarity with the strikers in principle, he admitted some confusion as to their identity.

"The hard thing in this British strike from an American standpoint, is to look at an Englishman and judge from the way he is working, whether he is on strike or not."

(see PROSPERITY, WORK)

EPITAPH

Few have the luxury or foresight to write their own epitaphs. Will Rogers planned ahead. On June 15, 1930, he was attending Tremont Temple Baptist Church, and the minister, James Brougher, called on Will to say a few words. Will took advantage of this opportunity to lay the groundwork for his epitaph. He said:

"When I die, my epitaph or whatever you call those signs on gravestones is going to read: 'I joked about every prominent man of my time, but I never met a man I didn't like.' I am so proud of that I can hardly wait to die so it can be carved. And when you come to my grave you will find me sitting there, proudly reading it."

Newspapers printed Will's statement and after his death in 1935 his wishes were carried out.

He is buried at the Will Rogers Memorial in Claremore, Oklahoma, on land he purchased for retirement. The inscription simply says: "I never met a man I didn't like."

(see HUMOR, ROGERS)

EQUALITY

Equality begins in the belly. "The Lord so constituted everybody that no matter what color you are," said Will, "you require the same amount of nourishment."

EUROPE

"It is the open season now in Europe for grouse and Americans," Rogers cabled from London in 1926. "They shoot the grouse and put them out of their misery."

Will Rogers frequently commented on Europe's war debts to the United States. "Don't ever lay the fault on Europe for not paying us. They would start tomorrow if we would just loan 'em the money to do it on."

"One good thing about European nations: They can't hate you so bad they wouldn't use you.

"I would like to stay in Europe long enough to find some country that don't blame America for everything in the world that's happening to them—debts, depression, disarmament, disease, fog, famine, or frostbite. Now the birthrate is falling, so I am going to get out of here before we get blamed.

"The only way we would be worse with them was to help them out in another war."

Europe is supposed to be artistic, but if I had to judge I should place their financial ahead of their artistic ability. So in offering prayers for downtrodden races, I would advise you not to overlook the downtrodden tourist.

—*Weekly Articles:* June 27, 1926

There ought to be a law against anybody going to Europe till they had seen the things we have in this country.

—*Daily Telegrams:* August 14, 1930
(see INTERNATIONAL, TOURISTS, UNITED)

EXPLANATIONS

We are living in an age of explanations, and plenty of
'em too. No two things that's been done to us has been
explained twice the same way by even the same man.

—*Weekly Articles:* January 28, 1934

When you straddle a thing it takes a long time to explain
it.

—*Convention Articles:* June 29, 1924
(see FENCE STRADDLING)

EXPORTS

Will Rogers proposed an ingenious scheme for eliminating our national trade deficit: export our politicians.

"Now, nations are just so many men like these. Each
can produce something better and cheaper than the rest.
Maybe it's by nature, climate, talent, or thrift.

"Among the commodities, which we could prove we
excelled in is officeholders and politicians. Along with a
free market for our wheat, meat, cotton, and automobiles, we could send 'em all the politicians they need. For
instance, Russia some senators for some vodka, little Nicaragua some congressmen for some bananas.

"I tell you, the whole fool scheme is worth trying, just
for the sake of this last part. If we can furnish the world
with our politicians, we can compete with 'em."

F

FAME

"We have statues built to every person who had a good press agent during their lives," Will Rogers remarked.

In the age of publicity fame itself is suspect. "The more people study about you, nowadays," said Will, "the less they think of you."

(see CHRIST, HEROES, PUBLICITY)

FAMILY TREE

In response to a request from the Daughters of the American Revolution, Will Rogers tried to trace his family tree, but he got lost on a lower limb. "We don't hardly know what to trace our birth to," he confessed. "I started to have my ancestors looked into one time, and they got back one generation and had one of the family up on a limb for horse stealing, and I asked them to discontinue."

(see ANCESTORS)

FANATIC

A fanatic is always the fellow that is on the opposite side.

—*Radio Broadcasts*, June 18, 1930
(see ANARCHIST)

FARMERS

Farmers are learning that the relief they get from the sky beats what they get from Washington.

—*Daily Telegrams:* June 4, 1934

FASHIONS

In 1930 women's hemlines peaked far above the knees and began to fall again. Will Rogers was an acute observer of fashion trends and women's legs.

"You see according to law, fashions must change every year, sometimes every month, and in order to change dresses' style, you have to either go up or down, the crossways change don't count, or show much. So if you can only change one way or the other and you have been going one way for years, why it stands to reason that the worm must turn sometimes, even if it's a silk worm. Well, skirts had just gone so high there wasn't anything to 'em, and the material people put up a howl. Men had just about lost interest in 'em, or below 'em."

So the skirts had to come down.

(see KNEES, LONG SKIRTS)

FATHER'S DAY

Many fathers dread Father's Day and some men avoid fatherhood altogether so they won't have to deal with it. Will Rogers offered this suggestion for Father's Day:

"No flowers, no fuss—just let him use the car himself

and go where he wants to. But we will never live to see such a contented day."

(see HOLIDAY, LABOR DAY)

FENCE STRADDLING

Both parties adopted an ambiguous platform on the Prohibition question during the 1928 conventions, trying not to offend anyone. Will Rogers came forward and offered a fence-straddling slogan he hoped would be acceptable to all parties:

Wine for the rich, beer for the poor
And moonshine liquor for the prohibitionist.

(see EXPLANATIONS, MILLS)

FICTION

Congress has got more fiction in it in a day than writers can think of in a year.

—*Weekly Articles:* May 12, 1929

FILIBUSTER

A filibuster in the senate prompted Will Rogers to comment: "The name is just as silly as the thing itself. It means that a man can get up and talk for fifteen or twenty hours at a time, just to keep some bill from coming to a vote, no matter about the merit of this particular bill, whether it's good or bad.

"There is no other body of lawmakers in the world that has a thing like it. Why, if an inmate did that in an asylum they would put him in solitary confinement. And, mind you, if any demented person spoke that long there would be something in his speech you would remember,

82

for he, at least, had to be smart or he would never have gone crazy. These just mumble away on any subject.

"Imagine a ball player standing at bat and not letting the other side play, to keep from having the game called against him; or an actor, the first one in a show, talking all night to keep the rest from going on. You know how long he would last. It's against all the laws of American sportsmanship, never mind the parliamentary part of it.

"One senator threatened to read the Bible into the record as part of his speech, and I guess he would have done it if somebody in the Capitol had had a Bible."

(see CONGRESS, SENATE)

FINANCES

We will never get anywhere with our finances till we pass a law saying that every time we appropriate something we got to pass another bill along with it stating where the money is coming from.

—Daily Telegrams: February 12, 1932
(see GOVERNMENT SPENDING, TAXES)

FIREWORKS

When the Fourth of July and a Sunday come together there just ain't nothing to do on Monday but send flowers.

—Daily Telegrams: July 6, 1931

FIRST PAYMENT

Don't make the first payment on anything. First payments is what makes us think we were prosperous, and the other nineteen is what showed us we were broke.

Daily Telegrams: July 9, 1930

FISHING

When President Coolidge took off for a fishing holiday, Will Rogers figured he would go fishing too. "I am not going to fish for 'em like he did though," said Will, observing that the president had very little luck in attracting fish. A natural-born country boy, Will Rogers knew the secrets of country life: "I am just going out on the porch and call 'em and cook the first ten that comes."

FIXING THINGS

Things in our country are not ever fixed, they just wear themselves out.

—*Daily Telegrams:* March 25, 1934

FLYING

Will Rogers may not have known he would die in a plane crash, but he loved to fly, especially at night.

"Ah, say, fly over a big city at night! Daytime is like slumming compared to seeing a big lighted city from the air at night."

There was only one problem with sightseeing from the air. "Yes, sir, a plane is a great place to see anything, only the wings are right under where you want to look and you can't see anything."

FOOD

Yours for corn bread, chitlins, and turnip greens.

—*Daily Telegrams:* May 15, 1927
(see BEANS, CHILI)

FOOTBALL

Football in South America is almost as violent as political revolution, Will Rogers noted during a tour of Peru.

"After a soccer game in Lima, Peru, five were killed. They only kill ten in a revolution down there, so two games equal one revolution.

"Up here we don't kill our football players. We make coaches out of the smartest ones, and send the others to the legislature."

(see LATIN AMERICAN REVOLUTIONS, URUGUAY)

FORD, HENRY

Assessing the great impact of Henry Ford on his sixty-sixth birthday, Will wrote this tribute to the father of the Automobile Age:

"Great educators try to teach people, preachers try to change people, but no man produced through the accepted channels has moved the world like Henry Ford. He put wheels on our homes, a man's castle is his sedan. Life's greatest catastrophe is a puncture. Americans don't fear the Lord as much as they do the next payment. Everybody is rushing to get somewhere, where they have no business, so they can hurry back to the place where they should never have left.

"So good luck, Mr. Ford. It will take a hundred years to tell whether you have helped us or hurt us, but you certainly didn't leave us like you found us."

(see AUTOMOBILE AGE)

FOREIGN AFFAIRS

"Who is the next country that wants their affairs regulated?" Will Rogers asked. Dismayed the United States Marines were interfering with governments all over the world, Rogers proposed America's next foreign adventure be staged in Nicaragua, as Nicaragua was closer to home and more convenient.

"If Nicaragua would just come out like a man and

fight us," he said, "we wouldn't have to be hunting away off over in China for a war.

"America could hunt all over the world and not find a better fight to keep out of," he said, than the one in China.

"It had just become almost impossible for a country to have a nice home-talent little revolution among themselves, without us butting in.

"Now if there is one thing that we do worse than any other nation, it is try and manage somebody else's affairs.

"We are liable to get a bad kick back from a lot of this high-handed stuff we are pulling. We are riding a high horse.

"Between our missionaries and our oil men, we are just about in wrong all over the world."

There's one thing no nation can accuse us of—that is secret diplomacy. Our foreign dealings are an open book—generally a check book.

—*Weekly Articles:* October 21, 1923
(see BUSYBODIES, INTERNATIONAL AFFAIRS, RIDING HIGH)

FOREIGN RELATIONS

We got too many relations with 'em now. It's great to be friendly with a foreign nation, but it's terribly expensive.

—*More Letters:* November 20, 1931

My business is not to increase our foreign relations but abolish 'em entirely.

—*More Letters:* November 20, 1931
(see INTERNATIONAL RELATIONS, TOURISTS)

FOURTH OF JULY

"We have killed more people celebrating our Independence Day," Will Rogers lamented, "than we lost fighting for it."

(see FIREWORKS)

FRANCE

France protested the terms of repayment of their American loans after the First World War and kept renegotiating more favorable terms. "We thought we had it settled at about five cents on the dollar," Will noted. "But now we find they think we were too severe, so the chances are we will pay them something and call it even."

A bunch of American tourists were hissed and stoned yesterday in France, but not until they had finished buying.

—Daily Telegrams: August 2, 1926
(see EUROPE, TOURISTS)

FREEDOM

A delegation of senators and congressmen will be the ones to decide just how far advanced you are in intelligence and how many years away from freedom, it won't be the people that will do that.

—More Letters: April 30, 1932, p. 172
(see LIBERTY, VOTE)

FRIENDS

You got to sorter give and take in this old world. We can get mighty rich, but if we haven't got any friends, we will find we are poorer than anybody.

—Weekly Articles: June 1, 1930

FUNNY

Will Rogers could see humor in everything. "Everything is funny," he said, "as long as it is happening to somebody else."

FUTURE

Actual knowledge of the future was never lower, but hope was never higher. Confidence will beat predictions any time.

—*Daily Telegrams:* September 19, 1933
(see CONFIDENCE, KNOWLEDGE)

G

GALLSTONES

While visiting Bluefield, West Virginia, during a lecture tour in 1927, Will Rogers was suddenly afflicted with severe stomach pains.

"Ordinarily when a pain hits you in the stomach in Bluefield, West Virginia, you would take it for gunshot wounds," Rogers explained. But this turned out to be something more serious.

Returning home to Beverly Hills, Will went to see his physician, Dr. Percy White, who diagnosed the ailment as gallstones. A second opinion was called for, and furnished. According to Rogers' recollection, Dr. White "phoned for what seemed like a friend, but who afterwards turned out to be an accomplice." The accomplice was a surgeon named Dr. Clarence Moore, whom Will described fondly as "the most famous machete wielder on the western coast."

Will asked what the doctor advised. The doctor advised surgery.

Later Will realized he needn't have asked. "Imagine

asking a surgeon what he advises! It would be like asking [President] Coolidge, 'Do you advise economy?' "

Just before Will Rogers was wheeled into the operating room he dictated his daily newspaper telegram. "I am in California Hospital, where they are going to relieve me of surplus gall," he wrote gallantly. "Let the stones fall where they may."

Rogers' illness turned out to be more serious than anyone anticipated and he nearly died. As always the humorist made light of his experiences and wound up writing a book about his gallstone adventures, *Ether and me, or "Just Relax."*

His condition was grave for several days after the operation. During his long recuperation Will Rogers was cheered by hundreds of telegrams from all over the country. Even President Coolidge, who had been the butt of many of Rogers' barbs, sent a get-well card.

A grateful Rogers remarked, "People couldn't have been any nicer to me if I had died."

(see OPERATION)

GAMBLING

Will Rogers suggested gambling as an alternative to taxation for raising revenue for the state.

"Monaco has the right idea. Fix a game where you are going to get it, but the fellow don't know you are getting it. A fellow can always get over losing money in a game of chance, but he seems so constituted that he can never get over money thrown away to a government in taxes. In other words, he will bet you on anything, but he won't pay it to you in taxes."

(see HORSES, TAXES, WALL STREET)

GENERATION

The trouble with this generation is they are getting too wise. That is they are getting too wise about things which they ought not to get wise about, and learning none of the things that might be any good to 'em afterwards.

—*Weekly Articles:* January 6, 1929

GENTLEMEN

Will Rogers sometimes opened his public speeches this way: "Gentlemen and Democrats."

It's easy to define a gentleman, a gentleman is to my way of thinking a man that can play golf and don't say so.

—*Weekly Articles:* August 10, 1930
(see DEMOCRAT, ENGLISH GENTLEMAN)

GERMAN SENSE OF HUMOR

During a performance in Berlin in 1906 Will Rogers was standing on stage when he noticed a uniformed German fireman hovering in the wings. Thinking it might be an amusing gag, Will roped the fireman, demonstrating considerable roping skill, catching him in a loop, pinning his arms to his sides, and pulling him onto the stage.

He expected laughter, he got stunned silence.

The manager of the music hall rushed on stage and apologized to the audience, saying the American performer's rope had slipped.

Will wrote home: "In Germany they have cultivated everything they got, but humor."

(see HUMOR, MISSED TRICK)

GOD

"Our religious beliefs are many, but one belief is universal with all, and that is that there is some divine being higher than earthly," Will responded to a questioning of his beliefs. "We can speak to Him in many devious ways, in many languages, but He sees us all in the same light, and judges us according to our actions, as we judge the actions of our children different because we know they are each different."

GOLF

"People ask what's the matter with this country," said the gum-chewing cowboy philosopher. "Nothing, only there is millions got a putter in their hand when they ought to have a shovel."

But golf is a good escape from life's responsibilities. "I guess there is nothing that will get your mind off everything like golf will. I have never been depressed enough to take up the game, but they say you can get so sore at yourself that you forget to hate your enemies.

"Golf is the only game in the world where it takes longer to explain than it does to play. You play it in two hours, and it takes the other twenty-two alibiing for what you didn't do."

I often wonder how they distinguished a gentleman in the old days when there was no golf.

—*Weekly Articles:* January 21, 1923
(see GENTLEMEN, HIGH STANDARD OF LIVING)

GOLF PARTNER

Then there is a pardner, or accomplice, who plays along with you. You are not sent out for company but to annoy each other. If it wasn't for watching what he was doing you could do pretty good.

—*Weekly Articles:* December 29, 1929
(see GENTLEMEN, HIGH STANDARD OF LIVING)

GOOD INTENTIONS

"All we have to do to get in bad is just to start out on what we think is a good-Samaritan mission, and we wind up in the pesthouse," wrote Will Rogers in a public letter to the president.

"We mean well, but the better we mean the worse we get in."

(see FOREIGN RELATIONS, INTERNATIONAL RELATIONS, MARINES)

GOOD MAN

Personally I think this is the right year for a good man to be defeated in.

—*Daily Telegrams:* November 2, 1930
(see ELECTIONS)

GOOD OLD DAYS

The good old days with most of us was when we didn't earn enough to pay an income tax.

—*Daily Telegrams:* March 31, 1935

GOVERNMENT

We should never blame the government for not doing something, said Will Rogers. "It's when they do something is when they become dangerous."

(see LEGISLATIVE BODY)

GOVERNMENT, UNITED STATES

Will Rogers had a profound understanding of the American system of government and its intricate checks and balances. This is how he explained the relationship between the Senate and the House of Representatives:

"You see they have two of these bodies—Senate and Congress. That is for the convenience of visitors. If there is nothing funny happening in one there is sure to be in the other, and in case one body passes a good bill, why the other can see it in time, and kill it."

The government is supposed to manage the country's business, not manage the country's businesses. It is not qualified to do the latter. "You could transfer the Senate and Congress over to run the Standard Oil, or General Motors, and they would have both things bankrupt in two years," Will predicted. "No other business in the world could afford to carry such dead wood."

The problem with government is it's too political: "If we could just send the same bunch of men to Washington for the good of the nation, and not for political reasons, we could have the most perfect government in the world."

Will Rogers was realistic about the role of government: "Things in our country run in spite of government. Not by the aid of it."

(see GOVERNMENT SPENDING)

GOVERNMENTESE

Will Rogers mastered the language of twentieth-century government bureaucracy. He deciphered all the terms government officials employ to assure the public they are doing something when they are doing the opposite.

"Well, the conference met today," he wrote from London where he was attending an international conference, "and appointed a commission to meet tomorrow and appoint a delegation who will eventually appoint a sub-committee to draw up ways and means of finding out what to start with first."

(see CONFERENCE, ECONOMIC JARGON)

GOVERNMENT INTERFERENCE

If every man was left absolutely to his own method of righting his own affairs, why, a big majority would get it done. But he can't do that. The government has not only hundreds but literally thousands in Washington to see that no man can personally attend to his own business.

—*Weekly Articles:* April 17, 1932

GOVERNMENT OVERTHROW

The best time to overthrow a government, Will Rogers advised, was when their army was away from home.

"That's when all governments change hands, when the army is away trying to take care of somebody else."

(see FOREIGN AFFAIRS, WAR)

GOVERNMENT RELIEF

The whole idea of government relief for the last few years has been to loan somebody more money, so they could go further in debt. It ain't much relief to just transfer your debts from one party to another adding a little more into the bargain.

—*Weekly Articles:* November 27, 1932
(see DEBT, NATIONAL DEBT)

GOVERNMENT SPENDING

Government spending has run amuck in the twentieth century. "All you read about Washington is how they are

going to spend those billions of dollars. There hasn't
been even one suggestion as to where it was to come
from."

Even the cost of saving money through cost-cutting
programs has increased: "The Treasury Department has
saved some money, but it showed that it cost millions
more to save it than it did in the same department last
year, showing that even the cost of saving money has
gone up."

It costs ten times more to govern us than it used to, and
we are not governed one-tenth as good.

—*Daily Telegrams:* March 27, 1931

It must be marvelous to just belong to some legislative
body and just pick money out of the air.

—*Daily Telegrams:* February 28, 1935

There is not a man in the country that can't make a living
for himself and family. But, he can't make a living for
them and his government, too, the way his government
is living.

—*Daily Telegrams:* December 20, 1932

GRAFT

Public outcry over corruption in New York City led the
mayor to call "a hundred prominent citizens to discuss
graft with him."

Will Rogers had no objection to this plan, he even approved it. After all, it would make no sense for the
mayor to "call in a hundred poor men to discuss graft, as
they would have no technical knowledge of the subject."

The conference on graft was held, but no decision was
made. "These one hundred met and adjourned, without
adopting any resolution to either halt or increase it," reported Will. "It seemed everyone was satisfied as it is.

"The way we do things, always have done things and always will do things, there just has to be so much graft. We wouldn't feel good if there wasn't. We just have to get used to charging so much off to graft just like you charge off so much for insurance, taxes, or depreciation."

(see CORRUPTION, DEMOCRATIC CORRUPTIONS, REPUBLICAN)

GREATNESS

"You must judge a man's greatness by how much he will be missed," said Will Rogers.

"It's great to be great but it's greater to be human."

I admire any man that can rise above his surroundings.

—*Radio Broadcasts*, May 18, 1930

GROUND HOG DAY

I don't know what the ground hog saw, but we didn't even see the ground all day.

—*Daily Telegrams:* February 2, 1934

GUESTS

William Randolph Hearst once invited Will Rogers down to San Simeon for one of the millionaire's famous week-end parties. The host had assembled a distinguished group of guests, of whom Rogers was the leading celebrity. Hearst took advantage of every opportunity to show off his star to the company, with the result that Rogers spent most of the weekend amusing the other guests.

The following week Hearst received a bill from Rogers for two thousand dollars for services as a professional entertainer. Hearst called Rogers on the phone and said heatedly, "I didn't engage you to come as an entertainer. I invited you as a guest."

"When people invite me as a guest," Will replied,

"they invite Mrs. Rogers, too. When they ask me to come alone, I go as a professional entertainer."

This charming story is an example of the kind of anecdote that sticks to celebrities. Both Will and Betty Rogers denied it ever happened.

(see ROGERS, BETTY)

GUNS

England's got a gun, France has got a gun, Italy's got a gun. Germany wants a gun, Austria wants a gun. All God's children want guns, going to put on the guns, going to buckle on the guns, and smear up all of God's heaven.

All these come from treaties that say, "I will have two guns, and you have one."

—*Daily Telegrams:* April 4, 1935

GUNBOAT DIPLOMACY

China is having a new war, and we are having trouble getting into it. We always have gunboats there, so if there is any shooting, why, one of our boats will be shot at and that gives us the usual alibi.

But this time it seems we only had one gunboat and it had to maneuver around for days before it could get in the line of fire.

—*Daily Telegrams:* August 3, 1930
(see FOREIGN AFFAIRS, MARINES)

GUN CONTROL

I see a lot of men are advocating letting everybody carry guns, with the idea that they will be able to protect themselves. In other words, just make a civil war out of this crime wave.

When you see a man coming and he looks like he

hasn't got as much as you and might want to rob you, why, just open up on him with your miniature Gatling gun. Wave it around in his general direction (your eyes can be shut if you prefer) and you will get him, or somebody else. He may start shooting at you thinking you are trying to murder him or rob him, so let every man protect himself—no policeman necessary—that is the slogan of these people.

—*Weekly Articles:* September 20, 1925

Can you imagine arresting a man in America for carrying a gun nowadays? Why, in Chicago there is pistol pockets put in your pajamas. There is thousands there that are faultlessly dressed in artillery that haven't got underwear on.

—*Weekly Articles:* March 30, 1930

Now we gather to disarm, when a gun has put every nation in the world where it is today. It all depended on which end of it you were—on the sending or receiving end.

—*More Letters:* March 12, 1932, p. 125

It's just not possible for me (3,000 miles away) to tell you what caliber gun to have in your house. You know your neighbors better than I do.

—*Daily Telegrams:* May 16, 1933
(see AUTOMATIC, CRIME, WOMEN MURDERERS)

H

HAMBURGERS

A good stiff sales tax on hamburgers today would have paid our national debt.

—*Daily Telegrams:* September 4, 1933
(see AMERICANS)

HAMILTON, ALEXANDER

"Alexander Hamilton was the man that originated the 'put and take' system into our national treasury," Will Rogers recounted. "The taxpayers put it in and the politicians take it out."

(see TAXES)

HARDING, WARREN

When Will Rogers was invited to the White House to meet President Harding, he vowed to make the president laugh.

"I told him I wanted to tell him all the latest political

jokes," Rogers recalled. "The president said, 'I know 'em, I appointed most of them.'

"I saw that I couldn't match humor with this man, so I called it a day."

(see COOLIDGE, ROOSEVELT, TAFT, WILSON)

HARVARD

Harvard, we always look to them for the freak things.

—*Weekly Articles:* June 30, 1929

HARVARD MAN

Seeing the results of the 1930 off-year congressional elections, Rogers pointed out Roosevelt as the rising star of the Democrats two years before his nomination:

"Looks like the Democrats nominated their president yesterday, Franklin D. Roosevelt. He is the first Harvard man to know enough to drop three syllables when he has something to say. Compared to me he is almost illiterate."

(see ROOSEVELT)

HAWAII

Hawaii is a backward place, observed Will Rogers. "Hawaii is the only place I know where they lay flowers on you while you are alive."

HEALING WATERS

Now, in my more or less checkered career before the more or less checkered public, I have been asked to publicly endorse everything from chewing gum, face beautifiers, patent cocktail shakers, ma junk sets, even corsets, cigarettes, and chewing tobacco, all of which I didn't use or know anything about. But I always refused. . . .

But, at last, I have found something that I absolutely

know no one else has something as good as, for an all-seeing nature put this where it is and it's the only one he had, and by a coincidence it is located in the town near the ranch where I was born and raised.

So I hereby and hereon come out unequivocally (I think that's the way you spell it) in favor of a place that has the water that I *know* will cure you. You might ask, cure me of what? Why, cure you of anything, just name your disease and dive in.

Claremore, Oklahoma, is the birthplace of this Aladdin of health waters.

Now you may say, "Oh, you boost it because you live there," but I don't want you to think so little of me that you would think I would misguide a sick person just for the monetary gain to my hometown. We don't need you that bad. The city is on a self-supporting basis without patients, just by shipping the water to Hot Springs, Ark.; Hot Springs, Va.; West Baden, Ind.; and Saratoga, N.Y.

It is located, this mecca of the ill, about 1,700 miles west of New York (either city or state, depends on whichever one you happen to be in). You bear a little south of west, after leaving New York, till you reach Sos McClellan's place, which is just on the outskirts of Claremore.

From the west, if you are afflicted and you are sure to be or you wouldn't have gone out there, why, Claremore is just 1,900 miles due east of Mojave, California, one of the few towns which Los Angeles has not voted into their cafeteria. You come east till you reach an oil station at a road crossing. You will see a lot of men pitching horseshoes. Well, that is the post office of Tulsa, Oklahoma, and the men are millionaires pitching horseshoes for oil wells, or for each other's wives.

Now, if you are living in the South and are afflicted with a cotton crop under a Republican administration, or with the Ku Klux Klan, or with the hook worm, we guarantee to rid you of either or all of these in a course of twenty-four baths.

I will admit that these waters have quite a peculiar

odor, as they have a proportion of sulphur and other un-
known ingredients, but visitors from Kansas City, who
are used to a stockyard breeze, take this wonderful water
home as a perfume.

Now, if you are in the North, and happen to get something the matter with you, we are 847½ miles south by
west from Gary, Indiana. We have cured hundreds of
people from Chicago, Ill., from gunshot wounds inflicted
in attempted murders and robberies. There is only one
way to avoid being robbed of anything in Chicago and
that is not to have anything.

—*Weekly Articles:* July 29, 1923
(see CHICAGO, ENDORSEMENT)

HEAVEN

Old New York, the so-called heartless city, houses some
great people in every denomination in the world, and I
can't see any difference in any of them. I haven't been
able to see where one has the monopoly on the right
course to heaven.

—*Weekly Articles:* May 24, 1925

HEROES

"Heroing is one of the shortest lived professions there
is," said Will Rogers, who somehow remained a hero until his death made him immortal.

"This thing of being a hero, about the main thing is to
know when to die. Prolonged life has ruined more men
than it ever made."

(see FAME, MOVIE HEROES)

HIGHER EDUCATION

Will Rogers reckoned higher education was as much a
racket as show business.

"We got so many educated now that there is not enough jobs for educated people," he complained.

"But none of these big professors will come out and tell you that our education might be lacking, that it might be shortened, that it might be improved. They know as it is now that it's a racket, and they are in on it.

"You couldn't get me to admit that making movies was the bunk either. None of us will talk against our own graft. We all got us our rackets nowadays.

"There is just about as much hooey in everything as there is merit."

The higher the education the higher priced drinks they become accustomed to.

—*Weekly Articles:* February 3, 1929
(see COLLEGE, MOVIES)

HIGH SOCIETY

You know there is a great tendency all over the country now to be highbrow. Everybody is four-flushing and pretending they are not what they really are, especially here in New York. More people should work for their dinner instead of dressing for it. Half the stiff bosom shirts worn nowadays, the laundry is due on them yet.

—*Weekly Articles:* February 25, 1923

HIGH STANDARD OF LIVING

"I think we put too much emphasis and importance and advertising on our so-called high standard of living," stated Will Rogers. "I think the 'high' is the only word in that phrase that is really correct. We sure are a-living high.

"Our children are delivered to schools in automobiles. But whether that adds to their grades is doubtful. There hasn't been a Thomas Jefferson produced in this country since we formed our first trust. Rail splitting produced an immortal president in Abraham Lincoln; but golf, with twenty thousand courses, hasn't produced even a good A Number-1 congressman."

—*More Letters:* June 2, 1928
(see GOLF)

HISTORY

History is the story told by the winning side. To illustrate this Will compared George Washington and the Indians. Washington "fought for his country against the invaders [Indians] and wound up with a flock of statues and a title of father-of-his-country. The old Apache chiefs went through more and fought harder for their country than George did, but George won, that's the whole answer to history.

"It's not what you do, but what did you get away with at the finish."

History ain't what it is; it's what some writer wanted it to be.

—*More Letters:* March 11, 1932

HISTORY MAKERS

All the speakers said, "we are making history." Well, I don't want to be disrespectful to either party, but I am just tired of seeing history made.

—*Weekly Articles:* June 29, 1928

HOLDING COMPANY

White collar criminals sometimes set up dummy corporations or holding companies. Will Rogers offered this definition: "A holding company is a thing where you hand an accomplice the goods, while the policeman searches you."

(see CRIMINALS, LAWYERS)

HOLIDAYS

If we could ever get vacations down to where you wasn't any more tired on the day one was over than on our regular work day it would be wonderful.

—*Daily Telegrams:* September 4, 1933
(see LABOR DAY)

HOLLYWOOD

"Compared to Hollywood, Sodom and Gomorrah were a couple of babes in the woods," said Will Rogers.

"In Hollywood you will see things at night that are fast enough to be in the Olympics in the day time."

Hollywood does have some redeeming features. One good thing about Hollywood is you can find anything there, good or bad. "If you want a couple of hundred real Arabs in a scene, you just let the casting department let it be known that you do and you get that many real Arabs. Anything under the sun you want, it's in Hollywood. I believe you could round up a hundred Eskimos and if you want the Wailing Wall in Jerusalem, you can get that with the original cast. In fact, the producers of the pictures will join in with the mob, the way business has been lately."

(see HOLLYWOOD REFORMS)

HOLLYWOOD REFORMS

Will Rogers explained why he no longer lived in Hollywood: "You see, when I left there a year and a half ago, they were cleaning up the morals of Hollywood and I had to get out."

HOLLYWOOD WEDDINGS

"It's kinder like Hollywood weddings," Will said. "I get a bundle of invitations every day to attend the weddings, but I would always rather wait a few weeks and take in the divorce."

HOME

Whenever Will Rogers returned to Oklahoma he felt he was returning home.

"On my way home to Oklahoma. What's happier, especially if people have forgot what you used to be?

"After all, there is nothing in the world like home. You can roam all over the world, but after all, it's what the people at home think of you that really counts.

"I am always going to do my best, no matter where I am, but it was the home folks that had been worrying me, and it's what worries everybody if they will admit it. There is a million towns in the United States, and a million communities. Pick out a million people and ask them where they would rather be thought well of, and they will say, 'Back home.'

"Gee, I am lucky, I fooled 'em at home."

(see CLAREMORE, OKLAHOMA)

HOME RUN

The boy on the sandlot gets just as big a kick out of a home run as Babe Ruth.

—*Weekly Articles:* October 26, 1930

HONESTY

Everybody praises honesty, but few can stand it. "Shrewdness in public life all over the world is always honored," Will commented, "while honesty in public

107

men is generally attributed to dumbness and is seldom rewarded."

HOOEY

Hooey is a nonsense word. It stands for nonsense that is called by fancier names. Hooey is almost never called what it is. Will Rogers called it hooey. He said, "There is just about as much hooey in everything as there is merit."

No nation likes hooey like we do.

—*Weekly Articles:* July 10, 1932

Viva hooey.

—*Daily Telegrams:* October 8, 1933
(see DIPLOMACY)

HOOVER, HERBERT

The Depression began during President Herbert Hoover's administration. The Democrats couldn't resist blaming him for the nation's economic woes.

"I always did want to see him elected," said Will Rogers. "I wanted to see how far a competent man could go in politics. It has never been tried before."

Rogers felt sympathetic toward Hoover, a competent administrator who had the misfortune of taking office in 1929, the year the stock market crashed.

"You'd think Hoover got up one morning, looked out the window, and said, 'This looks like a nice day for ruining the country, I think I'll do it today.'

"Prosperity—millions of people never had it under nobody and never will have it under anybody, but they all want it under Mr. Hoover. If the weather is wrong, we blame it on Mr. Hoover."

President Hoover was merely a scapegoat for an economic collapse that was a long time coming. "He arrived at the picnic when even the last hard-boiled egg had been consumed. Somebody slipped some Limburger cheese into his pocket and he got credit for breaking up the dance."

(see DEPRESSION, PRESIDENTS)

HORSES

Will Rogers was reluctant to bet on the horses. He had seen so many friends and acquaintances lose so much money at the racetrack, he began to suspect that the intelligence of horses had been underestimated.

"You know horses are smarter than people," he said. "You never heard of a horse going broke betting on people."

(see DOPEY, JOCKEY)

HUMANITARIAN

Will Rogers was skeptical of arms control as a means of peace-keeping.

"One fellow tries to stop the actual fight, we try to regulate the number of bullets he shall have after the fight starts. Take your pick as to who is the humanitarian."

—*Daily Telegrams:* February 28, 1933
(see ARMS TRADING, DISARMAMENT, GUN, TREATY)

HUMAN MATING HABITS

With the human race you may just as well throw your register book in the creek, for what the mating brings forth no human mind can guess, much less be certain of. You are just liable to have some fine old stock bring forth a family of human mutts as to produce an amateur Lincoln.

—*Weekly Articles:* August 4, 1929

HUMAN NATURE

It is human nature to want what we don't have more than what we have.

"A Ford car and a marriage certificate is the two cheapest things there is," declared Will Rogers. "We no more than get either one than we want to trade them in for something better."

Funny thing about human nature. When we ain't feeling so good ourselves, we always want to read about somebody that is worse off than we are.

—Daily Telegrams: December 9, 1930
(see DIVORCE, MARRIAGE PREDICTION)

HUMOR

The secret of his humor, explained Will Rogers, was simply to tell the truth. "I use only one set method in my little gags, and that is to try to keep to the truth. Personally, I don't like the jokes that get the biggest laughs, as they are generally as broad as a house, and require no thought at all. I like the one where, if you are with a friend, and hear it, it makes you think, and you nudge your friend and say: 'He's right about that!' I would rather have you do that than have you laugh—and then forget the next minute what it was you laughed at."

Telling the truth came naturally to Will Rogers. It was part of the naturalness of his public persona. He learned other secrets of success in the humor trade from experience. Experience with live audiences taught him to focus on current subjects.

"I have found out two things," he wrote in a 1917 article entitled, "The Extemporaneous Line." "One is that the more up-to-date a subject is the more credit you are given for talking on it, even if you really haven't anything very funny. But if it is an old subject, your gags must be funny to get over."

In his choice of current events, Will Rogers concentrated his humor on politics and international affairs. "I have written on nothing but politics for years," Will avowed. "You never heard me do a mother-in-law joke. It was always about national or international affairs."

Another discovery Rogers made is that his own original humor worked better than borrowed jokes or gags written by others. Will Rogers preferred to write his own original material.

"I would read the papers for hours, trying to find out a funny angle to the day's news, and I found that they would laugh easiest at the stuff that had just happened that day. A joke don't have to be near as funny if it's up to date.

"So that's how I learned that my own stuff, serving only strictly fresh-laid jokes, as you might say, goes better than anything else."

Perhaps the most endearing quality of Will Rogers' humor is that it is *good-natured*. It is ultimately kind and forgiving rather than harsh and judgmental. It is devoid of bitterness and hatred. "I have often said in answer to inquiries as to how I got away with kidding some of our public men, that it was because I liked all of them personally, and that if there was no malice in your heart there could be none in your gags, and I have always said I never met a man I didn't like.

"I don't think I ever hurt any man's feelings by my little gags. I know I never willfully did it. When I have to do that to make a living I will quit."

Every gag I tell must be based on truth. No matter how much I may exaggerate it, it must have a certain amount of truth.

—*Weekly Articles:* March 9, 1924

I have always noticed that people will never laugh at anything that is not based on truth.

—*Weekly Articles:* November 30, 1924

HUNGER

When the House of Representatives vetoed a hunger bill in 1931 to appropriate $15 million for hungry people, Will commented:

"They seem to think that it's a bad precedent to appropriate money for food—it's too much like the dole. They think it would encourage hunger."

HUNTING

Will was skeptical of the prowess of weekend hunters. "The deer season just opened," he observed. "A deer hunter in Ventura brought in his first man yesterday."

HUSBAND KILLING

Will Rogers recommended to wives considering killing their husbands that they try to arrange to do the killing on Long Island.

"The beauty about killing a husband on Long Island is that you draw a better class of people at the trial," he noted. "It's far enough away from New York that you don't get that ordinary bunch of court hangers-on. A murder trial out there draws what used to be known in the old days as 'carriage trade.' In other words they come in limousines. It's a pleasure to be sentenced to hang if you can get the right kind of audience to be present at the verdict."

I

IDEALS

High ideals are fine, said Will Rogers, "but they got to be about 33 percent plausible."

IDEAS

"Everything worthwhile is a good idea," stated Will, "but did you ever notice there is more bad ideas that will work than there is good ones?

"We have some good ideas, but most of 'em come too late to do us any good."

(see BIG IDEAS, COMMUNISM)

IGNORANCE

Everybody is ignorant, only on different subjects.

—*Weekly Articles:* August 31, 1924

The more ignorant you are, the quicker you fight.

—*Daily Telegrams:* August 11, 1929

113

INCOME TAXES

"This is becoming the richest, and the poorest country in the world," said Will Rogers. "Why? Why, on account of an unequal distribution of the money. How can you equalize it? By putting a higher surtax on large incomes, and that money goes to provide some public work, at a livable wage."

The idea of higher taxes for higher incomes flopped with the rich. They favored lower taxes on earned incomes.

"There is a tremendous movement on to get lower taxes on earned incomes. Then will come the real problem. Who among us on salary are earning our incomes?"

The income tax has made more liars out of the American people than golf has.

Even when you make one out on the level, you don't know when it's through if you are a crook or a martyr.

—*Weekly Articles:* April 8, 1923

The good old days with most of us was when we didn't earn enough to pay an income tax.

—*DTIV:* March 31, 1935

(see AMERICA, HEAD HUNTERS, TAXES, UNEMPLOYED)

INDEPENDENCE

Every nation is entitled to self-government. "I don't care how poor and inefficient a little country is," Will said, "they like to run their own business. Sure, America and England can run countries perhaps better than China, Korea, or India, but that don't mean they ought to. I know men that would make my wife a better husband than I am, but darn it, I'm not going to give her to 'em."

INDIANS

"They were very religious people that come over here from the old country. They were very human. They would shoot a couple of Indians on the way to every prayer meeting."

The New World belonged to the immigrants. The Indians were in the way of progress. They had to go. The government said so.

"Every time the government moved the Indians, they gave 'em the same treaty: 'You shall have this land as long as the grass grows and the water flows.'

"But finally they settled the whole Indian problem. They put the Indians on land where the grass won't grow and the water won't flow!"

What became of the Indians? We became them.

"Indians used to be wards of the government," said Will, "but now we all are. Everybody is an Indian."

Our record with the Indians is going to go down in history. It is going to make us mighty proud of it in the future when our children of ten more generations read of what we did to them. Every man in our history that killed the most Indians has got a statue built for him.

—Gulf radio broadcast, April 14, 1935
(see CHEROKEES, JACKSON, NATIVE AMERICANS)

INDIAN TALK

Will Rogers took exception to stereotyped Indian impressions. He pointed out that many Indians are more intelligent than ignorant white folks give them credit for. "Some of them are very highly educated. One night there was one of them coming out of Syd Grauman's Egyptian theater in Hollywood and Syd, the old showman, asked him in his best 'kosher' Indian language, 'How you likum heap big show?'

" 'It is a splendid production,' replied the brave. 'One

might say it is superior to the original of the French classicist. The star's characterization is indeed superb.' "

INDUSTRY

Industry. Industry has shown a slight gain since we wrote to you last week, but the expense of keeping tabs on whether it made a gain has overshadowed the amount of the actual gain.

—*Weekly Articles:* November 12, 1933

INHERITANCE TAX

Congress knocked the rich in the creek with a 72 percent income tax. Then somebody must have told 'em, "Yes, Congress, you got 'em while they are living, but what if they die on you to keep from paying it?"

Congress says, "Well, never thought of that, so we will frame one that will get 'em, alive or living, dead or deceased."

Now they got such a high inheritance tax on 'em that you won't catch these old rich boys dying promiscuously like they did. This bill makes patriots out of everybody. You surely do die for your country, if you die from now on.

—*Daily Telegrams:* March 23, 1931

I don't see why a man shouldn't pay inheritance tax. If a country is good enough to pay taxes to while you are living, it's good enough to pay in after you die. By the time you die, you should be so used to paying taxes that it would almost be second nature anyway.

—*Weekly Articles:* February 28, 1926

I would call that the nearest to a painless tax that could be invented. You don't pay it till you die and then you don't know it.

—*Daily Telegrams:* June 20, 1935

INSURANCE

Insurance companies have guys figure out the very day you will die. (In fact they won't insure till they have it investigated and find out.) Then you like a sucker go bet them you will live longer than that.

—*Weekly Articles:* February 24, 1929
(see LIFE INSURANCE)

INTERNATIONAL AFFAIRS

"There ain't anything that you find in one country," said Will Rogers, "that you don't find is being done just about as bad in your own."

INTERNATIONAL GOOD WILL

"There just ain't no animal such as international good will," Will Rogers remarked. "It just lasts until the loan runs out."

INTERNATIONAL NEWS

If any American correspondent sends any news home today, he has made it up.

—*Daily Telegrams:* January 22, 1930

INTERNATIONAL RELATIONS

The way Europeans talk about American aggressiveness, you'd think the last world war started in Tulsa.

Will Rogers abroad found that a favorite topic of conversation, especially in Europe, was how hated America is for being so pushy. "Everybody talks about how we are hated," he wrote in a published letter to President Coolidge in 1926.

"I would just casually, of course, admit that we were a band of highbinders, and were just waiting to get England or France up a back alley and knock 'em in the head and get what little they had left; and while they were discussing jubilantly the subject of our unpopularity I would, in order to keep up the conversation and not change the subject, just nonchalantly remark, 'Will you enumerate to me, in their natural order, the number of nations that you people can call bosom friends?'

This question quiets the quarrelsome foreigner considerably, Will discovered. "When you insist on a count, he finds that he not only could enumerate them on his fingers but he could count them on his fingers if he had been unfortunate enough to have both arms off."

Will Rogers urged Americans to be more tolerant of their European brethren: "Some of these nations have been hating each other for generations, while they are only just starting in hating us."

(see EUROPE, FOREIGN RELATIONS, TOURISTS)

INVENTIONS

"America invents everything, but the trouble is we get tired of it the minute the new is wore off," Will said.

"Every invention during our lifetime has been just to save time. Two hundred years from now history will record: America, a nation that conceived many odd inventions for getting somewhere, but could think of nothing to do when they got there."

INVESTIGATIONS

There were always congressional investigations going on in Will Rogers' time, not unlike today. Commissions would be appointed to investigate; then other commissions would be appointed to investigate the investigators. Each investigation would disagree with the conclusions of the previous investigation, and as a result of the lack of agreement, nothing would be done about the problem being investigated in the first place.

"What's the use of having a lot of statistics and data on something that you can't do?" asked Will. "It's like garbage: What's the use of collecting it if you ain't got nowhere to put it; you don't know what to do with it. Well, that's the way with commissions."

The investigations always took a long time but never led to anyone *doing* time. "The American people would trade ten investigations for one conviction."

There was one benefit to all the investigations, Will pointed out. "In Washington these days there are politicians acting honest now that never acted that way in their lives."

The only trouble about this suggesting that somebody or something ought to be investigated is that they are liable to suggest that you ought to be investigated. And from the record of all our previous investigations it just looks like nobody can emerge with their nose entirely clean.

I don't care who you are, you just can't reach middle life without having done and said a whole lot of foolish things.

If I saw an investigating committee headed my way, I would just plead guilty and throw myself on the mercy of the court.

—*Daily Telegrams:* December 28, 1934
(see KNOWLEDGE, RESIGNATION PROTOCOL)

INVESTIGATIONS RULE

They ought to pass a rule in this country in any investigations, if a man couldn't tell the truth the first time he shouldn't be allowed to try again.

—*Weekly Articles:* March 2, 1924
(see TESTIMONY)

INVESTIGATIVE COMMITTEES

The queerest investigation that has sprung up in Washington (and it has to go some to be queerer than some of the others) is one that happened lately. Mr. Wheeler who has been presiding questioner at one of the various investigations, was himself indicted up in his home state, and turned right around and caused an investigation to be made, and a committee formed to investigate where they got the ground to indict him on.

Now the people who had him indicted will appoint a committee to investigate where he found out that he was indicted. So we will go on as long as there is a man who will act on a committee.

—*Weekly Articles:* April 27, 1924
(see COMMISSIONS)

INVITATIONS

"I am Will Rogers and I have come to see the king."

During a visit to England, Will Rogers walked up to the gate of Buckingham Palace and announced to the guards he had come to see the king.

The guards were so appalled at his effrontery that they stood speechless as he continued: "You tell him that when the Prince of Wales was out my way, he told me to look up his old man sometime, so here I am."

Uncertain how to handle this impudent American half-breed, the guards consulted their superiors. The end result was that Will Rogers was admitted to Buckingham Palace, had a long chat with the king, and even stayed for lunch.

IRELAND

"The trouble with Ireland is the English landlords," said Will Rogers. "The best way to settle that is to make every English landlord go to Ireland and collect the rent personally. That would not only solve the problem but eliminate the landlords."

I have been in twenty countries and the only one where American tourists are welcomed wholeheartedly by everybody is in Ireland.

They don't owe us and they don't hate us.

—*Daily Telegrams:* August 1, 1926

Ireland treats you more like a friend than a tourist.

—*Daily Telegrams:* September 8, 1926
(see ENGLISH GENTLEMAN, MEXICO)

IRISH INDIAN

Will Rogers claimed to have Irish blood as well as Cherokee blood flowing through his veins. "These Irish, you got to watch 'em," he warned. "There was a few of 'em sneaked into Oklahoma and got mixed up with the Rogerses and the Cherokees, and I am a sort of an offshoot—an Irish Indian."

(see ANCESTORS, FAMILY TREE)

J

JACKSON, ANDREW

"To tell you the truth, I am not so sweet on old Andy," confessed Will Rogers at a gala Jackson Day dinner. "He is the one that run us Cherokees out of Georgia and North Carolina. Old Andy, every time he couldn't find anyone to jump on, would come back and pounce onto us Indians."

The Indians were glad to see Jackson move into the White House. "The Indians wanted him in there so he could let us alone for a while. Andy stayed two terms. The Indians were for a third term for Andy."

JACKSON LEGACY

He was the first one to think up the idea to promise everybody that if they will vote for you, why, you will give them an office when you get in, and the more times they vote for you the bigger the office you will give them. That was the real starting of the Democratic Party. It was called Democratic because you was supposed to get something for your vote.

Then the Republicans came along and improved on the Democrats and Jackson's idea by giving them money instead of promises of jobs. In that way you got paid whether your man was elected or not. So naturally that's why more people are Republicans than Democrats.

—*Weekly Articles:* February 5, 1928
(see DEMOCRATIC CORRUPTION, REPUBLICANS)

JAPANESE

The Japanese shouldn't criticize us for being lazy when their best chefs don't even bother to cook the fish before serving it. But not all Japanese workers are lazy, explained Will Rogers, ambassador-at-large.

"The Japanese are a good race of people in a lot of ways. We may just as well admit it; we can't compete with them when it comes to work. A clock and a bed are two things that a Jap farmer never used in his life. A Jap will raise a crop while the American will be telling his neighbor over the back fence what he is thinking about putting in this year."

Don't ever call a Japanese a "Jap." Now, I didn't know that till I got over here; I just thought that it was about like Englishmen calling us "Yanks"; even if you come from Alabama, the English don't know but what you are a Yank. But this Jap business is a serious matter with them.

—*More Letters:* March 12, 1932

Japan is civilized now. They have a navy. We don't send any more missionaries there now. Any nation is a heathen that ain't strong enough to punch you in the jaw.

—*Weekly Articles:* February 6, 1927

They got everything we got, and if they haven't you show it to 'em and they will make it.

—*Weekly Articles:* January 17, 1932

123

JEFFERSON, THOMAS

All of 'em will claim they are running on the real Democratic ticket. I expect Thomas Jefferson was about the very last real Democrat.

—*Daily Telegrams:* May 13, 1935

JEFFERSONIAN PRINCIPLES

The Democrat will miss his supper to explain to you what Jeffersonian principles are. He don't know what they are, but he has heard 'em spoken of so often in speeches that he knows that no speech is complete without wishing that we would return to those principles and the only thing that keeps us from not returning to them is that very reason we don't know what they were.

—*Weekly Articles:* December 2, 1928

JOBS

Will proposed a slogan for those who were in favor of jobs for the unemployed: "The slogan will be: 'I believe every man should have a job, but not mine.' "

(see LABOR, SOFT JOB, UNEMPLOYMENT)

JOCKEY

Will Rogers was not much of a gambler. When he bet on the horses, he usually lost. But he did not blame it on the horses; he blamed it on the jockeys. The horses, he said, were honest.

"Lincoln went down in history as Honest Abe, but he never was a jockey," said Will. "If he had been a jockey he might have gone down as just Abe."

(see GAMBLING, HORSES, LINCOLN)

JOKES

"There are only a few original jokes," Will said in response to a question about humor, "and most of them are in Congress."

(see CONGRESS, HUMOR)

JOKE SUBJECTS

An unwritten law ... you must never tell a joke about a little fellow. They can't stand it. But always tell it on the big fellow. That's why they are big.

—Weekly Articles: August 2, 1925
(see CONGRESS, HUMOR)

K

KANSAS

Being from Oklahoma, Will Rogers could not resist the temptation to poke occasional fun at the neighboring state of Kansas.

"The only way you could tell a citizen from a bootlegger in Kansas," he said, "was the bootlegger would be sober."

KILLERS

Killing is becoming a cold-blooded business, almost impersonal.

"The fellow that kills you nowadays, why, he don't have it in for you, he don't even know you. You are not even pointed out to him till just before he bumps you off. That's all a business, done through an agency, just like any other agency. They can furnish killers for 'singles' or 'double murders' or 'group.' You get a rate if you want to put several out of commission. It's cheaper to have it all done at once. It's very little more trouble to shoot down a group, than it is one.

"Oh, we are living in progress."

(see CRIME, MURDERS)

KNEES

Anne Pennington, one of the dancing stars of Ziegfeld's Follies, was said to have the world's most attractive knees.

"Now almost every part of the human anatomy has gained fame in some way or another," observed Will. "We speak of beautiful arms, necks, heads, feet, body, hands, nose, eyes, and ears, but do you know out of 120 million knees we have never heard a word about one of them, only two belonging to little Anne Pennington."

Anne Pennington and Will Rogers would appear together on the same bill. "I had my gum and Anne had her knees," he recalled. "When she wanted to disguise herself and not be recognized in public she used to cover up her knees and no one ever knew her."

Will said he never forgot the impact of Anne Pennington's knees on an audience. "I used to do a dance with her in the Follies and I could black up some nights, or send in a double, and let him do it for me, and I would never be missed. For when Anne's knees were on the stage, why, your audience never looked up."

(see FASHIONS)

KNOWLEDGE

The Lord split knowledge up among his subjects about equal. The so-called ignorant is happy. You think he is happy because he don't know any better. Maybe he is happy because he knows enough to be happy.

The smart one knows he knows a lot. That makes him unhappy because he can't impart it to his friends. Discontent comes in proportion to knowledge.

—*Weekly Articles:* May 11, 1930

L

LABOR

"Labor. We can confidentially report to our clients that labor is not laboring," Will Rogers confided to the country in his syndicated column. "As to the cause of not laboring, it's generally rumored around here among our source of information that labor is not laboring because labor hasn't got a job."

(see ENGLISH GENTLEMAN, SOFT JOB, UNEMPLOYMENT, WELFARE)

LABOR DAY

Every holiday ought to be named Labor Day.

—*Daily Telegrams:* September 4, 1933
(see HOLIDAYS)

LABOR LEADERS

Labor leaders are ex-laborers, Will noticed. "Labor leaders don't do any laboring after they are able to lead."

LAME DUCK

A lame duck is a man that didn't bring home enough "loot" from the National Treasury to warrant his re-election.

—*Weekly Articles:* February 23, 1931

LARCENY

There is two types of larceny, petty and grand, and the courts will really give you a longer sentence for petty than they do for grand. They are supposed to be the same in the eyes of the law, but the judges always put a little extra on you for petty, which is a kind of a fine for stupidness. "If that's all you got you ought to go to jail longer."

—*Weekly Articles:* April 22, 1928

LATIN AMERICA

Will commented on the death of a Central American dictator: "For a Central American dictator, he died a natural death—he was shot in the back."

LATIN AMERICAN REVOLUTIONS

The dumbest guy in the world knows that the minute a Latin American country has a revolution that is just the opening of a series of 'em. You know we got the wrong impression of a revolution. They was raised on 'em down there. They love 'em. It's their only relaxation. Sure, people get killed sometimes. If it's a first-class, grade A revolution, they may lose about as many as we lose over a weekend by trying to pass somebody on a turn.

—*Daily Telegrams:* September 6, 1931
(see FOOTBALL, URUGUAY)

LAW

It's terrible to have a law telling you you got to do something. But you ain't going to do it unless there is.

—*Daily Telegrams:* May 31, 1935

LAW SCHOOLS

Will Rogers was alarmed at the growing number of law school graduates. He predicted that the crime rate would rise in proportion to the increase in the number of lawyers looking for work.

"Thousands of students just graduated all over the country in law. Going to take an awful lot of crime to support that bunch."

LAWYERS

Will Rogers made some cruel remarks about lawyers—-he told the truth about them.

He said lawyers had made crime more profitable for criminals. "The first thing they do now if they are taking up crime as a profession (even before they buy the gun) is to engage their lawyer. He works on a percentage. He acts as their advance agent, too, he picks out the banks they are to rob. Bar associations invented the word 'ethics,' then forgot about it."

Law is complications and complications are law. If everything was just plain, there wouldn't be any lawyers.

—*Daily Telegrams:* February 14, 1935

Everytime a lawyer writes something, he is not writing for posterity, he is writing so that endless others of his craft can make a living out of trying to figure out what he said. 'Course, perhaps he hadn't really said anything. That's what makes it so hard to explain.

—*Weekly Articles:* July 28, 1935

The minute you read something and you can't understand it, you can *almost* be sure that it was drawn up by a lawyer. Then if you give it to another lawyer and he don't know just what it means, why then you *can* be sure it was drawn up by a lawyer. If it's in a few words and is plain and understandable only one way, it was written by a nonlawyer.

—*Weekly Articles:* July 28, 1935

If it weren't for wills, lawyers would have to work at an essential employment. There is only one way you can beat a lawyer in a death case. That is to die with nothing.

—*Weekly Articles:* May 31, 1925

I have always noticed that any time a man can't come and settle with you without bringing his lawyer, why, look out for him.

—*Weekly Articles:* January 14, 1923
(see LAW SCHOOLS, WILLS)

LEADERSHIP

This would be a great time in the world for some man to come along who knew something.

—*Daily Telegrams:* September 21, 1931
(see EDUCATION, POLITICIANS, PRESIDENT)

LEARNING

"A man learns by two things," said Will. "One is reading. The other is association with smarter people."

(see BELIEFS, KNOWLEDGE)

LEGISLATIVE BODIES

One whiff of the English House of Lords and Will Rogers telegrammed from London on February 10, 1930:

"See some of these other legislative bodies, and it makes you appreciate our boys. You know they are the nicest fellows in the world to meet. I sometimes really wonder if they realize the harm they do."

LEGISLATURE

Will Rogers offered to perform for the legislature at half price during the 1927 spring season. "I do this not for the legislature's sake, but I feel that the same time that I take up theirs is keeping them from doing any harm against the people in the way of laws, so I really do it to help out the people.

"One thing you can always feel assured of in addressing a legislative body, that is you certainly are not taking up any of their time. You are not keeping them from anything. So remember, half rates for lawmakers. This is an ad."

We cuss the lawmakers. But I notice we're always perfectly willin' to share in any of the sums of money that they might distribute.

—Radio Broadcasts, April 7, 1935

There's nothing will upset a state economic condition like a legislature. It's better to have termites in your house than the legislature.

—Radio Broadcasts, March 31, 1935

Never blame a legislative body for not doing something. When they do nothing, that don't hurt anybody. When they do something is when they become dangerous.

—*Daily Telegrams:* November 23, 1929
(see CONGRESS, GOVERNMENT)

LETTER WRITING

Will Rogers received many letters but wrote few replies. He didn't even write thank-you notes for all the gifts he received. "They must think I am a fine mess that they don't hear from me about it," he said, apologizing for his poor correspondence habits.

"Well, they ought to just know what a poor hand I am at writing. About twice a year I will have batches of letters pile up that I keep saying I will answer, and maybe I do and I send 'em off and get lots of 'em back saying the people are dead."

LIBERAL

A liberal is a man who wants to use his own ideas on things in preference to generations who, he knows, know more than he does.

—*Weekly Articles:* February 4, 1923

LIBERTY

"Liberty don't work as good in practice as it does in speeches," observed Will Rogers. People are quick to complain about any loss of liberty, he pointed out, but rarely do they want to take the initiative to *increase* liberty—their own or anyone else's. "Everybody is running around in circles, announcing that somebody's pinched their liberty. Now the greatest aid that I know of that anyone could give the world today, would be a correct definition of 'liberty.' What might be one class's liberty might be another class's poison. I guess absolute liberty couldn't mean anything but that anybody can do anything they want to, any time they want to. Well, any half-wit can tell you that wouldn't work. So the question arises, How much liberty can I get away with?

"Well, you can get no more liberty than you give! That's my definition, but you got perfect liberty to work out your own."

(see CHINA, FREEDOM, VOTE)

LIFE

What constitutes a life well spent, anyway? Love and admiration from your fellow men is all that any one can ask.

—*Weekly Articles:* August 9, 1925
(see WILL ROGERS)

LIFE INSURANCE

Life insurance is a great thing. It's the only way we have of being remembered after we are gone. The extent of your memory depends on how long the money lasts.

—Radio broadcast for Unemployment Relief, 1933
(see INSURANCE)

LINCOLN, ABRAHAM

"Lincoln made a wonderful speech one time: 'That this nation under God shall have a new birth of freedom and that government of the people, by the people, for the people shall not perish from this earth.'

"Every time a politician gets in a speech," Will Rogers observed, "he digs up this Gettysburg quotation. He recites it every Decoration day and practices the opposite the other 364 days.

"Every politician always talks about him, but none of them ever imitate him."

Papers today say, "What would Lincoln do today?" Well, in the first place, he wouldn't chop any wood, he would trade his ax in on a Ford. Being a Republican he would vote the Democratic ticket. Being in sympathy with the underdog he would be classed as a radical progressive. Having a sense of humor he would be called eccentric.

—*Daily Telegrams:* February 12, 1934
(see OHIO)

LINDBERGH, CHARLES

Infatuated with aviation, Will Rogers was a great admirer of Charles Lindbergh, the first nonstop transatlantic solo flier.

Rogers met Lindbergh when the pilot visited San Diego in September, 1927, four months after the historic flight, and the two men struck a life-long friendship. Rogers visited Charles and Anne Morrow Lindbergh and their nineteen-month-old son at their home in Englewood, New Jersey, only two weeks before the boy was kidnapped in one of the most highly publicized crimes of the century.

"Why don't lynching parties widen their scope and take in kidnappings?" wrote Rogers in his daily telegram, expressing the national outrage. He was furious not only at the kidnapping itself but at the society that could foster such crimes.

"A father who never did a thing that didn't make us proud of him. A mother who though only the wife of a hero, has proven one herself. At home or abroad they have always been a credit to their country. They have never fallen down. Is their country going to be a credit to them? Will it make him still proud that he did it for them? Or in his loneliness will a thought creep into his mind that it might have been different if he had flown the ocean under somebody's colors with a real obligation to law and order? America goes further into debt, and the debt is to the Lindberghs."

After the Lindbergh child was found murdered—a crime for which the German-born carpenter Bruno Hauptmann was convicted and executed in 1936—the grieving parents were invited by Will Rogers to spend time in seclusion on his ranch, away from the press and popping flashbulbs and the peering public eye. The Lindberghs accepted his kindly invitation, remaining undisturbed on Rogers' ranch for two weeks.

When Will Rogers died with Wiley Post in a plane crash off Point Barrow, Alaska, on August 15, 1935, Charles Lindbergh called Betty Rogers and said he would like to take responsibility for flying the bodies back home from Alaska. Betty gratefully accepted Lindbergh's offer.

LINGERIE

Lord, we have all spent half our life looking at "Laungerie" ads.

—Weekly Articles: May 20, 1928

LITTLE NATIONS

The whole thing as I see it all over the world today is that the little nations has got no business being little.

—Daily Telegrams: September 10, 1933
(see NATIONS)

LIVING TOGETHER

"Two can live as cheap as one," said Will Rogers, repeating a popular truism. "That, next to law enforcement, is the biggest bunk slogan ever invented. Why, two can't even live as cheap as two, much less one."

LOAN

A man has to be mighty careful nowadays or he will burn up more gasoline trying to get a loan than the loan is.

—*Daily Telegrams:* May 17, 1931
(see BANKERS)

LOBBYIST

A lobbyist is a person that is supposed to help a politician to make up his mind—not only help him but pay him.

—*Weekly Articles:* August 25, 1929

LOBBYIST INVESTIGATION

California had a bill in to investigate lobbying, and the lobbyists bought off all the votes and they can't even find the bill now. Putting a lobbyist out of business is like a hired man trying to fire his boss.

—*Daily Telegrams:* April 5, 1935

LOCAL

We are sure getting sucked into a lot of things for the sole benefit of a local community, to be paid for by everybody.

—*Weekly Articles:* February 5, 1933

LONG, HUEY

One of the most colorful political figures of Will Rogers' era was Huey Long, the Louisiana governor who proposed a share-our-wealth program to provide financial security for every American.

Huey Long declared himself a presidential candidate in 1934.

"He found me and pinned a button on me, called EV-ERY MAN A KING, and it said everybody was to divide up their wealth. I am working with him on a percentage," said Will, who was always optimistic.

"Up to now nobody has divided, but we will get 'em. In fact I think the taxes will get 'em before Huey and I do."

An assassin got Huey Long. He was shot on the steps of the Louisiana State capitol by Dr. Carl Weiss in September, 1935, a month after Will Rogers' fatal plane crash.

LONG SKIRTS

When skirts began to get longer again during the Depression, Will Rogers proclaimed it a democratic development. "Every girl gets an even break till she hits the beach," he said.

"You see short skirts was made for certain figures. Long skirts mean democracy, there is no privileged classes. Society is not rated on its curves as it has been. You got to get by with your head now instead of under-pinning."

(see FASHIONS, LONG SKIRTS)

LOS ANGELES

Los Angeles in 1931 was not the crime capital it is today. But Will Rogers saw its great potential.

"Los Angeles, which has been in the bush league as far as racketeers are concerned, is getting right up in fast company. We pulled off a double header of a murder here a couple of weeks ago that would do credit to a Chicago or any of the big timers. The racketeers are mixed up with phases of the city government just like a regular Class A City. The killer walked away as usual."

(see AUTOMATIC, CRIME, KILLERS)

LUCK

"Last year we said, 'Things can't go on like this,' " sighed Will, "and they didn't. They got worse."

LUNATICS

Twelve mental patients escaped from an institution in Beverly Hills in the summer of 1930. Will Rogers took a keen interest in the breakout.

"Headlines in all the papers say: AUTHORITIES HAVING TROUBLE ROUNDING UP TWELVE ESCAPED LUNATICS. The main trouble is in recognizing 'em. I bet they get a different twelve back in."

M

MAJORITY

This country is not where it is today on account of any man. It is here on account of the big normal majority.

—*Weekly Articles:* February 22, 1925

MAN

Everything the Lord has a hand in is going great, but the minute you notice anything that is in any way under the supervision of man, why it's cockeyed.

—*Weekly Articles:* April 17, 1932

MARINES

You can't pick up a paper without seeing where the Marines were landed to keep some nation from shooting each other, and if necessary we shoot them to keep them from shooting each other.

—*Weekly Articles:* July 5, 1925

(see FOREIGN AFFAIRS, INTERNATIONAL AFFAIRS)

MARRIAGE PREDICTION

Walter Winchell, the famous broadcast journalist of the early days of broadcasting, was well known for predicting who was going to get married. One day Will Rogers asked him the secret of his unerring accuracy of marriage prediction.

"I asked him how it was he knew when people were going to get married, and when they were going to be divorced.

"Well, for instance marriage. He said he watched the divorce first, that was to give him a line on who was to get married. That there never was a divorce without at least a 50 percent marriage being in the offing. So he watched 'em before they was divorced to see who they would marry after the divorce. He says that marriage is a habit and divorce is a necessity.

"Then of course the minute he finds out who is marrying, it don't take a bit of thinking or figuring on who will be divorced. In fact he seemed kinder astonished at me, that I was so dumb as to not know who would be divorced. 'Why the ones that got married.'

"Well, as stupid as I am I had never thought of that, but that's just what he does, he just watches the marriage notices, and then announces the divorces after that.

"Course you got to work on a certain class of people to do that, but that is the class of people that he works on."

MARX, GROUCHO

Will Rogers, Jr., accompanied his father to the Democratic convention in 1932 to see Roosevelt nominated. A number of celebrities were in attendance. Bill recalled late one night seeing his father Will Rogers, Carl Sandburg, and Groucho Marx, all sitting together in a hotel room playing guitars and singing songs.

Will Rogers held a high opinion of Groucho Marx and respected his musical ability. As Will put it: "Groucho can play as good on the guitar as Harpo can on the harp, or Chico on the piano, but he never does. He is really what I call an ideal musician. He can play but don't."

(see VIOLIN)

MASS PRODUCTION

"If the other fellow sells cheaper than you, it is called 'dumping,' " Will explained. "Course, if you sell cheaper than him, that's 'mass production.' "

Why the thought never entered our head that we wasn't the brightest, wisest, and most accomplished people that ever was on this earth. Hadn't we figured out mass production? Couldn't we make more things than anybody? Did the thought ever enter our bonehead that the time might come when nobody would want all these things we were making? No, we had it all figured out that the more we made the more they would want.

—*Weekly Articles:* March 27, 1932

MAYORS

Will Rogers claimed that his removal from office as mayor of Beverly Hills occurred because he took a controversial moral stand that challenged cherished local customs.

"When I was thrown out as mayor of a certain alleged town on account of being called a Puritan when I came out against polygamy, I took defeat without an alibi, which proved I had none of the earmarks of a politician. I was immediately made president of the Ex-Mayors Association of America. There is an organization that will grow as long as there is an honest election."

142

I am the only mayor that never made a mistake. I never made a decision.

—*Weekly Articles:* February 27, 1927

An ex-mayor never dies. He lives just to get back in office to spite the people.

—*Weekly Articles:* September 4, 1927
(see BEVERLY HILLS)

MEETING

When a meeting ain't running right, why, the thing to do is to adjourn, reorganize, and meet some time when the ones that are against you don't know you are going to meet.

—*Weekly Articles:* March 31, 1929

MEMOIRS

Every year publishers publish the latest memoirs of those prominent personages who have recently lost their power or reputation or both. Will Rogers offered this definition of *memoirs:*

" 'Memoirs' . . . means when you put down the good things you ought to have done, and leave out the bad ones you did do."

There ain't nothing that breaks up homes, country, and nations like somebody publishing their memoirs.

—*Daily Telegrams:* December 23, 1934

MEN'S FASHIONS

I am telling you men are watching their styles. That's why they all look so funny.

—*Weekly Articles:* May 20, 1928

MERGERS

We are living in an age of mergers and combines. When your business is not doing good you combine with something and sell more stock.

—*Weekly Articles:* March 23, 1930

Merger on top of merger. Get two nonpaying things merged and then issue more stock to the public.

—*Weekly Articles:* November 27, 1932

A high-class bootlegger makes friends with a politician before he does with a customer; in fact that was one of the first big mergers—big money, politics and bootleggers.

—*Daily Telegrams:* August 8, 1929

MEXICO

The part of Mexico that adjoins the United States is the least appealing part of Mexico, mainly mesquite brush. "Nature so provided that the worst part of Mexico adjoins us. If it hadn't been, we would have taken any good part long ago," said Will Rogers.

"We could never understand why Mexico wasn't just crazy about us. We have always had their goodwill, oil, coffee, and minerals at heart.

"Up to now our calling card to Mexico or Central America had been a gunboat or violets shaped like Marines.

"We couldn't figure out why they didn't appreciate the fact that they had been shot in the most cordial manner possible.

"We couldn't realize their attitude in not falling on our necks and blessing us for giving them the assistance of our superior knowledge of government.

"Every nation must have its legalized form of gambling. We have our Wall Street. Mexico gives you a more even break. They have roulette, also a percentage of your losings go to the government. They are a primitive race. They put government above broker.

"I like Ireland and Mexico better than any other countries. They both got humor, and while they both think they take life serious, they don't. They will joke with you, sing with you, drink with you, and, if you want, fight with you—or against you, whichever you want— and I think if they like you well enough they would die with you."

I also have no humorous cracks about Mexico being lazy. If they are any lazier than us, which I doubt, but if they are, and can make a living at it, why, then I give them credit of being the smartest nation on earth. For our own educational system is to teach our youth to learn something so that he will feel assured he won't have to do any manual labor through life. So if Mexicans can abstain from physical work without having to go to school twelve or fourteen years to learn how not to work, then I claim that's a national asset.

—More Letters: May 19, 1928

Mexicans are fine people. They don't do everything our way or like we do. But why should they? Maybe their way is best, who knows?

—Weekly Articles: January 15, 1928
(see IRELAND, IRISH INDIAN)

MEXICAN-AMERICAN RELATIONS

They said there were fewer Americans being killed there than ever. Sure, they will keep on being killed till they get the last one.

—Convention article: July 3, 1920

MILITARY DEFENSE

Will Rogers offered this advice to the Secretary of Defense:

"I told our secretary that I wished we had the biggest navy in the world, the biggest army, and by all means the biggest air force, but have it understood with the taxpayers that they are only to be used to defend the home grounds. Be ready for it, and then just stay home."

Get us a good navy, and a good army and more aeroplanes than anybody, and just say, "Yes we got 'em, but they are only to be used on the home grounds, now lay off us."

—*Weekly Articles:* December 9, 1928
(see ARMED FORCES, PEACE, WAR)

MILLIONAIRES

A man can make a million over night and he is on every page in the morning. But it never tells who gave up the million he got. You can't get money without taking it from somebody.

—*Weekly Articles:* June 1, 1930

MILLS, OGDEN

Will Rogers was asked to speak in support of Congressman Ogden Mills's candidacy for re-election to Congress. At a rally at New York's Town Hall on October 26, 1922, Will obliged the congressman with a classic campaign speech.

First Will attacked the congressman's opponent. He admitted he did not know his candidate's opponent, but assumed he was a scoundrel and a tool of special interests.

Will then confessed he did not actually *know* his own candidate. That is why he was "more apt to say something good of him than any one else."

146

While many candidates took up politics with questionable motives, Mills was wealthy before he went into politics, said Will—"not as wealthy as now, but rich."

Mills was handicapped by being educated at Harvard, said Will, but he was the only candidate who owned a silk hat and could get past the front door of a Fifth Avenue residence without delivering something.

"A living wage for bootleggers" was Mills's platform, Will announced, and free medical examinations for those who drank the stuff they sold.

Mills, shocked by Rogers' speech, sat through it without cracking a smile. However, he was re-elected despite Will Rogers' support.

MISSED TRICK

Will Rogers never missed a trick on purpose—until he discovered it was a secret of success as a performer: not the unintentionally missed trick but the *intentionally* missed trick.

One of the rope tricks Rogers performed in his vaudeville act involved jumping with both feet inside a spinning loop. It was not Rogers' most difficult trick, not by a long shot, but one night he missed the trick and broke the loop. He picked up his rope and apologized to the audience, "Well, got all my feet through but one."

This comeback brought the house down. Rogers was so gratified by the audience reaction that he incorporated the missed trick into his act every night.

MISSIONARIES

Same thing wrong with the missionaries. They will save anybody if he is far enough away and don't speak our language.

—*Daily Telegrams:* March 22, 1932

MODERN PROGRESS

Now that is what they call changing with the times, or modern progress. Everything must change. If a thing used to be good, now it must be bad. They tell you we are living in a fast age. We are—*if* we can live.

—*Weekly Articles:* May 31, 1925
(see PROGRESS)

MODESTY

Will Rogers was a modest man. His natural modesty prevented him from taking full credit for all his historic accomplishments.

"From my earliest birth I was always doing things and letting other people get the credit," he wrote in the author's note of *Letters of a Self-Made Diplomat.*

"I started the Spanish-American War in '98. But I never said anything. I just sit back and let the *Maine* get the credit of it. I was the one who told Roosevelt to call his regiment the Roughriders, even if there wasn't a horse nearer Cuba than Lexington, Kentucky.

"I didn't do much backstage management until I advised Roosevelt to go ahead and run for vice president, that something would turn up. We split over Taft [who weighed 300 pounds], I wanted him to reduce and Roosevelt didn't."

MOMENTOUS TIMES

Everybody is always talking about what momentous times we're living in, except Will Rogers. "Now what is momentous about 'em?" he asked. "Time is time, momentous things happen to individuals, not to everybody at once. What might be momentous to one would just be wasting time to another."

(see HISTORY MAKERS)

MONEY

"There had never been a time in our history when as many fools are making money as now," observed Will Rogers just after the stock market crashed in 1929. He wondered if that might have had anything to do with it.

Some men will do anything for a dollar—except work.

"Men will do things every day for money that all the spirit in the world you try to assemble can't make 'em do," said Will.

"Now, I am no philanthropist. I am hard to separate from money; if I killed two birds with one stone I would want the stone back."

All I know is it's easier to print than to make by work.

—Daily Telegrams: March 22, 1935

You can't make a dollar without taking it from somebody.

—Weekly Articles: October 2, 1932

People that pay for things never complain. It's the guy you give something to that you can't please.

—Weekly Articles: January 3, 1926

We got to get some other kind of distribution of money. The rich never had as much, and the poor as little.

—Weekly Articles: December 28, 1930

Everybody likes to make a dollar his way, but if he finds he is not allowed to make it his way, why, he is not going to overlook the chance of making it your way.

—Daily Telegrams: December 15, 1933

Everybody nowadays is suggesting ways of getting prosperous on somebody else's money.

—Daily Telegrams: February 17, 1931

(see DISTRIBUTION, WEALTH, WISHES)

MONKEY BUSINESS

There is still a lot of monkey in us. Throw anything you want into our cage and we will give it serious consideration.

—*Daily Telegrams:* June 25, 1935

MORNING

The distinguished ranks of early risers include some of history's greatest achievers or overachievers, including Benjamin Franklin (who said, "Early to bed and early to rise makes a man healthy, wealthy, and wise"). Will Rogers believed that the early morning hours were essential to constructive thinking. He expressed his early morning philosophy in *More Letters of a Self-Made Diplomat:* "I think that early morning, say from seven to eight, was meant for sleeping. That's when I do all my heavy thinking—is when I am sleeping from seven to eight A.M."

MOSES

The minute a thing is long and complicated it confuses. Whoever wrote the Ten Commandments made 'em short. They may not always be kept, but they can be understood. They are the same for all men. Some industry can't come in and say, "Ours is a special and unique case. You can't judge it by the others."

Moses just went up on the mountain with a letter of credit and some instructions from the Lord, and He just wrote 'em out, and they applied to the steel men, the oil men, the bankers, the farmers, and even the United States Chamber of Commerce. And he said, "Here they are, Brothers, you take 'em and live by 'em, or else."

I expect there is a lot of lessons in the Bible that we could learn and profit by and help us out, but we are just so busy doing nothing we haven't got time to study 'em out. But in Moses' time the rich didn't gang up on you and say, 'You change that commandment or we won't play.'

—*Weekly Articles:* March 17, 1935
(see BUSINESS)

MOSQUITOS

When Will Rogers learned from an entomologist that male mosquitos do not bite, make noise, or lay eggs, he urged a campaign for birth control among female mosquitos.

"Get that, the males are harmless, they don't bite, buzz, or lay eggs," he wrote in an article on February 24, 1929. "It makes me proud I am a male. That fellow Kipling had it write when he wrote (or maybe it was Shakespeare, or Lady Astor, or somebody over there) 'The female of the species is more deadly than the male.' Women denied it then and there was a great mess raised about it. But this Jersey entomologist has finally got the dope on 'em."

Will recommended pamphlets on birth control be distributed among the female mosquitos. "Show them that they are not only doing their part but they are going over their quota. Teach them that the days of the big families in mosquitos are past, that what we want is fewer and better mosquitos. Try and get 'em to move out of Jersey and to Fifth and Park Avenue, New York, and let 'em see there that being prolific in offsprings is only for the lower classes.

"Don't try to kill off the females. Educate 'em up to modern ways. They are not so crazy about laying eggs, it's just because they think it's their duty to do it."

But how do you tell the female mosquitos from the males? That is the question. "If he bites you he is a her, and if he sings, he is a her. Watch him and see if he lays an egg, then it's a her. But if he just sits around all day and don't do anything, why about the only conclusion we can come to is that it is a he. Don't kill him, he

151

does no harm, he just sits and revels in the accomplishments of his wife."

MOTHERS

My own mother died when I was ten years old. My folks have told me that what little humor I have comes from her. I can't remember her humor but I can remember her love and understanding of me. Of course, the mother I know the most about is the mother of our little group. She has been for twenty-two years trying to raise to maturity four children, three by birth and one by marriage. While she hasn't done a good job, the poor soul has done all that mortal human could do with the material she had to work with.

—Radio Broadcasts, May 11, 1930

Mothers are the only race of people that speak the same tongue. A mother in Manchuria could converse with a mother in Nebraska and never miss a word.

—Radio Broadcasts, May 11, 1930

I doubt if a charging elephant, or a rhino, is as determined or hard to check as a socially ambitious mother.

—Daily Telegrams: May 10, 1932
(see ROGERS, BETTY)

MOTHER'S DAY

"It's a beautiful thought," Will commented on Mother's Day, "but it's somebody with a hurting conscience that thought of the idea."

MOVIES

"I was in pictures before they were referred to press agents as an art," reminisced Will Rogers in an article published August 22, 1926. "I was in Hollywood away back, when some of these big stars now were just learning to get married."

His place in motion picture history belonged to its pioneering phase: "In other words, I am what you call a pioneer. I am all right in anything while it's in its crude state, but the minute it gets to having any class, why, I am sunk. After anything begins to take itself seriously, I have to gradually drop out, sometimes suddenly."

With a modesty uncharacteristic of a movie star, Will Rogers explained his contribution to the development of the film medium. "You see, pictures have to undergo a poor, or what Will Hayes would call 'mediocre,' stage, before they can get to be big. Well, there is the stage that I assisted the great film industry through. The minute they commenced to getting better, why, my mission had been fulfilled."

The motion picture industry was two decades old when Will Rogers made his film debut in 1918. It was a silent feature called *Laughing Bill Hyde,* a Samuel Goldwyn production based on a novel by Rex Beach. The author's wife had seen Will Rogers performing for the Ziegfeld Follies and decided he would be perfect for the lead role. The comedian expressed doubts about his ability to perform without a live audience, but agreed to do it.

The film received enthusiastic reviews. "Those inclined to believe that all of the magnetic Rogers personality is in his conversation will realize their mistake if they see this picture," wrote a *New York Times* critic. "The real Will Rogers is on the reels."

Goldwyn offered Rogers a two-year contract at triple his Ziegfeld wages, an offer Rogers found irresistible. He moved his family to Beverly Hills in 1919 and made twelve pictures before the contract expired. In 1921 Goldwyn left the studio and Will Rogers suddenly found himself without a contract. He made three movies with his own money—*Fruits of Faith, The Ropin' Fool,* and *One*

Day in 365—well received by critics but not financially successful.

A man who hated borrowing, Rogers found himself deeply in debt. His initial experience in Hollywood left him a wiser but not a richer man. "If a loan is made for a moving picture," he explained, "the president of the bank wants to write the story for you. The directors want to know who the leading lady is, and if they could, they would keep her as collateral."

Will Rogers learned from firsthand experience how hard it is to please everybody in a medium that is designed to please as many as possible:

"Producers decided to make fewer and worse pictures. . . . The decency code people said, 'They got to be cleaner!' The exhibitors say: 'If you get them too clean, nobody is interested in them!' The novelists say: 'What's the use of selling them a story, they don't make the story they buy!' The scenario staff says: 'It reads good, but it won't photograph!' The so-called intellectual keeps saying: 'Give us something worthwhile in the movies, that we can think about!' The regular movie fans say: 'Give us something to see, never mind think about. If we wanted to think, we wouldn't go to the movies!' "

Rogers continued occasionally acting in silent films until 1927, but most of his energy was channeled into writing his columns and lecturing. The advent of talking pictures in 1927 was what made movie stardom inevitable for Will Rogers. So much of his appeal as a performer lay in his words and artful delivery that silent film could not give vent to his comic genius.

In 1927 the first full-length feature film with sound, *The Jazz Singer*, was released by Warner Brothers. By 1929 Will Rogers was successfully launched on a new film career with his first talkie, *They Had to See Paris*. What followed was a series of wholesome family films—*A Connecticut Yankee in King Arthur's Court, David Harum, The Chairman, State Fair, Life Begins at Forty*, and others—in which Will Rogers played a character similar

154

to himself, a likable common man speaking out against corruption and villainy.

Will Rogers the movie star was the ultimate personification of the perennial comic type known as the rube—the native American rustic who outwits the sophisticated city slicker—the man with the hoe who wins out over the man with the hokum.

Rogers made three films a year for $110,000 apiece until he signed a contract in 1930 with Fox Film Corporation obligating him to six films for a total of $1,125,000, an astronomical sum during the Depression. By 1933 Will Rogers was ranked second in the *Motion Picture Herald*'s official list of the top ten box-office stars. In 1934, his best year of all, Will Rogers topped the list. In 1935, the year of his death in the Alaska plane crash, he slipped back to second place below the rising child star Shirley Temple.

"We try to make moving pictures as good as we can," Rogers explained as spokesman for an American art form still struggling to find itself somewhere between commerce and culture. "Bad pictures are not made with a premeditated design. It looks to you sometimes we must have purposely made 'em that way, but honest, we don't. A bad picture is an accident, and a good one is a miracle."

I don't know a thing about the motion picture business.

—*Weekly Articles:* June 13, 1926

They notify me the night before we start what it's to be, if they know by then themselves.

—*Weekly Articles:* June 16, 1935

MOVIE ADS

All I know is just what I read in the moving picture ads, and say boy what an education it is! I thought the underwear ads in the magazines were about the limit in presenting an eyeful, but these movie ads give you the same thing without the underwear. Even I myself appeared in a nightgown in *A Connecticut Yankee,* so on the billboards it would add a touch of romantic glamour, to say nothing of a smattering of sex appeal.

Mind you, you mustn't let the ad have anything to do with what you see on the insides. You are liable to see the wildest stuff facing you on the billboards, and then go inside and everybody is dressed as Eskimos all through the picture.

So the big problem of the movies now is to deliver up to what the lithograph makers and ad writers have shown on the outside.

In other words, that branch of the industry has outstripped the production end. We just can't seem to get 'em as wild as they show 'em on the outside. We got to get wilder people.

—Weekly Articles: May 17, 1931

MOVIE AUDIENCES

If so many of 'em are not looking at our pictures as used to, we are mighty grateful to those that are. If they are not looking at us it's because they are wise to us, and that's about the way it is with everything else.

—Weekly Articles: April 17, 1932

MOVIE BUSINESS

It's just like fishing, we never know when the public is going to bite. With all their unfailing judgment, the public has bit at some bad ones, so we keep on having a supply of them on hand, hoping that ours might be the sucker picture they would go for.

—Weekly Articles: October 2, 1932

156

MOVIE HEROES

"The average life of the movie hero," said Will, "is till he is found out."

(see HEROES)

MOVIE LIFE

"The average life of the movie," said Will, "is till it reaches the critic."

MOVIE OPENING

When Will Rogers' *Connecticut Yankee*—an adaptation of the Mark Twain classic—opened in 1931 he had high hopes for it. He felt it was not as bad as his other films.

"We turned out a little movie here a short time ago, and from reports it seemed to be pretty good, that is for mine."

Will was in New York when *Connecticut Yankee* opened, nervously awaiting news from Betty.

"I received a wire from my wife from California saying the picture had opened and I could come home, that's all the wire said. So you see we got two comedians in the family."

(see ROGERS, BETTY)

MOVIE STARS

At the start of 1935, the last year of his life, Will Rogers was still a screen star at fifty-five. But he knew the days of stars were numbered.

"When your beauty has deserted you, when you are getting old you have to resort to pure skill or trickery," he wrote in February, 1935. "I kinder take up the trickery.

"Now in the old days just looks alone got me by. I had the main love interest in my pictures stepping out to keep ahead of me. The Lord was good to me in the matter of handing out a sort of a half-breed Adonis profile (well, it was a little more than a profile that you had to get). Straight on I didn't look so good, and even sideways I wasn't too terrific, but a cross between a back and a three quarter view, brother I was hot. The way my ear (on one side) stood out from my head, was just bordering on perfect.

"That rear view give you just the shot needed.

"You see all screen stars have what they call their better angles. These women have just certain cameramen to shoot them, they know which way to turn 'em, and how to throw light on 'em.

"Well, they don't pay much attention to lighting with me, the more lights go out during a scene, the better."

MOVIE TECHNOLOGY

No art form has undergone so many technological transformations as motion pictures. Will Rogers lived through the transformation from silent film to talking pictures as a movie star.

"Talking pictures hit us at a time when we was as dumb as a rabbit, color photography showed up our red noses and gray hair, and to sink us entirely some guy in Washington yesterday got a patent on an apparatus that will register 'smell in the movies.' Now we not only got to look colorful, act good, talk good, but our personal odor has got to be above suspicion.

"A criticism will read: 'Popular John Gilbert appeared here last night in *Love 'Em and Destroy 'Em*. His speaking voice in the lower registers is pleasing, he has dark spots under his eyes, and a bluish bruise on his left thigh, he acts marvelous, but why don't he do something about his halitosis?"

(see TALKING PICTURES)

MOVIE TITLES

"They just can't think of enough suggestive titles to go around," Will Rogers explained the painstaking process of movie title selection.

"They bring every big writer out here from New York and England and have them in an office just thinking all the time on titles that will lead you to expect you are going to see on the inside about four of the most prominent commandments broken, right before your eyes. But there is just so many of these titles and every company is fighting to get 'em.

"Few of the best that have been turned in by the highest priced writers up to now is *The Old Love Nest, Home in Name Only, The Birthplace of Folly, Devilment Galore among the Honeysuckles, What Took Place under the Old Roof, The Gal Pays the Mortgage with Body and Soul, The House Is Old But the Carryings On Is New And Spicy. The Gangster's Birthplace Is As Far As We Know.*"

They will film the Lord's Supper and when it is made, figure out that it is not a good release title and not catchy enough, so it will be released under the heading, *A Red Hot Meal*, or *The Gastronomical Orgy*.

—*Weekly Articles:* October 13, 1929

MOVIE VIOLENCE

When gangster movies came in fashion, cowboy movies seemed old-fashioned. The cowboy philosopher preferred cowboy pictures but agreed they were old-fashioned.

"We have run the old cowboy trying to save the sheriff's daughter, right back to the dairy farm. No modern child wants to learn how to shoot a .45 Colt. He wants to know how to mow 'em down with the old Browning machine gun."

MUNICIPAL ELECTIONS

Our municipal election run true to political form. The sewer was defeated but the councilman got in.

—*Daily Telegrams:* June 3, 1931

MURDERERS

Americans are more fascinated by the lives of murderers than the lives of great leaders or luminaries. "Right now we know more about Mrs. Ruth Judd's life than we do about Lincoln's, Washington's, Napoleon's, or Greta Garbo's," Will noted in November, 1931, alluding to the latest celebrity murderer.

Mrs. Judd received a lot of notoriety because she chose to stuff her victim in a trunk. "You can kill all the people you want in this country and not attract any attention, but if you kill 'em and put 'em in a trunk, why, you become famous. It's how you dispose of a dead body that makes you sensational in this country and how many dead bodies you did create."

Will's advice to aspiring murderers: "Don't figure out who you are going to kill, figure out how you are going to kill 'em."

MURDERS

Whatever kind of murder you want, why, just write to your favorite tabloid and they will, if you get ten signers, have the murder for you.

—*Weekly Articles:* June 30, 1929

You know what has been the cause of the big increase in murders? It's been the manufacture of the automatic pistol. In the first place there is no skill or nerve required in using it.

—*Weekly Articles:* September 20, 1925
(see AUTOMATIC, GUN CONTROL, WOMEN MURDERERS)

MURDER SUICIDES

Following the latest murder trials in the newspapers, Will pointed out a high percentage of murder-suicides.

"Why is it that an attempted suicide that is going to kill somebody else along with himself," Will asked, "why is it they never miss the other party but are poor shots on themselves? You would think as close as they are to themselves that they couldn't miss. But they most generally do. They seem to be able to hit everybody else they shoot at but themselves."

MUSSOLINI, BENITO

When an Irish woman attempted to assassinate Italian dictator Benito Mussolini in Rome in 1926, Will Rogers wrote about the event irreverently in his nationally syndicated daily column, poking fun at fascism—not knowing that two months later he would meet Mussolini.

"An Irish woman shot at Mussolini in Rome and hit him in the nose. It looked for a minute like Italy would be saved. So that's the advantage of having a Roman nose in Rome. Even photographers will tell you you must never shoot a man's profile. The shooting demonstrated one thing, and that was that you could shoot Mussolini in the head without hitting his brains. So they are not as extensive as he has led us to believe.

"It only shows that you can dictate to men, but you can't dictate to women.

"I tell you the world owes women a terrible lot, and one of our greatest debts to them is for shooting some of the men. If we can just improve their marksmanship we can improve civilization.

"People think there is a lot of shooting going on in the United States nowadays, but I tell you there is not half as much as there ought to be. About every fourth fellow you meet nowadays ought to be shot."

Two months after publishing this humorous squib, in

June, 1926, Will Rogers found himself in Italy at a racetrack—for reasons that can be explained, but the explanation is omitted here—when Mussolini appeared. Rather than try to avoid him, Will Rogers insisted on being introduced to him. They had a brief chat that Will remembers well. The great dictator asked Will what impressed him most about Italy.

"Well, I knew that everybody had always told him that it was the 'marvelous development that had taken place in the last three years.' But I told him that it was two things—he seemed very interested—one was the amount of automobiles meeting and neither one ever knowing which side the other was going to pass him on, and yet nobody ever got hit, and the other thing was the amount of bicycles ridden, and I never saw anyone ever fixing a puncture."

Mussolini laughed.

"But you could tell he was disappointed," Will recalled. "I was the only one that had not noticed the 'marvelous improvement in the last three years.'"

N

NAME-DROPPING

At the 1928 Republican convention in Kansas City, Will Rogers remarked: "If you eliminate the names of Lincoln, Washington, Roosevelt, Jackson, and Wilson, both parties' political conventions would get out three days earlier."

(see LINCOLN, WASHINGTON, ROOSEVELT, JACKSON, WILSON)

NATION

"What we forget is that every nation has to look at things from their own angle, not our angle," said Will Rogers, ambassador-at-large.

"So every nation is equally cuckoo. It all depends on who is looking at us."

(see FOREIGN RELATIONS, INTERNATIONAL RELATIONS)

NATIONAL AFFAIRS

Now is one of the best times in the world for us to fight among ourselves. It will at least keep us out of some bigger devilment.

—*Daily Telegrams:* February 14, 1934
(SEE FOREIGN RELATIONS, INTERNATIONAL RELATIONS)

NATIONAL ANTHEM

"It will take America two more wars," Will Rogers predicted, "to learn the words to our national anthem."

NATIONAL DEBT

"We owe more money than any nation in the world," said Will. "When is the time to pay off a debt if it is not when you are doing well? All Government statistics say that 70 percent of every dollar paid in the way of taxes goes to just the keeping up of interest and little dab of amortization of our national debts. In other words, if we didn't owe anything our taxes would only be less than one third what they are today.

"I bet tomorrow if you started a political party and had this as its platform, 'No taxes are to be paid at all. We will borrow money on our national resources for all current expenses.' Remember the slogan, 'No taxes as long as we can borrow.'

"Well, I bet you would have the biggest political party in America.

"Start a society on the following platform: 'Everybody try to borrow all you can personally, and save up nothing. Leave your children plenty of debts.' Say you wouldn't get ten to join that. You would be arrested for being crazy. But you will let the coming generation pay 70 percent (of each dollar they pay in) just for what you borrowed during your generation.

"No sir, you let a politician return home from Washington and announce, 'Boys, we lowered your taxes. We had to borrow the money to do it, but we did it.' Say, they would elect him for life. While me on my platform would be thrown to the wolves as an infidel.

"Most folks say, 'Well, our children seem to think they are smarter than we are, so if they are, the chances are that their children will be smarter than they are, so if they are that smart why maybe they can think of some substitute for money that they can pay off their national debt with, and they will wonder why we didn't have a bigger one.'

"There is a change coming over the country anyhow. People have just got to get more used to debt. Let's all let the fellow we owe do the worrying and the United States will be the happiest land on earth."

(see DEBT)

NATIONAL HEALTH CARE

One thing that a poor person should never be even expected to pay for is medical attention, and not from an organized charity, but from our best doctors. But your doctor bill should be paid like your income tax, according to what you have. There is nothing that keeps poor people poor as much as paying doctor bills.

—*Weekly Articles:* July 13, 1930
(see DOCTORS, TAXES)

NATIONAL HONOR

The honor roll of nations reads like a roster of the world's greatest weapons merchants. "It is funny, Senator," Will wrote to Senator Borah in 1932, "what a respect and a national honor a few guns will get you, ain't it?"

(see ARMS, DISARMAMENT, GUNS, PATRIOT)

NATIONALISM

It's the same the world over; every nation is trying to live more and more within itself; each nation is going in the hole and pulling the hole in after it.

—*More Letters:* April 30, 1932, p. 173

NATIONS

It's awful hard for three nations to entirely agree on how the other three will be run by them.

—*Daily Telegrams:* April 11, 1935

No nation has a monopoly on good things. Each one has something that the others could well afford to adopt.

—*Weekly Articles:* November 30, 1930

Nations are just like individuals. Loan them money and you lose their friendship.

—*Weekly Articles:* January 11, 1925

Nations are like a lot of women with their babies. Each thinks that theirs is the best.

—*Daily Telegrams:* April 27, 1933

Why don't they let every nation go ahead and do what it wants to?

—*Weekly Articles:* December 9, 1928

NAVAJOS

Will visited Navajo territory in 1924:

"They struck oil on the Navajo's land three years ago. I foolishly asked how often they get their payment for their oil royalty. Well, they hadn't any yet. They took a million of it to build a bridge across the Little Colorado River so tourists wouldn't have to drive so far around to see the Grand Canyon. The Navajos paid for the bridge and there has never been a Navajo crossed it yet. If the Indians' oil royalties hold out they will have enough to build the Boulder Dam for the whites."

(see CHEROKEES, INDIANS, NATIVE AMERICANS)

NATIVE AMERICANS

The final tragedy of the Native Americans is that they are becoming "uncivilized" under the influence of the whites. "I tell you it's awful hard to stay civilized in this country nowadays," Will said, speaking from personal experience.

The combined efforts of the missionary, the schoolteacher, and the bootlegger were taking their toll on the Native American. "Now," said Will sadly, "he is as unreliable as his white brother."

Consider history:

"Why were the pilgrims allowed to land anywhere? That's what we want to know. Now I hope my Cherokee blood is not making me prejudiced, I want to be broadminded. But I am sure it was only the extreme generosity of the Indians that allowed the pilgrims to land. Suppose we reverse the case. Do you reckon the pilgrims would ever let the Indians land? What a chance! Why, the pilgrims wouldn't even allow the Indians to live, after the Indians went to the trouble of letting 'em land."

(see CHEROKEES, INDIANS, NAVAJOS)

NATURAL

Being "natural" was a trade secret of Will Rogers' success as a public performer. "Natural" was his trademark. The challenge was to "stay natural" despite the distractions and temptations of success.

"If I can stay natural I will be a hit," he wrote from a movie set in London in 1926. He felt his success in the movies depended on his playing a "natural" role—himself.

"If I can just get cast in a picture now where the part is a lecturer going around the country trying to reform all the politicians, why I will have another natural part on my hands."

(see MOVIES, SMALL TOWN)

NATURAL RESOURCES

Will Rogers warned we are using up our natural resources without replenishing them: "We are going along at top speed, because we are using all ours up just as fast as we can. If we want to build something out of wood, all we got to do is go cut down a tree and build it. We didn't have to plant the tree. Nature did that before we come. Suppose we couldn't build something out of wood till we found a tree that we had purposely planted for that use. Say, we never would get it built.

"We are certainly setting pretty right now. But when our resources run out, if we can still be ahead of other nations then will be the time to brag; then we can show whether we are really superior.

"You know Americans have been getting away pretty soft up to now. Every time we needed anything, why it was growing right under our nose. Every natural resource in the world, we had it. But with them getting less, and debts getting more, there is going to be some work going on in this country some day."

(see AMERICA, PROSPERITY, WORK)

NEVADA

"Nevada—it's freedom's last stand in America," Will Rogers affirmed. "Yet they don't do one thing that other states don't do.

"Every state in the union gambles as much as Nevada

does, but they were smart enough to pass a law and get some tax money out of it.

"If Wall Street paid a tax on every 'game' they run, we would get enough revenue to run the government on."

(see SOFT JOB, WALL STREET)

NEVADA DIVORCE

Arkansas lowered its divorce requirements in 1931 and Will Rogers told what happened next: "Nevada heard about it and called a special session of their legislature and says: 'We will give you one in six weeks, and if any other state goes under that time, we will give you a divorce, marriage, and another divorce all for the same time, and price. In other words, that's our business. We have built it up to what it is today. If there had been no Reno, you would still have been living with the same old gal. So, remember, we are the state that will divorce you, even if we have to do it by telegraph."

(see DIVORCE, MARRIAGE PREDICTION)

NEW CARS

Every year there was excitement generated by the auto makers attending the new models.

Will Rogers claimed to have the inside dope on the new 1928 Ford from Mr. Henry Ford himself, who allegedly met with him over lunch.

"Before I left I got the specifications of the new car," Will recounted. "At that time it was not out. But he gave me the dope on it. Here are some of the 'specs.'

Wheel Base	Twenty feet running and folds up to three feet when parked.
Gear	10 percent of advertised rate, and 2 percent of Chamber of Commerce figures.
Rear Axle	Will bend or break as occasion demands.
Weight	Deceiving.
Finish	Natural Mud.
Tires	Just as good as rubber.
Cooling System	Frigidaire.
Transmission	That's a big word, but it's in there.
Body	Perfect 36.
Horn	Alto or Soprano.

"Special equipment includes wheels, engine, fenders, and seats, if you care to sit down."

NEWPORT

Newport is a great old place. If you are not a sailor or a millionaire you feel out of place here.

—*Daily Telegrams:* July 23, 1928

NEWS SHORTAGE

During the Depression in 1931 there was an occasional news shortage. Will Rogers noticed the lack of news and reported to the public: "There just ain't no news and now some of our big men predict that there will be a turn for the better, that there will be news coming our way any day now. They claim that news is just around the corner, and that it will be on us before we know it. They claim that there has been times like this before, and the press has come out of it, and that it will do it again. But never has there been as general a shortage of news all over the world as there is now."

The press corps, of course, was always hopeful for a new war. "Nothing revives interest in the press like a good war. It don't necessarily have to be local, it can be foreign if it's a good one."

But the world wasn't ready for the next war quite yet. So still no news.

"You see the trouble nowadays is that no one can think of anything new to do. Everything that is done has been done before, so there is no news in it.

"It may be years before there is much news. It's going to take a new generation of people to make new news."

(see YOUNG FOLKS)

NEWSPAPER FUNNIES

"The funnies occupy four pages of the paper and editorials two columns," noted Will Rogers. "That proves that merit will tell."

NEWSPAPERS

The news that's *not* fit to print is what makes the newspapers.

—*Weekly Articles:* August 2, 1925

NEWSPAPER WOMEN

Will Rogers was invited to speak at a convention of newspaper women.

"The newspaper women of all the papers formed a Newspaper Woman's Club and they give a big ball and I was asked to announce the acts. You know, women are doing all the writing on newspapers and magazines now.

"We had there women writers that cover everything. It would have been the greatest place in the world for some woman to have shot her husband. There were women murder writers that can tell from the smoke the caliber pistol used. Then there were the fashion editors that could have described her chemise frock while she did the shooting. Then the sob sister squad who could have almost made you feel sorry she only had one husband to shoot."

(see HUSBAND KILLERS, WOMEN MURDERERS)

NEW YORK

"Another innocent bystander shot in New York yesterday," Will noted one night at the Follies. "You just stand around this town long enough and be innocent and somebody is going to shoot you. One day they shot four. That's the best shooting ever done in this town. Any time you can find four innocent people in New York in one day you are doing well even if you don't shoot 'em.

"That really was quite an event to shoot an innocent person in New York City. It takes better shooting than you think. You know policemen in New York are never taught to aim; they are instructed just to shoot up the street any way. No matter who they hit it will be someone that should have been hit before. They very seldom hit the one originally intended, but they most always get a worse one."

New York is so situated that anything you want, you can get in the very block you live in. If you want to be robbed, there is one living in your block; if you want to be murdered, you don't have to leave your apartment house; if you want pastrami or gefilte fish, there is a delicatessen every other door; if it's female excitement you crave, your neighbor's wife will accommodate you.

The whole of New York City, where 80 percent of our wealthy people are in storage, if you turned 'em loose in Canada on their own resources, it would be fifty years before one would get far enough away from Toronto to discover Lake Erie.

—*More Letters:* November 20, 1931
(see GRAFT, HEAVEN, OKLAHOMA)

NEW YORKERS

But we got to be tolerant, for these New Yorkers are likable rascals even when they are skinning you.

—*Daily Telegrams:* May 1, 1933

NEW YORK WRITERS

Those New York writers should be compelled to get out once in their lifetime and get the "folks" angle.

—*Weekly Articles:* December 18, 1932

NICARAGUA

"If Nicaragua would just come out like a man and fight us, we wouldn't have to be hunting away off over in China for a war."

Will urged the United States to find a more convenient war, closer to home. "Stop Nicaragua while there is still time," he said, attempting to rally American military forces. "Join the navy and help find Nicaragua."

Eventually the U.S. government did manage to stir up some war in Nicaragua. The American public always eventually gets tired of war in Nicaragua. "We are even getting tired of continually fighting with Nicaraguans," Will observed in 1931. "We always have to take them on when there is no bigger bait."

War in Nicaragua is holding on pretty good. Our original assertion that it was only a few rebels that were dissatisfied has kinder been disproved. The rebels must of had a majority when they started out or else we couldn't have killed as many as we have.

—*Weekly Articles:* November 27, 1927

How in the world did we find out where Nicaragua is anyway? Everytime you pick up a paper "the American Marines have landed at Nicaragua." There has been more Marines landed in Nicaragua than there has at the Brooklyn Navy Yard.

—*Weekly Articles:* December 5, 1926

Here is a fellow that is sending me a book, *The Looting of Nicaragua*. It's in answer to, "Why are we in Nicaragua, and what in ____ are we doing there? by congressman-at-large Will Rogers."

—*Weekly Articles:* February 19, 1928

NIGHTCLUBS

"I see where New York is going to make their nightclubs close at three in the morning, and the people are kicking about it," observed Will. "Well, I say they ought to close 'em. Anybody that can't get drunk by three A.M. ain't trying."

(see BEER, RUSSIAN VODKA)

NOMINATION

Will Rogers' name was placed into nomination at the 1932 Democratic convention. He was present at the convention, but had fallen asleep and had to be awakened and informed of what had happened.

"A tornado of approval swept the stadium," wrote one reporter, "but Rogers would have slept right through this moment of glory had not colleagues of the press punched him in the ribs. He came out of the trance dazed but smiling, and let out a long, loud laugh when he heard what had happened."

Will later confessed that he had indeed dozed off. He excused himself in this way: "The whole thing came on me so sudden and I was so sleepy. I had been taking opiates all night. No man can listen to thirty-five nominating speeches and hold his head up. And I am sure some of these that did the nominating can never hold theirs up again."

Will Rogers received the twenty-two votes from the leader of the Oklahoma delegation, Alfalfa Bill Murray, who threw his twenty-two votes "to that sterling citizen, that wise philosopher, that great heart, that favorite son of Oklahoma, Will Rogers.' "

Will expressed a desire to keep the twenty-two delegates and later lamented their loss. Thinking the excitement was over, Will dozed off again and when he woke someone else had been nominated—Franklin Delano Roosevelt. "And what do I do—go to sleep and wake up without even the support of the Virgin Islands. They not only took my votes but they got my hat and typewriter."

Will waxed philosophical about the whole ordeal of being nominated for president. "Now what am I? Just another ex-Democratic presidential candidate. There's thousands of 'em. Well, the whole thing has been a terrible lesson to me and nothing to do but start in and live it down."

(see ROOSEVELT, RESIGNATION, WITHDRAWAL)

NOSE JOBS

With all the practice they get, any woman that can't find her nose without a mirror should not be allowed to have a nose. Suppose the man of the species (who is usually more dumb than the female) had to take out a mirror to find his nose every time he wanted to blow it! Suppose he had lost his mirror! His nose would have to go blowless.

Noses are receiving entirely too much attention anyway. You can hardly pick up a paper nowadays without the story of some prominent person having the contour of his or her nose reassembled. In the old days you used to be born with an appendix and a nose, and you went through life practically ignorant of the shape of either.

Now the appendix in a bottle has replaced the family Bible as an exhibit in the home, and a nose that has not been overhauled, don't *nose* nothing.

There are today in New York City more doctors removing superfluous noses than there are dentists removing teeth. Every nose has a doctor all its own. They are landscaping noses just like flower gardens. If an architect has not drawn up a blue print of your nose you are as old-fashioned as red flannel underwear. I haven't had mine charted yet, as the face gardener said it would take more than a readjusted nose to do me any good. In fact, he said my nose was about the only thing on my face that seemed to be properly laid out.

—*Weekly Articles:* September 7, 1924
(see TEETH)

NUDE

Will Rogers was often surrounded by scantily clad Follies. He liked to tease women about their fashions, especially the showy attire that revealed a lot of female flesh. "It's awful hard to tell when a woman is nude nowadays and when she is fully clothed," he said. "If the worse come to the worst she could always say it was an evening dress."

(see FASHIONS, LONG SKIRTS)

NUDISTS

"If it really is a religion with these nudist colonies," said Will with a chill, "they sure must turn atheists in the winter time."

OBSERVATION

"People's minds are changed through observation and not through argument," was Will Rogers' observation.

(see ARGUMENT)

OFF YEARS

It's an off year in politics and all off years are Democratic years.

—*Daily Telegrams:* December 31, 1929

OHIO

"Ohio claims they are due a president as they haven't had one since Taft," remarked Will Rogers. "Look at the United States, they haven't had one since Lincoln."

(see LINCOLN, PRESIDENTS)

OKLAHOMA

The born New Yorker who lives in Ohio has been trying to get up a Society of New Yorkers out there, but you can't incorporate with only one member. I, myself, belong to the Oklahoma Society in New York. We meet every year in a member's single room at the Mills Hotel—all four of us. Now judge for yourself which is the best state.

—*Weekly Articles:* January 28, 1923
(see NEW YORK, NEW YORKERS, OHIO)

OKLAHOMA PROGRESS

If Oklahoma does in the next twenty-two years what we have in the last, why, New York will be our parking space, Chicago our arsenal, New Orleans our amusement center, and Los Angeles segregated for Elk and Shriner conventions.

—*Daily Telegrams:* September 18, 1929

OKLAHOMA SEASONS

Our people don't move with the seasons, hunting a different climate. Our climate changes with our seasons. Why, we throw away more climate that we don't need in one year than you have charged your customers with! We don't sell climate; it goes with the purchase of land, just as the darkness or the light. We don't have to throw in a Gulf Stream or a trade wind or a canceled state income tax or a movie contract or a catfish. There are no remnant sales in Oklahoma. California has to irrigate, Florida has to fertilize. Now it hardly seems right, does it, that the Lord would take both those off an Oklahoman's hands? We don't have to depend on a dam; nor Chile for nitrates. You just throw anything out in Oklahoma and all you have to do is come back and harvest it.

—"How To Be Funny," May 29, 1926
(see HOME)

OLD MAN

"A young man, he just thinks," reflected Will. "But an old man, when he thinks, he is supposed to be pondering."

(see BIOGRAPHY 1935)

OLD REPUBLICIANS

When Hoover was running for re-election in 1932, there were many prominent Republicians who downplayed the Great Depression.

"Passed the Potter's Field yesterday and they was burying two staunch old Republicans," said Will, "both of whom died of starvation, and the man in charge told me their last words were, 'I still think America is fundamentally sound.' "

OPERATION

Will Rogers claimed he once had a joke surgically removed. It was when he had an operation to remove his gallstones. He wrote about the experience in *Ether and Me*.

Realizing he might not survive the procedure, Will gave some thought to his last words. He wanted to go out with a clever remark.

"So I thought all night of a good joke; and just before they operated, I was going to pull this joke and then they would all laugh hilariously and say, 'Well, old Will wasn't so bad at that.'

"So I got ready to pull the joke, and there was one fellow standing behind—he's the fellow you can't see, that's going to knock you out; he's the fellow that's got a jar of ether in his hand—well, I was all ready to set the world laughing uproariously when this old boy just gently slipped that nozzle right over my mouth and nose both.

"I wanted to tell him, 'Just a minute!' And I started to reach up and snatch it off, and a couple of men enlisted as interns, but who in reality were wrestlers on vacation, had me by each hand. Out I went, and from that day to this I have never been able to think of that joke. It was the best one I ever had.

"I don't know what they operated on me for, but they certainly took out that joke."

(see GALLSTONES)

OPINION

Will Rogers discovered that people who agreed with his opinions thought he was brilliant, whereas those who disagreed with his opinions thought he was an ignorant fool.

"My lack of humor, lack of English, lack of good taste, and all the other things they accuse me of, is a lot of bunk," he wrote in rebuttal to his critics. "Let the same things be said in favor of their opinion, and I would be a great guy."

If I don't see things your way, well, why should I?

—*Weekly Articles:* December 18, 1932

ORGANIZED CRIME

Lots of people think that all this racketeering and bootlegging and corruption is just a fly-by-night affair, run on a slipshod haphazard way. Well, you never were more wrong in your life. You know as a matter of fact there is nothing as old as crookedness. It started away back when Eve used some political and sex influence on poor old, dumb Adam to get him to gnaw on a forbidden apple. Old Cain slew Abel, or vice versa, I don't know which. But anyhow it was an argument over the spoils. So you see on account of its age it's not a fly-by-night industry. Meanness has always been better organized and conducted than righteousness.

—*Weekly Articles:* July 6, 1930
(see CRIMINALS, CRIME AND PUNISHMENT)

OVERPOPULATION

We are raising too many people. There ain't enough jobs to go round, and there ain't enough business to go round.

—*Daily Telegrams:* March 23, 1930
(see MOSQUITOS, POOR PEOPLE)

P

PACKER, ALFRED

Will Rogers wrote a tribute to the first American convicted of cannibalism, Alfred Packer, who devoured some of his starving fellow companions on the Donner party expedition in Colorado in 1847.

Will pointed out Packer's educational background helped prepare him for his destiny as a cannibal. "Packer was a Harvard graduate," Will said. "What I am getting at is that the only case of a person willfully devouring human flesh was by the alumni of the great Harvard, so Harvard has not only produced the least understandable English in our fair land, but produced the only living cannibal."

Packer's occupation also prepared him for cannibalism. "He was a lawyer, that of course seems natural, their profession is an offshoot of the cannibal profession."

There was one other thing on Packer's résumé that seemed to be a special qualification: "I forgot to tell you he was the son of a missionary, and in his youth spent some time in the South Sea Islands. That's how he acquired his taste. A missionary, a lawyer, a Harvard graduate."

Those are the three best qualifications for cannibalism in the United States.

(see HARVARD, LAWYERS, MISSIONARY)

PAGEANT

Will Rogers, being a celebrity, was forced to participate in many pageants, often accompanied by nearly naked dancing girls.

"It's an unwritten law that you can't put a girl on a float with any clothes on. In fact here is the ingredients of a 'pageant.' You first pick a cold night, then have plenty of places all over the 'float' for girls to stand, but don't let 'em have anything on. That's the first ingredient of a 'float rider' is to be totally naked. Now she must be able to smile through the snow and sleet.

"What she is doing up there, or what she is to represent must never enter her head any more than it does the man that arranged it. She is just up there to act naked, and hope that she is not frostbitten by the end of the journey. They are not really 'pageants.' They are early stages of pneumonia.

"A 'pageant' is a collection of bare skin, surrounded by plenty of electric light bulbs."

(see PARADES, NUDE)

PALL BEARER

Will Rogers was scheduled to introduce a speaker at a theater in Hollywood. Before he went on stage he received a warning from his wife Betty.

"My wife was so afraid that I in my long-winded way would monopolize the whole evening, she said, 'Now remember tonight, you are just a pall bearer, you are not the corpse, and it's the corpse they are interested in.' "

(see MOVIE OPENINGS; ROGERS, BETTY)

PARADES

"There is two things that tickle the fancy of our citizens, one is let him act on a committee, and the other is promise him to let him walk in a parade."

Will Rogers was hard pressed to explain the American fondness for parades.

"There is nothing as overestimated as a parade of any kind. It don't draw crowds, the people that are lined along the sidewalk are just trying to get to the other side. That's all. Nobody is interested in the parade."

To make parades interesting Will recommended including horses.

"You get 'em all dressed up and put 'em on a horse, and then a parade means something. Even if the parade don't interest you, you can always watch it to see how many fall off."

(see HORSES, POLO SPILLS)

PARKING

It's getting so a man that has a car now walks further than he ever did in his life, walking back from where he parked it at.

—*Weekly Articles:* December 27, 1925

PARKING VIOLATIONS

"Fourteen thousand people were fined last year for parking more than six inches from the curb," said Will Rogers. "Two murderers were convicted, and then released as insane."

(see CRIMINALS)

PARTY

"If we didn't have two parties, we would all settle on the best men in the country and things would run fine," said

Will. "But as it is, we settle on the worst ones and then fight over 'em.

"I really can't see any advantage of having one of your party in as president. I would rather be able to criticize a man, than to have to apologize for him.

"You know the more you read and observe about this politics thing, you got to admit that each party is worse than the other. The one that's out always looks the best."

If a man could tell the difference between the two parties he would make a sucker out of Solomon for wisdom.

—*Weekly Articles:* November 11, 1928

They are always telling, "What my party has accomplished." Now as a matter of fact any time a man says that he is insulting the intelligence of his audience, for no party can put over one sprig of legislation without the aid of some members of the other party.

—*Weekly Articles:* July 1, 1928

I have not aligned myself with any party. I am just sitting tight waiting for an attractive offer.

—*Weekly Articles:* November 11, 1923

I generally give the party in power, whether Republican or Democrat, the more digs because they are generally doing the country more damage, and besides I don't think it is fair to jump too much on the fellow who is down. He is not working, he is only living in hopes of getting back in on the graft in another four years, while the party in power is drawing a salary to be knocked.

—*Weekly Articles:* November 9, 1924
(see CORRUPTION, POLITICS, PRESIDENTS)

PARTY CONVENTION

I don't believe there is over three or four ideas at any given convention.

—*Weekly Articles:* July 1, 1928

PARTY FOUNDERS

Republicans and Democrats keep referring to the respective founders of their parties, "not to pay tribute to his memory, but to put over some party hooey," Will explained. "The man in the grave if he could hear it, would get up and denounce the whole affair. It's 'Lincoln and the great Republican party, and Jefferson and the great Democratic party.' Neither man would know his party if he came back today, and neither one would admit it if he did know 'em."

(see HOOEY, JEFFERSON, LINCOLN, NAMEDROPPING)

PARTY HISTORY

The main thing to make 'em cut out is the so-called "history of the party." They always start out, "This party has always since its early birth been the party of right. The other party has been cockeyed all their life. Noah when he founded our party, had both sides to pick from right and wrong, and he wisely chose right, and right we have ever remained, so it is a principle born in us to uphold the weak against the strong. This great party had its birth in virtue, its youth in righteousness, and is spending its old age in holiness."

—*Weekly Articles:* July 1, 1928

(see DEMOCRATIC CORRUPTIONS, REPUBLICANS)

PARTY PLATFORM

Party platforms are prepared at each party's convention and then ignored. Reporting on the 1928 Democratic convention, Will did not claim to have read the platform—he was too honest a man to make such an idle boast—but he said he did know of a man who actually did read it. "The platform I will discuss later," he telegrammed from Houston on June 29: "A man read it last night, perhaps the last man that will ever read it."

(see ECONOMIC JARGON, IDEAS, THEORIES)

PARTY POLITICS

Party politics is the most narrow-minded occupation in the world. A guy raised in a straight jacket is a corkscrew compared to a thickheaded party politician.

All you would have to do to make some men atheists is just to tell them the Lord belonged to the opposition political party. After that they could never see any good in Him.

—*Weekly Articles:* March 29, 1925

There is a hundred things to single you out for promotion in party politics besides ability.

—*Weekly Articles:* October 14, 1928

(see DEMOCRATS, REPUBLICANS)

PATRIOTISM

Any man is a bandit if he is fighting opposite you and licking you most of the time. If you are fighting against him, that's patriotism. The difference between a bandit and a patriot is a good press agent.

—*More Letters:* April 30, 1932, p. 172

(see ANARCHIST, HISTORY; WASHINGTON, GEORGE)

PEACE

"Peace is like a beautiful woman," said Will Rogers, "it's wonderful, but has been known to bear watching."

You can't get nothing without trying, and if no effort is made toward peace, why, we can't expect any.

—Weekly Articles: October 20, 1929

They want peace, but they want a gun to help get it with.

—Weekly Articles: February 9, 1930

If we pulled together as much to put over a siege of peace as we do a spell of war, we would be sitting pretty.
   Peace is kinder like prosperity. There is mighty few nations that can stand it.

—Daily Telegrams: November 12, 1930

People talk peace, but men give their life's work to war. It won't stop till there is as much brains and scientific study put to aid peace as there is to promote war.

—Daily Telegrams: May 31, 1929

The greatest contribution to peace in the world would be an international clause, "Any nation can have a nice little revolution any time it sees fit, without any outside aid or advice from America or England."

—Weekly Articles: August 20, 1933

I don't care how little your country is, you got a right to run it like you want to. When the big nations quit meddling then the world will have peace.

—Daily Telegrams: August 9, 1933
(see DIPLOMATS, INTERNATIONAL AFFAIRS, WAR)

PEACE CONFERENCE

Every war has been preceded by a peace conference. That's what always starts the next war.

—*Weekly Articles:* July 22, 1923
(see CONFERENCE, WAR)

PERU

Peru is the Inca country. In fact every country has become the Inca country—red inka. Excuse me for that one, but remember we are flying at 13,000 feet. It's the altitude that makes you light-headed.

—*Daily Telegrams:* October 15, 1932

PESSIMISTS

The summer before the stock market crash of 1929 there were many pessimists saying the country was going downhill. People looked to the Senate for leadership. When the Senate adjourned for summer vacation without having done anything, Will Rogers said it was good news.

"Come on, downtrodden, let's finally give some cheers! The Senate met and adjourned in three minutes. That will knock the pessimists in the head that think this country is not improving.

"But—and there is always a 'but' to all good news—they are going to meet again. So we can't hope for this continued prosperity."

(see AMERICA, CONGRESS, SENATE)

PHILOSOPHY OF LIFE

The philosopher Will Durant asked Will Rogers to contribute to his book *Living Philosophies*. This is how Will Rogers expressed his philosophy of life:

"I can't tell this doggone Durant anything. What all of

us know put together don't mean anything. We are just here for a spell and pass on. Any man that thinks civilization had advanced is an egotist. We have got more toothpaste on the market and more misery in our courts than at any time in our existence. So get a few laughs and do the best you can.

"Don't make an ideal to work for, that's like riding toward a mirage of a lake. When you get there it ain't there. Believe in something for another world, but don't be too set on what it is, and then you won't start out that life with a disappointment. Live your life so that whenever you lose, you are ahead."

(see ADVICE, CIVILIZATION, LIFE, PROGRESS, SUCCESS)

PICNIC

You can't have a picnic lunch unless the party carrying the basket comes.

—*Daily Telegrams:* January 21, 1932

PLACES

Will Rogers traveled the world and came to the conclusion that all places, like all people, are ultimately equal.

"You see the Lord in His justice works everything on a handicap basis. California having the best of everything else must take a slice of the calamities (earthquakes). Even my native Oklahoma (the Garden of Eden of the West) has a cyclone. Kansas, while blessed with its grasshoppers, must endure its politicians. New York with its splendors has its Wall Street, and Washington, the world's most beautiful city, has a lobbyist crawling out to attack you from every manhole.

"So every human and every place is equal after all."

(see EQUALITY, KANSAS; WASHINGTON, D.C.)

PLANS

My plan is to end all plans. It's to do away with all plans. This country has been planned to death.

—*Radio Broadcasts*, April 21, 1935

POLICE

All they do nowadays is give you a ticket. Policemen are not policemen any more, they are just process servers. You shoot a man nowadays and they hand you a ticket telling you to please appear in court Monday at ten o'clock. If you can't come, send your chauffeur.

There are a thousand policemen to see that you don't park your car, where there is not one to see that your baby is not kidnapped, or your home broken into. Every man on the street can have an automatic pistol in every pocket, and there is nobody to see that he don't, but you let his taillight be out and he will be thrown in jail for life.

—*Weekly Articles:* May 31, 1925
(see AUTOMATIC PISTOL, CRIME, ROBBERY)

POLITICIANS

As a comedian Will Rogers sometimes resented all the unfair competition he was receiving from politicians. "With every public man we have elected doing comedy, I tell you I don't see much of a chance for a comedian to make a living. I am just on the verge of going to work. They can do more funny things naturally, than I can think of to do purposely."

Most politicians simply did not realize the harm they were doing: "Politicians are doing the best they can according to the dictates of no conscience."

Be a politician—no training necessary.

—*Weekly Articles:* April 12, 1925

But a politician is just like a pickpocket; it's almost impossible to get one to reform.

—*Weekly Articles:* March 25, 1923

A politician is just like a spoiled kid. If he feels that his stick of candy is not the longest, why, he will let out a yap that will drown out the neighborhood.

—*Weekly Articles:* August 17, 1930

You can't help but like 'em, and they are always smarter than the people that elect 'em.

—*Weekly Articles:* September 4, 1932
(see CONGRESS, ELECTIONS, HUMOR)

POLITICS

Politics was Will Rogers' subject, a subject as big as humanity, which was his theme.

"You never heard me on a mother-in-law joke," he said. "I have written on nothing but politics for years.

"I read politics, talk politics, know personally almost every prominent politician; like 'em and they are my friends, but I can't help it if I have seen enough of it to know there is some baloney in it.

"Every four years we have politics. Every seven years some people have the itch, in a malaria country every other day people are scheduled to have a chill, every forty years France and Germany fight, and there is just hundreds of these calamities that hit us every once in a while. But of all of them I think politics is really the most dangerous.

"You have to discount about 90 percent of what each side says."

"Common sense is not an issue in politics; it's an affliction. Neither is honesty an issue in politics. It's a miracle.

"Politics and self-preservation must come first, never mind the majority of the people. A legislator's thoughts are naturally on his next term more than on his country.

"Another trouble with politics, it breeds politics. So that makes it pretty hard to stamp out. The only way to do it is at the source. We got to get birth control among politicians."

Politics is the best show in America.

—*Weekly Articles:* December 18, 1932

Politics has got so expensive that it takes lots of money to even get beat with nowadays.

—*Daily Telegrams:* June 28, 1931

You know the platform will always be the same, promise everything, deliver nothing.

—*Weekly Articles:* July 8, 1928

You yourself know that about all there is to politics is trading anyway.

—*More Letters:* June 2, 1928

This country has gotten where it is in spite of politics, not by the aid of it.

—*Daily Telegrams:* November 1, 1932

Time has only proven one thing, and that is that you can't ruin this country even with politics.

—*Weekly Articles:* November 4, 1928

Ninety percent of the people in this country don't give a damn. Politics ain't worrying this country one tenth as much as parking space.

—*Weekly Articles:* January 6, 1924

(see CONGRESS, ELECTIONS, PRESIDENT)

POLO

I was fifty-one Saturday, and played Sunday (after coming from Sunday school). I didn't play good, but I had as much fun missing, as the others did hitting. I am going to play till my whiskers get tangled up in the horse's tail.

—*Daily Telegrams:* October 26, 1930

POLO SPILLS

The Prince of Wales received a lot of publicity for falling off his horse during polo exhibitions. When Will Rogers took up the sport in middle age the same thing happened to him.

"Now I want it distinctly understood that I did not take up polo for any social prestige, or to make myself pointed out as a man about town. If I was the champion player of the world, I still couldn't drink a cup of tea without a saucer."

Two days after taking up the sport Will experienced the thrill of hitting his first ball. "Finally I got so every once in a while I would hit the ball. But it seemed like every time I hit the ball it would get mad at me and go in an opposite direction.

"Well, finally I got to playing in practice games, more for the comedy I would cause than through any good I might do my side. If the purple and whites had a game I might wear a purple jersey, but in reality I would be playing with the whites."

Then came his first tournament held at Coronado Beach.

"I was on a new pony who suddenly reared up and fell back on me. There he was, a laying across my intermission, my head was out on one side and my feet on the other; that was all you could see. When he got up I knew for the first time how the prince must have felt.

"Well, everything goes okay for two more periods. I am on a friend's horse and coming lickety-split down the field, when for no reason at all the horse crosses his front legs and starts turning somersaults. They picked me up just south of Santa Barbara.

"The crowd all said, 'Oh, that's Will Rogers the comedian. He does that for laughs.' The papers next day all said, COMEDIAN SPILLS OFF HORSE TWICE AT POLO GAME.

"Now I will admit there was not quite the same publicity given to all my various falls, as to those of the prince. But the hurt was just as bad. Everybody that reads about it had been kidding me about being the local Prince of Wales of America. But what I want to know from some of these newspaper riders is what I am supposed to do in case the horse falls.

"Are the prince and I supposed to fall with the horse, or are we supposed to stay up there in the air until he gets up, and come back up under us?"

(see MISSED TRICK, PRINCE OF WALES)

POOR PEOPLE

There is one rule that works in every calamity. Be it pestilence, war or famine, the rich get richer and the poor get poorer. The poor even help arrange it.

—*Daily Telegrams:* October 31, 1929

POWER

Those that are in are trying to stay in, and those that are out are trying to get in, and that's about all there is to the game.

—*Weekly Articles:* June 3, 1928

PRAYER

Will was somewhat surprised to hear the sound of prayer at the 1920 Democratic Convention.

"There is somebody praying," he said to President Wil-

195

son, who happened to be with him at the time (according to Will's account).

The president, Will said, sighed and said, "Yes, even a Democrat needs a little religion every four years."

The trouble with our praying is, we just do it as a means of last resort.

—*Weekly Articles:* May 11, 1930
(see REPUBLICAN CONVENTION)

PRESIDENT-ELECT

"A president-elect's popularity is the shortest lived of any public man's," Will stated. "It only lasts till he picks his cabinet."

PRESIDENTIAL CAMPAIGN

Because of his great popularity Will Rogers was repeatedly urged to run for president. He expressed reluctance. In 1928 he dismissed a delegation of his would-be supporters: "We are used to having everything named as presidential candidates, but the country hasn't quite got to the professional comedian stage."

The high office of president of the United States has degenerated into two ordinarily fine men being goaded on by their political leeches into saying things that if they were in their right minds they wouldn't think of saying.

—*Daily Telegrams:* November 1, 1932

PRESIDENTIAL CANDIDATES

Now if there is one thing that America should be interested in, it should be some scheme for eliminating presidential candidates.

—*Weekly Articles:* January 22, 1928
(see CANDIDATES)

PRESIDENTIAL RUNNERUP

Politics is the only sporting event in the world where they don't pay off for second money; a man to run second in any other event in the world it's an honor. But any time he runs second for president it's not an honor; it's a pity.

—*Daily Telegrams:* October 29, 1927

PRESIDENTIAL TERM

Will Rogers offered one serious recommendation for improving the quality of U.S. presidential leadership: a six-year term.

"A president should hold office six years, with no re-election. Stop this thing of a president having to lower his dignity and go trooping around asking for votes to keep him there another term. He has to do it, naturally, but a six-year term with no re-election will be the remedy. Six years gives him time to do something."

PRESIDENTS

"Being great as president is not a matter of knowledge, or farsightedness," said Will Rogers, "it's just a question of the weather, not only in your own country but in a dozen others.

"If the president does nothing else but keep our army and navy at home, we can forgive him for not giving us rain, lower taxes, and an inflated stock market.

When you're president, half the people think you're wrong all the time, and most of the rest think they could do a better job.

"Here we all are, we can't handle our own little affairs, and yet we start yapping about 'what the president ought to have done.'

"Now, if I was a president and wanted something I would claim I didn't want it. For Congress has not given any president anything that he wanted in the last ten years. Be against anything and then he is sure to get it.

"Take it all in all it's a tough life, this being president and trying to please everybody—well, not exactly everybody, but enough to re-elect.

"This president business is a pretty thankless job. Washington and Lincoln didn't get a statue until everybody was sure they were dead."

We shouldn't elect a president; we should elect a magician.

—*Daily Telegrams:* May 26, 1930

Presidents become great, but they have to be made presidents first.

—*Daily Telegrams:* October 22, 1933

They do love to be president. It's the toughest job in the world, but there is always 120 million applicants.

—*Weekly Articles:* October 23, 1932
(see COOLIDGE, HARDING, ROOSEVELT, SENATE, WILSON)

PRICE

I am a great believer in high-priced people. If a thing costs a lot it may not be any better, but it adds a certain amount of class that the cheap thing can never approach; in the long run it's the higher-priced things that are cheapest.

—*Letters of a Self-Made Diplomat:* May 20, 1926

PRINCE OF WALES

"The Prince of Wales is here now," Will Rogers acknowledged the latest visit from our distant relatives known as the royal family, "and everybody has put on her best nose and is trying to see him."

Will noticed the prince was getting some bad press. "I see where he won a booby prize at some affair on the boat and the papers have been kidding him about it, and belittling the accomplishment. I want to tell you that with the stiff competition one has nowadays, it is hard to win a booby prize in any line. It's no credit for a person to win a prize where he has real merit to display, because he has no opposition, but it's hard to win a booby prize as there is so many boobies."

(see POLO SPILLS, QUEEN)

PRISON

"Our big problem is this discontent in our prisons," Will Rogers said, referring to the latest prison riot. "Hardly a day passes that prisoners show some little outward sign of uneasiness, such as shooting a few guards, burning some buildings, and giving some hint publicly that they want to participate in this era of prosperity through which we are struggling to make both ends meet.

"It just looks like the boys in there don't appreciate how fortunate they are to have no installment payments to make.

"This may be a radical suggestion, but couldn't they fix some way where the guards carried the guns instead of the prisoners?"

(see CRIMINALS, CRIME & PUNISHMENT)

PROFESSIONALS

Anything to be done right has got to be done by people that make their living at it, like football.

—*Weekly Articles:* December 29, 1929

PROFESSIONS

The banker, the lawyer, and the politician are still our best bets for a laugh. Audiences haven't changed at all, and neither has the three above professions.

—*Weekly Articles:* August 11, 1935
(see BANKERS, LAWYERS, POLITICIANS)

PROGRESS

Suppose around twenty-five years ago when automobiles were first invented, that, say, Thomas Edison, had gone to our government, and he had put this proposition up to them: "I can in twenty-five years time have every person in America riding quickly from here to there. You will save all this slow travel of horse and buggy.

"But," says Mr. Edison, "I want you to understand it fully, in order to accomplish it and when it is in operation it will kill fifteen to twenty thousand a year of your women and children and men."

"What! You want us to endorse some fiendish invention that will be the means of taking human life! How dare you talk of manufacturing something that will kill more people than a war? Why, we would rather walk from one place to another the rest of our lives than be the means of taking one single child's life."

But as it is, we go right on. Build 'em faster and get better roads. So we can go faster and knock over more of them. This is the age of progress.

Live fast and die quick.

—*Weekly Articles:* April 4, 1926
(see AUTOMOBILE AGE, CLOSE CALLS, FORD, SPEED)

PROHIBITION

Will Rogers thought Prohibition unwise. What would the prohibitionists prohibit next? "I see where they now propose to stop cigarettes first and then profanity. They are going to have a rough time with that profanity, cause as long as there is a prohibitionist living there will be profanity."

Will said alcohol interests were actually behind the Prohibition laws. "Personally I think the saloon men put this prohibition through, as they have sold more in the last year than in any ten previous years before."

Something good could be said for Prohibition, Will said: "Well, Prohibition is better than no liquor at all."

(see BEER, NIGHTCLUBS, VODKA)

PROMISES

Every candidate in the race on all sides have had enough promises to elect 'em unanimously.

—*Weekly Articles:* November 6, 1932
(see POLITICIANS, TAXES)

PROSPERITY

"We are better off than any nation. Why?" asked Will Rogers. "Why just because we work more. Prosperity is based on just what you produce and if you don't produce much you are just out of luck.

"We would all be mighty prosperous in this country; all we need is just some money to practice it with."

There is nothing that sets a nation back as far in civilization as prosperity.

—*Daily Telegrams:* April 2, 1933

Prosperity don't divide the two parties, for under either administration the poor get poorer and the rich get richer.

—*Weekly Articles:* September 30, 1928
(see MONEY, POOR PEOPLE, WORK)

PUBLIC APPROVAL

There is no country in the world where a person changes from a hero to a goat, and a goat to a hero, or vice versa, as they do with us. And all through no change in them. The change is always with us.

It's not our public men you can't put your finger on. It's our public. We are the only fleas weighing over a hundred pounds. We don't know what we want, but we are ready to bite somebody to get it.

—*Daily Telegrams:* June 19, 1935

PUBLICITY

We are living in an age of publicity. It used to be only saloons and circuses that wanted their name in the paper, but now it's corporations, churches, preachers, scientists, colleges, and cemeteries.

—*Daily Telegrams:* June 23, 1931

The greatest publicity and interest in the world is to be told about something, not to have read about it.

—*Weekly Articles:* July 14, 1929
(see HEROES)

PUBLIC OFFICE

"You know, I truly believe that our public men in high office want to do something worthwhile for us," Will Rogers surmised, "but they just can't think of anything to do."

(see NEWS SHORTAGE)

PUBLIC OFFICE SEEKER

Once a man wants to hold a public office he is absolutely
no good for honest work.

—*Weekly Articles:* March 22, 1925
(see CONFERENCES, FOREIGN POLICY, POLITICIANS)

PUBLIC SERVICE

"They are always yapping about 'public service,' " said
Will. "It's public jobs that they are looking for."

QUEEN

When the Queen of England visited the United States in 1926, Will Rogers observed how our democracy bows to royalty. "This queen, you can imagine the many quiet laughs she has had at democracy on this trip. Society trying to get to say they met her, and the yokels trying to get to say they saw her."

(see INVITATION, PRINCE OF WALES)

R

RAILROAD ACCIDENTS

Railroad accidents were not rare occurrences during World War I. Will Rogers commented on them regularly in his nightly routine with the Ziegfeld Follies. One day the New York, New Haven, and Hartford Railroad, a line with a particularly poor safety record, suffered a wreck in which fifty lives were lost.

"I see where the NYNH&H have started in on their spring drive," announced Will that night during his rope and patter act. The next day a railroad executive warned Ziegfeld that his comedian should not make any reference to the company.

Will Rogers acknowledged this demand diplomatically during the next evening's performance: "One of our railroads have started in on their spring drive," he said, adding: "You see, I did not mention the name of any railroad in that, which ought to please the official who tried to censor my material. I did not say one word about the NYNH&H."

Rogers could not resist a last parting shot at the railroad company: "It is one railroad where you see friends bidding each other good-bye at their depots just as though they were going to war."

RANCHES

In the West there is a tendency to call everything a "ranch."

"Now you have heard of 'ranches.' Everything out here that is not an apartment is a 'ranch.' If you got twenty feet in your back yard it's a 'ranch.' If you got an old avocado bush (no matter if it bears or not) why it's an 'avocado ranch.' "

In California "everything big enough to spread a double mattress on is a 'ranch.'

"We even call mine a 'ranch,' " Will confessed, "and there is nothing on it but an old polo field, a few calves to rope, and some old cow ponies."

Will Rogers' Malibu ranch is now a national historic landmark and park open to the public.

(see CALIFORNIA, COWBOY)

READING

"I forget everything I read," Will admitted. "I haven't got any more memory than a billy goat, and I forget about nine tenths of what I read, and get the other tenth wrong. But it makes me think that I am sorter doing something when I am reading."

The important thing in reading, according to Will, was to get more than one point of view. Rogers' reading regimen was simple and well-balanced: "I do a lot of newspaper reading, then at the end of the week I have to do a lot of magazine reading, for it contradicts what the papers have said all week. Then by that time come the monthlies, and they fog the issue up more than ever."

(see CONFUSION, EDUCATION, KNOWLEDGE, WORRY)

REAL ESTATE

At the peak of his career Will Rogers was earning more than half a million dollars a year. He invested most of his fortune in real estate, for he loved to own land.

One of his first major investments was the purchase of some oceanfront beach property in Santa Monica for $20,000. It turned out to be adjacent to some property that William Randolph Hearst was acquiring for his mistress, Marion Davies. At Hearst's behest, a real estate agent dropped by and asked Rogers what he wanted for it.

Rogers replied, "Forty thousand."

"Absurd!" muttered the agent as he stalked off. A few days later the agent returned and announced that Mr. Hearst was willing to pay the $40,000.

Rogers shook his head. "The price has gone up to eighty thousand dollars," he said.

Once again the real estate agent stamped out of the room, muttering angrily. Ultimately Will Rogers sold the land to Hearst for $100,000.

"I got to get me some more of that beach," Will declared after the deal was sealed. In time he came to own two miles of Santa Monica beachfront. The property was worth many millions on the real estate market before it was converted into Will Rogers Beach, a state park.

(see WASHINGTON, GEORGE)

REAL ESTATE AGENTS

When Will Rogers moved to California in 1919 to begin a two-year contract with Goldwyn Studio he had his first skirmishes with California real estate agents.

"I arrived in Beverly Hills just in time to keep real estate men from plotting off and selling my front yard.

"You buy lots in Los Angeles with the same frequency you would newspapers in other towns. After buying it, you put it back in the hands of the agents again, for

don't think you are going to get away with that lot. It has
to be sold three or four more times that day. Why, every
lot out here has its own agent. Agents get rich out here
just off the various commissions on one lot. If an agent
handles two lots he opens up a branch office and has an
assistant."

REBATE

Overpaying his income taxes one year by mistake, Will
Rogers repeatedly tried to claim a rebate—to no avail.
His letters to the Internal Revenue Service went unan-
swered. A one-sided correspondence with the IRS continued for months until the form for the next year's tax
return arrived. In the space marked deductions, Rogers
made this entry: "Bad debt, U.S. government—$40,000."

RELATIVES

Nobody can fall out and get as sore at each other as kin-
folks.

—*Daily Telegrams:* November 23, 1934

RELIGION

Not long before his death, Will Rogers wrote an answer
to a minister who solicited the cowboy philosopher's
philosophy for use in an inspirational sermon.

"I was raised predominantly a Methodist," Will replied, "but I have traveled so much, mixed with so many
people in all parts of the world, I don't know just now
what I am. I know I have never been a nonbeliever. But
I can honestly tell you that I don't think that any one religion is *the* religion.

"You hear or read a sermon nowadays, and the biggest
part of it is taken up by knocking or trying to prove the
falseness of some other denomination. They say that the

Catholics are damned, that the Jews' religion is all wrong, or that the Christian Scientists are a fake, or that the Protestants are all out of step.

"Now, just suppose, for a change they preach to you about the Lord and not about the other fellow's church, for every man's religion is good. There is none of it bad. We are all trying to arrive at the same place according to our own conscience and teachings. It don't matter which road you take.

"Hunt out and talk about that good that is in the other fellow's church, not the bad, and you will do away with all this religious hatred you hear so much of nowadays.

"The Lord put all these millions of people over the earth. They don't all agree on how they got there, and 90 percent don't care. They all do agree on one thing—and that is that the better lives you lead the better you will finish."

(see CHURCH, CHRISTIANITY, GOD, HEAVEN, SERMON)

RELIGIOUS FEUDING

There is no argument in the world carries the hatred that a religious belief does.

—*Weekly Articles:* January 20, 1924

REPENTANCE

"American people like to have you repent," said Will, observing the latest public fall from grace, "then they are generous."

(see CRIME AND PUNISHMENT)

REPUBLICANS

"The Democrats and the Republicans are equally corrupt—it's only in the amount where the Republicans excel.

"The difference between a Republican and a Democrat is the Democrat is a cannibal—they have to live off each other," Will Rogers explained, "while the Republicans, why, they live off the Democrats.

"The Republicans always looked bad three years out of four. But the year they look good is election year. A voter don't expect much. If you give him one good year he is satisfied.

"Everything that is put through during a Republican administration is always referred to as 'our legislation,' and all that come off during the Democrats as 'our policies.' Now neither one can even pass a motion to adjourn without some aid from the other side."

Republicans controlled the White House through the Roaring Twenties and when the economy collapsed in 1929 the Republicans were blamed by the Democrats. By the 1932 election the Republicans were on the defensive and the Roosevelt Democrats were on the offensive.

"The Republican says, 'Things could have been worse.' The Democrats say, 'How?' Democrats are attacking and the Republicans are defending. All the Democrats have to do is promise what they would do if they got in. But the Republicans have to promise what they would do and then explain why they haven't already done it."

Will Rogers never met a Republican he didn't like and as far as he could tell Republicans had only one flaw. "The whole trouble with the Republicans is their fear of an increase in income tax, especially on higher incomes. They speak of it almost like a national calamity. I really believe if it come to a vote whether to go to war with England, France, and Germany combined, or raise the rate on incomes of over $100,000, they would vote war."

Republicans, they take care of big money, for big money takes care of them.

—*Weekly Articles:* September 20, 1931

The Republicans have always been the party of big business. The Democrats of small business. So you just take your pick. The Democrats have their eye on a dime and the Republicans on a dollar.

—*Weekly Articles:* April 29, 1928

You know it takes nerve to be a Democrat. But it takes money to be a Republican.

—*Weekly Articles:* February 10, 1929
(see DEPRESSION)

REPUBLICAN CONVENTION

"The Republican convention opened with a prayer," Will Rogers reported from the 1928 affair in Kansas City. "If the Lord can see his way clear to bless the Republican party the way it's been carrying on, then the rest of us ought to get it without even asking for it."

I am being paid to write something funny about this Republican convention. That's funny. All a fellow has to do to write something funny on a Republican convention is just write what happened.

—*Convention Articles,* June, 1920

This convention would have been over a week ago if they had taken four words out of the dictionary: 'the great Republican party.'

—Comment on 1928 Republican Convention, Kansas City
(see NAMEDROPPING, PRAYER, WOMEN SPEAKERS)

REPUBLICAN SLUSH FUNDS

"The Democrats are investigating the Republican slush fund," Will reported. "And if they find where it's coming from, they want theirs."

(see DEMOCRATIC CORRUPTIONS)

RESIGNATION

During his mock presidential campaign of 1928, candidate Will Rogers made only one pledge:

"If elected I absolutely and positively agree to resign. That's my only campaign pledge or slogan, Elect Rogers and He Will Resign.

"That's offering the country more than any candidate has ever offered it in the entire history of its existence."

(see NOMINATION, UNOFFICIAL PRESIDENT, WITHDRAWAL)

RESIGNATION PROTOCOL

The first sign of an impending resignation is a firm denial.

Commenting on one such instance in the newspapers, Will predicted: "I suppose by the time this reaches an eager public that he will have resigned, as I see where he says he 'won't quit under fire!' That is the usual remarks before leaving."

(see INVESTIGATIONS)

REVOLUTIONARY

It's a mighty hard thing to tell nowadays whether an idea is revolutionary, or downright conservative.

—*Daily Telegrams*, June 12, 1934
(see CONSERVATIVE)

REVOLUTIONS

There is one thing in common with all revolutions (in fact they are pretty near like wars in that respect): nobody ever knows what they are fighting about.

—*Daily Telegrams*: March 4, 1935
(see WAR)

RIDING HIGH

We are riding mighty, mighty high in this country. Our most annoying problem is, "Which car will I use today?"

We are just sitting on top of the world. For every automobile we furnish an accident. For every radio sold we put on two murders. Three robberies to every bathtub installed. Building two golf courses to every church. Our bootleggers have manicures and our farmers have mortgages. Our courts are full, our jails are full, our politicians are full.

Truly, Rome never saw such prosperity.

—*Daily Telegrams:* April 24, 1930
(see AMERICA, ROME)

RIGHT OR WRONG

It takes years in this country to tell whether anybody is right or wrong. It's a case of just how far ahead you can see.

—*Weekly Articles:* November 17, 1929
(see ARGUMENT)

ROBBERY

Robbing is one profession that certainly has advanced in this country. And the remarkable thing about it is that there is no schools or anything to learn you to rob. No other line, outside of drinking, can show the progress that robbing has in the last five years. We spend billions of dollars on education, and we are no smarter today than thirty years ago, and we spent nothing to foster robbing, and here it is one of the most skilled industries we have. So it sometimes makes you think what's the use learning people anything, anyway. Let 'em alone, and they will progress quicker.

—*Weekly Articles:* April 25, 1926
(see CRIME AND PUNISHMENT, GOVERNMENT INTERFERENCE, EDUCATION)

ROBBERY TAX

Supply and demand regulate robberies the same as it regulates anything else. The supply of people who have money to be robbed of will never exceed the demand to rob them. In other words, as soon as there is a man has a dollar there is a robber to take it. But they will never stand a tax.

—*Self-Made Diplomat to His President*, p. 196
(see CRIME, TAX ON MURDERS)

ROGERS, BETTY

"The two finest things that can happen to a man is to have a good wife and to know that he's accepted by the people he comes from," said Will Rogers. He was speaking from experience.

He had to go out of state to find the wife. He found her in Arkansas, a state known for its "scenery, vacation land, fertility, beautiful women. I traded a wagon bed full of hickory nuts for one of the prettiest ones in the state at Rogers, Arkansas, twenty-four years ago," he wrote in 1933. "I expect with the Depression on like it is, a gunnysack would get you one now. But not as good one as I got."

You know, there ought to be some kind of star given to any woman that can live with a comedian.

—*Radio Broadcasts*, May 11, 1930
(see MOVIE OPENING, PALLBEARER)

ROGERS, WILL

Will Rogers was beloved for the gentleness of his humor and his unsentimental acceptance of human nature for what it is.

"You know I have often said in answer to inquiries as to how I got away with kidding some of our public men, that it was because I liked all of them personally, and that if there was no malice in your heart there could be none in your gags, and I have always said I never met a man I didn't like."

(see HUMOR; BIOGRAPHY)

ROGERS HOTEL

Informed that the Will Rogers Hotel in his hometown of Claremore, Oklahoma, had been named after him, he was delighted. "I know now how proud Christopher Columbus must have felt when he heard they had named Columbus, Ohio, after him."

ROME

"We call Rome the seat of culture—but somebody stole the chair."

Will Rogers, like the great nineteenth-century American humorist Mark Twain, enjoyed deflating European cultural pretenses. He refused to be awed by Rome when he visited the Eternal City in 1926 as roving ambassador-at-large.

In a published letter to President Coolidge, Rogers asserted that Rome "has no more culture than Minneapolis or Long Beach, California. They live there in Rome amongst what used to be called culture, but that don't mean a thing. Men in Washington you know yourself, Calvin, live where Washington and Jefferson and Hamilton lived, but as far as the good it does them, they might just as well have the Capitol down at Claremore, Oklahoma—So, you see, association has nothing to do with culture."

Will was saddened to learn from the tour guides that ancient "Rome had senators. Now I know why it declined."

The ancient Romans impressed Will Rogers as being a

particularly cruel and bloodthirsty people. Those old Romans, he said, "loved blood. What money is to an American, blood was to a Roman. A Roman was never so happy as when he saw somebody bleeding. That was his sense of humor. Where we like to see you lose your hat, they loved to see you leave a right arm and a left leg in the possession of a tiger.

"Rome has more churches and less preaching in them than any city in the world. Everybody wants to see where Saint Peter was buried, but nobody wants to try to live like him.

"The whole of Rome seems to have been built, painted, and decorated by one man; that was Michelangelo. If you took everything out of Rome that was supposed to have been done by Michelangelo, Rome would be as bare of art as Los Angeles."

(see AMERICA, MUSSOLINI, RIDING HIGH)

ROOSEVELT, FRANKLIN D.

"Don't worry too much," was Will Rogers' advice to the newly elected President Roosevelt in a personal telegram sent after the 1932 landslide.

Rogers urged President Roosevelt not to be afraid to smile, saying a smile in the White House again would "look like a meal to us."

And he told the president not to be afraid to "have a good time. Too many of our presidents mistake the appointment as being to the Vatican and not to just another American home. Just don't get panicky. All you have to do is manage 120 million hoodlums."

Will Rogers was closer to FDR than to any other president, but he didn't let that stop him from poking fun. "He is a particular friend of mine and for many years standing, he and his whole family, but I have to start making a living out of the fool things that he and those

Democrats will do. I am not worried, I know they will do plenty of them."

(see HARVARD MAN)

RUMOR

Rumor travels faster, but it don't stay put as long as truth.

—*Weekly Articles:* March 9, 1924

RUNNING

The trouble with America is they are not "running" minded, we are "riding" minded.

—*Weekly Articles:* July 17, 1932

RUSSIA

In 1926 Will Rogers went to Russia to see for himself what all the fuss was about. Warned by friends at the last minute not to take any written materials with him across the Russian border, Rogers threw away the names and addresses of all the Russians he might have visited.

"Well, they throwed such a scare into me that I stripped myself down till I didn't have a single piece of paper about me but my passport. I tore up two handfuls of cards that people had given me of people in Russia to look up." But when he got to Moscow, Rogers discovered that he had nowhere to go.

"Now as a consequence of getting rid of all those cards and addresses, I don't have a soul in the world to go to. And as for the next popular illusion: 'Oh, they will take care of you; they will just take you and show you just what they want you to see; you won't be allowed to see anything.' Well, I tell you, I was so lonesome . . . it was humiliating to me. I wanted to hire my own detective and have him watch me, just to keep up the popular tradition."

Will Rogers wrote a book about his 1926 visit to Russia, *There's Not a Bathing Suit in Russia.* "I am the only person that ever wrote on Russia that admits he don't know a thing about it," he declared proudly. "On the other hand, I know just as much about Russia as anybody that ever wrote about it."

There's no income tax in Russia, but there's no income.
—*Radio Broadcasts*, April 7, 1935

RUSSIAN COMMUNISM

"You see, the communism they started out with in Russia, you know, the idea that the fellow that was managing the bank was to get no more than the man that swept it out, that talked well to a crowd, but they got no more of that than we have. Everybody gets what he can get, and where he can get it; and it takes about two to watch one, and then four to watch those two.

"Russia under the czar was very little different from what it is today," Will reported, "for instead of one czar, why, there is at least a thousand now. Any of the big men in the Party holds practically czaristic powers.

"Siberia is still working. It's just as cold on you to be sent there under the Soviets as it was under the czar.

"The only way you can tell a member of the Party from an ordinary Russian, is that the Soviet man will be in a car."

(see COMMUNISM, IDEAS, THEORIES)

RUSSIAN GOVERNMENT

"What they need in their government is more of a sense of humor," Will said, "and less of a sense of revenge."

RUSSIAN SEX EQUALITY

You have heard of equality of sex in Russia. That's not so. The women are doing the work.

—*Daily Telegrams:* August 28, 1934

RUSSIANS

A Russian just loves misery, and he wants to get as many in on it as he can. He wants to share it among friends as well as foes.

—*Weekly Articles:* December 28, 1930

RUTH, BABE

"They offered Babe Ruth the same salary President Hoover gets," Will said of the famous Yankee slugger in 1930. "He should have more. He can't appoint a commission to go to home plate and knock the home runs; he has to do it himself."

(see BASEBALL, COMMISSIONS, HOME RUN)

S

SALARY

Nobody can live on one salary any more.

—Daily Telegrams: October 19, 1929

SALES TAX

Will Rogers preferred sales tax to income tax. "A tax paid on the day you buy is not as tough as asking you for it the next year when you are broke. It's worked on gasoline. It ought to work on Rolls Royces, cigarettes, lipstick, rouge, and Coca-Cola.

"The idea that a tax on something keeps anybody from buying it is a lot of hooey. They put it on gasoline all over the country and it hasn't kept a soul at home a single night or day. You could put a dollar a gallon on and still a pedestrian couldn't cross the street with safety without armor."

(see HOOEY, TAXES)

SAPS

We are a good-natured bunch of saps in this country.

When the president is wrong we charge it to inexperience.

When Congress is wrong we charge it to habit.

When the Senate is right we declare a national holiday.

When the market drops fifty points, we are supposed not to know it's through manipulation.

When a bank fails we let the guy go start another one.

When a judge convicts a murderer that's cruelty.

When enforcement officers can't capture it fast enough to fill orders, that's good business.

Everything is cockeyed, so what's the use kidding ourselves.

—*Daily Telegrams:* June 30, 1930
(see AMERICANS, BANKERS, CRIME AND PUNISHMENT, CRIMINALS)

SAVING

"Everybody is saying that the trouble with the country is that people are saving instead of spending," Will commented during the Depression. "Well, if that's advice I am Einstein.

"Spending when we didn't have it puts us where we are today.

"Saving when we have got it will get us back to where we was before we went cuckoo.

"If there was ever a time to save, it's now. When a dog gets a bone he don't go out and make the first payment on a bigger bone with it. He buries the one he's got."

(see DEBT, ECONOMIC CRISIS, NATIONAL DEBT)

SCHOOLS

This modern education gag has sure got me licked. I can't tell from talking to 'em what it's all about.

All the kids I know, either mine or anybody's, none of 'em can write so you can read it, none of 'em can spell so you can read it. They can't figure and don't know geography.

Everybody has swimming pools, but nobody has got a plain old geography. Gymnasiums to the right of you, and tennis courts to the left of you, but not a spelling book in a carload of schools.

Then they got another gag they call "credits." If you do anything thirty minutes twice a week, why you get some certain "credit." Maybe it's lamp shade tinting, maybe it's singing, maybe it's a thing they call "music appreciation." That used to drive my cowboy son Jim pretty near nuts.

Some of 'em you get more "credits" for than others. If a thing is particularly useless, why it give you more "credits." There is none at all for things that we thought constituted school.

Some of these days they are going to remove so much of the "punk and hooey" and the thousands of things that the schools have become clogged up with, and we will find that we can educate our broods for about one-tenth the price and learn 'em something they might accidentally use after they escaped.

But us poor old dumb parents, we just string along and do the best we can, and send 'em as long as we are able, because we want them to have the same handicaps the others have.

We don't know what it's all about. We just have to take the teachers' word. They all think education is our salvation, but the smarter a nation gets, the more wars it has. The dumb ones are too smart to fight. Our schools teach us what the other fellow knows, but it don't teach us anything new for ourselves. Everybody is learning just one thing, not because they will know more, but because they have been taught that they won't have to work if they are educated.

—*Weekly Articles:* July 31, 1932

Is there nobody here teaches reading, or writing, or arithmetic, or some of the old-fashioned things that Lincoln struggled along with to the presidency?

—*Weekly Articles:* May 16, 1926
(see EDUCATION, TEACHING, WORK)

SCIENTISTS

Scientists are a peculiar breed, Will Rogers said. "They can tell you just to the minute when something is going to happen ten million miles away and none of them has ever been smart enough to tell you what day to put on your heavy underwear.

"A scientist is a man that can find out anything, and nobody in the world has any way proving whether he ever found it out or not, and the more things he can think of that nobody can find out about, why the bigger scientist he is."

(see KNOWLEDGE)

SEASICKNESS

A seasick Will Rogers sent the following radiogram to President Coolidge on April 30, 1926:

My Dear President: Will you kindly find out for me through our Intelligence Department who is the fellow that said a big boat didn't rock. Hold him till I return.
Yours feeble but still devotedly,
WILLROG
That's code name for Will Rogers.

SELFISHNESS

There ain't but one thing wrong with every one of us in the world, and that's selfishness.

—*Daily Telegrams:* March 10, 1935

SENATE

"All I can say about the U. S. Senate is that it opens with a prayer, and closes with an investigation."

The primary purpose of the Senate was to prevent passage of useful legislation. "Anything that has to pass by that Senate is just like a rat having to pass a cat convention, it's sure to be pounced on, and the more meritorious the scheme is the less chance it has of passing."

The Senate and the president have never been able to get along. It's a great American tradition for them to quarrel.

"Distrust of the Senate by presidents started with Washington who wanted to have 'em courtmartialed. Jefferson proposed life imprisonment for 'em, old Andy Jackson said 'to hell with 'em' and got his wish. Lincoln said the Lord must have hated 'em for he made so few of 'em. Teddy Roosevelt whittled a big stick and beat on 'em for six years. Taft just laughed at 'em and grew fat. Coolidge never let 'em know what he wanted so they never knew how to vote against him."

Will Rogers preferred the Senate to any of the other shows in politics. "I will stay with the Senate. I know those backwards, cause that's the way they are generally going."

Men in America live, hope and die trying to become president. If they can't make it, they accept the booby prize and go in the Senate.

—*Weekly Articles:* October 16, 1932
(see INVESTIGATIONS)

SENATE COMMITTEES

Statistics have proven that the surest way to get anything out of the public mind and never hear of it again is to have a Senate committee appointed to look into it.

—*Weekly Articles:* February 10, 1924

SENATE DIARY

Diary of the Senate trying to find $2 billion that it already had spent, but didn't have:

Monday	Soak the rich.
Tuesday	Begin hearing from the rich.
Tuesday afternoon	Decide to give the rich a chance to get richer.
Wednesday	Tax Wall Street sales.
Thursday	Get word from Wall Street: Lay off us or you will get no campaign contributions.
Thursday afternoon	Decide we are wrong on Wall Street.
Friday	Soak the little fellow.
Saturday	Find out there is no little fellow. He has been soaked until he drowned.
Sunday	Meditate.
Next week	Same procedure, only more talk and less results.

SENATE HEARINGS

One of the charming customs of the Senate is to hold hearings and summon expert witnesses from all over to testify their knowledge. But nothing ever comes of it.

"What does the Senate do with all the knowledge they demand from other people?" Will Rogers wanted to know. "They never seem to use it."

(see INVESTIGATIONS, KNOWLEDGE, TESTIMONY)

SENATORS

Senators spend most of their time talking.

"There is no race of people in the world that can compete with a senator for talking," attested Will Rogers, who was no slouch of a talker himself. "If I went to the Senate, I couldn't talk fast enough to answer roll call.

"If a distinguished foreigner was to be taken into the Senate, and not told what the institution was, and he heard a man rambling on, talking for hours, he would probably say: 'You have lovely quarters here for your insane, but have you no warden to see they don't talk themselves to death?' "

In addition to talking, senators are engaged in trade and travel. "A senator learns to swap his vote at the same age a calf learns which end of its mother is the dining room.

"All senators travel a lot. They all try to keep away from home as much as they can."

Will Rogers had mixed feelings about senators. "They are a kind of a never-ending source of amusement, amazement, and discouragement. When you see what they do officially you want to shoot 'em, but when one looks at you and grins so innocently, why you kinder want to kiss him."

The only way to keep a governor from becoming senator is to sidetrack him off into the presidency.

—*Convention Articles:* June 8, 1920

SERIES

It was the fashion among all the great authors of the 1920s to publish books in series. When Will Rogers published *Letters of a Self-Made Diplomat to His President* in 1926 he threatened to follow it up with more volumes.

"All the big writers nowadays are fetching out their books in volumes, or a series of volumes rather," he wrote in his preface. "The day of the 'one book man' is gone, the same as the day of the 'one gun man' in the movies was limited. The advantages of double barrel over the old single barrel breech loading books is numerous. In the first place you can always say in the second volume what you forgot to say in the first book. Or, more handy still, you can use it for denial purposes. I hope to be like a good bookkeeper: when my volumes are finished my accusations and denials will balance so even that I haven't really said a thing.

"More ideas haven't lengthened books—it's easy-working typewriters that have done it. Writing today is based on endurance not thought, and I am going to give my public the advantage of a wonderful physical constitution while it's at its peak. I know when you read this volume you will say: 'I want volume number two, it must be better.' "

(see READING)

SERIOUSNESS

Will Rogers learned a lesson in absolute seriousness from the perennial populist William Jennings Bryan, whom he met at the 1924 Republican convention. They arrived together.

"Bryan and I had no sooner got in the hall than they commenced to pray," Will reported June 11, 1924. "The prayer was very long, but, of course the parson may have known his audience and their needs better than me.

"Then Mr. Bryan turned to me and said: 'You write a humorous column, don't you?'

"I looked around to see if anybody was listening and then I said: 'Yes, sir.'

"He said: 'Well, I write a serious article, and if I think of anything of a comical or funny nature, I will give it to you.' "

Will was very flattered by this offer. "I thanked him and told him: 'If I happen to think of anything of a serious nature, I will give it to you.' "

Later Will had second thoughts: "When he said he wrote seriously, and I said I wrote humorously, I thought afterward we both may be wrong."

Nothing is so funny as something done in all serious-ness. The material on which the congressional record is founded is done there every day in all seriousness.

—*Weekly Articles:* June 8, 1924
(see HUMOR)

SERMON

A preacher from Simpson Methodist Church in Minneap-olis wrote to Will Rogers saying he intended to do a ser-mon on the cowboy philosopher, asking if Will would contribute something to it.

"I can honestly tell you that I don't think that any one religion is the religion," Will wrote in reply. "Which way you serve your God will never get one word of argument or condemnation out of me.

"There has been times when I wished there had been as much real religion among some of our creeds as there has been vanity, but that's not in any way a criticism."

Will concluded his letter by saying he hoped the preacher wouldn't be too persuasive in his sermon. "I heard a fellow preach one time on Jesse James, the out-law, and I left the church wanting to hold up everything and everybody I run into.

"So if you are such a persuasive preacher, you are lia-ble to turn out a flock of Swedish comedians up around Minneapolis. Don't make the life too rosy, for with the politicians horning in, our comedian business is over-crowded as it is."

(see PHILOSOPHY OF LIFE, POLITICIANS, RELIGION)

SEX APPEAL

Will Rogers felt it was cheating for a political candidate to take advantage of sex appeal in order to get elected. In his brief run for president in 1928 he vowed *not* to use his sex appeal.

"We may alienate the entire female vote, but there will be no effort for sex appeal. Of course, if it unconsciously manifests itself, we can't help it."

(see NOMINATION, RESIGNATION, WITHDRAWAL)

SEXUAL POLITICS

"Democratic women want birth control of Republicans," reported Will, "and Republican women want equal corruption for both sexes."

SHAW, GEORGE BERNARD

Will Rogers admired British playwright George Bernard Shaw and the way Shaw could stir a crowd with his words. "Bernard Shaw stopped over just long enough to make one speech in Bombay, India, started a war and one hundred Indians killed each other," Will telegrammed January 10, 1933. "That's what I call good speech making. The only enthusiasm any of our speakers can rouse is a demand to kill the speaker."

(see SPEAKER REFORM, SPEECHES)

SIGHTSEEING

If you want to have a good time, I don't care where you live, just load in your kids, and take some congenial friends, and just start out. You would be surprised what there is to see in this great country within 200 miles of where any of us live. I don't care what state or what town.

—*Weekly Articles:* August 31, 1930
(see PLACES)

SISTER

When his sister Maud died in 1925, Will Rogers attended her funeral. "Some uninformed newspapers printed: MRS. C.L. LANE, SISTER OF THE FAMOUS COMEDIAN WILL ROGERS.'

"They were greatly misinformed. It's the other way around. I am the brother of Mrs. C. L. Lane, the friend of humanity. And I want to tell you, all these people who were there to pay tribute to her memory, it was the proudest moment of my life that I was her brother."

SKILL

"There is skill in anything if you practice it long enough," said Will. "Spitting at a crack don't get much recognition among the arts, but you just try to hit one some time and you will never laugh at another spitter again."

SMALL TOWN

"You bet your life I am small-town," declared Will Rogers, "and listen, that is what I am going to stay is small-town."

Will always had a feeling for small-town life and re-gretted its passing. "Just reading these late census reports and it shows that the small town is passing. We not only ought to regret it, we ought to do something to remedy it. It was the incubator that hatched all our big men, and that's why we haven't got as many big men as we used to have. Take every small-town–raised big man out of business and you would have nobody left running it but vice presidents."

(see COUNTRY BOY, NATURAL)

SMART ALECK

They say all children reach a smart-aleck age some time. Well, our whole country is in that stage now. Every man, every denomination, and every organization wants things their way. It's just one of those things we got to pass through, and we will look back and feel ashamed of ourselves afterward.

—*Daily Telegrams:* December 10, 1931

SOCIALISTS

"If socialists worked as much as they talked," said Will, "they would have the most prosperous style of government in the world."

SOCIETY

What is society? Society is any band of folks that kinder throw in with each other, and mess around together for each other's discomfort. The ones with the more money have more to eat and drink at their affairs, and their clothes cost more, and so that's called high society.

—*Weekly Articles:* August 10, 1930
(see HIGH SOCIETY)

SOCIETY TALK

When you have to be told what to say when you meet anyone, you are not the one to meet them.

—*More Letters:* January 8, 1927

SOFT JOB

Sometimes we don't realize how soft we have it. In the summer of 1930 Will Rogers was working on a picture at Tahoe Tavern, and "a fellow come up and wanted me to help get him into some soft job in the movies. I asked him what he was doing and he said he was 'house detective in the big hotel in Reno where all the divorcées live.'

"I said, 'Brother, you must be hard to please. John Barrymore is not doing as well as you. But if you are going to give the job up consult me, I'll change with you.' "

(see WORK)

SPEAKER REFORM

A veteran of many dull conferences and conventions, Will Rogers suffered through more than his share of long speeches. He offered this suggestion for the reform of public speakers:

"Make every speaker, as soon as he tells all he knows, sit down. That will shorten your speeches so much you will be out by lunch every day."

Another recommendation for speaker reform is to "not allow one man to repeat what some other man had already said. That would cut it down to just one speech at each convention."

The spectacle of the 1924 Democratic convention gave Will another idea for reforming public speakers. "I want to go down and take my rope, and when the speaker has said enough, rope him, and drag him back to his delegation. I will be a bigger help to my country in that way than any way I can think of."

(see SPEECHES)

SPEECHES

The best speeches are short speeches. Short speeches usually go over better. At the 1924 Democratic convention in New York, Will Rogers observed, one guy from Montana, Maloney, forgot his speech and didn't say anything. He was the hit of the day. They applauded for five minutes. That should have been a tip to the other speakers.

232

Maloney can remain proud of himself for the rest of his life, for he had by far the best speech at the New York convention.

"There is only one speech any speech maker in the world can make to a hungry audience and be heard, and that is 'Dinner's ready, come and get it, or we will throw it out!' "

SPEED

There was never such a demand for speed, for less reason. There is not one of us that couldn't walk where we are going and then get there earlier than we have any business.

—*Daily Telegrams:* April 28, 1933

SPIRITUALISTS

Us ignorant people laugh at spiritualists, but when they die they go mighty peaceful and happy, which after all is about all there is to living, is to go away satisfied.

—*Daily Telegrams:* July 7, 1930
(see AFTERLIFE, SUCCESS)

ST. PAUL, MINNESOTA

Somebody with a sense of humor built it and Minneapolis right close together, and then they moved away to watch the fun. If either city could find the fellow that did it his life wouldn't be worth as much as bank messengers in Chicago.

—*Weekly Articles:* November 8, 1925
(see CHICAGO, DETROIT)

STALIN ERA

Every government in the world today has more discontented people than usual, but I think there is less complaint by the subjects in Russia than anywhere else. That is, they don't complain as long.

Russia hasn't today in her borders what you would call a constant critic. You simply say your say and then you are through. Russia is a country that is burying their troubles. Your criticism is your epitaph.

Here lies the body of Boris Ogimsky; he said Stalin, the dictator, wouldn't last, but he outlived Himsky.

—*Daily Telegrams:* November 25, 1930
(see COMMUNISM, RUSSIAN COMMUNISM)

STATES

We haven't got a state in our whole union but what has some great advantages that no other state possesses.

—*Weekly Articles:* January 8, 1933
(see PLACES, SIGHTSEEING)

STATESMAN

"I was born on Election Day, but never was able to get elected to anything," Will Rogers acknowledged. "I am going to jump out some day and be indefinite enough about everything that they will call me a politician, then run on a platform of question marks, and be elected unanimously, then reach in the treasury and bring back my district a new bridge, or tunnel, or dam, and I will be a statesman."

Just raid the national treasury enough and you will soon be referred to as a "statesman."

—*Daily Telegrams:* November 4, 1930

Imagine a man in public office that everybody knew where he stood. We wouldn't call him a statesman, we would call him a curiosity.

—*Daily Telegrams:* February 28, 1933

STATISTICS

"We are always reading statistics and figures," Will Rogers reflected. "Half of America do nothing but prepare statistics for the other half to read.

"Everything is figured out down to a gnat's tooth according to some kind of statistics. Course nobody knows if the figures are right or not, you have no way of checking up on 'em.

"Numbers don't get you nothing. It's individuals that get you something."

(see ECONOMIC JARGON, INSURANCE)

STOCK MARKET

The market not only operates O. P. M. (other people's money) but O. P. R. (other people's rumors). So the only thing can break the stock market is a fact.

—Daily Telegrams: October 24, 1933
(see BIG BUSINESS, MERGERS, WALL STREET)

STOCK MARKET CRASH

A few days after the stock market crashed in 1929, on Halloween, Will Rogers telegrammed his most famous financial advice: "Don't gamble; take all your savings and buy some good stock, and hold it till it goes up, then sell it. If it don't go up, don't buy it."

(see DEPRESSION)

SUBWAY TRANSPORTATION

"We had quite a panic here the other day in New York, in the subway," Will told the crowd at Ziegfeld's Follies. "Several people were trampled on and crushed. The cause of the trouble was that someone hollered out: 'Here is a vacant seat!' "

(see NEW YORK, NEW YORKERS)

SUCCESS

When you are satisfied you are successful. That's all there is to success is satisfaction.

—*Weekly Articles:* July 29, 1928
(see FORTUNE, GREATNESS)

TAFT, WILLIAM HOWARD

President William Howard Taft, the twenty-seventh president (1909–1913), was the heaviest man ever to serve in the White House, tipping the scales at 335 pounds.

"President Taft, what a lovely old soul," Will wrote of him. "Fat and good-natured. He always seemed like he was one of us. He was our great human fellow because there was more of him to be human."

(see MODESTY)

TALKING

"I don't suppose there ever was a time when everybody knew as little about what they were talking about as they do today," remarked Will Rogers.

"Nobody wants his cause near as bad as he wants to talk about his cause."

Rogers admitted he was partially to blame for all the talk.

"I have talked more and said less in the past year in New York than any man outside of public life.

"I don't care how smart you are, if you say something you are liable to say something foolish and the smarter you are, and the longer you talk the more fool things you will say."

(see INVESTIGATIONS, KNOWLEDGE, SPEECHES)

TALKING PICTURES

Talking pictures came in 1927 and Will Rogers was one of the few movie stars who made the transition successfully.

"And speaking of the movies, they are going full blast out here, all 'noisies.' Everybody that can't sing has a double that can, and everybody that can't talk is going right on and proving it.

"You meet an actor or girl and in the old days where they would have just nodded and passed by, now they stop and start chattering like a parrot. Weather, politics, Babe Ruth, anything just to practice talking, and they are so busy enunciating that they pay no attention to what they are saying.

"Everything is 'enunciation.' I was on the stage 23 years and never heard the word or knew what it was.

"It's going to make pictures about twice as human," Will predicted. "For a while they will lose part of their audience, for with this new intelligence coming in so sudden there is going to be a lot of movie fans that can't stand it.

"If you have missed anybody around their old haunts in the East and have no idea where they are, they are right here in Beverly Hills trying to get into the talkies, and the ones that were in 'em are trying to learn to talk."

(see CALIFORNIA, MOVIES)

TARIFF

"The U. S. Senate just passed the tariff bill," Will telegrammed on April 6, 1930. "Everlasting life and perpetual motion are the only other two things now that we have to look forward to.

"Tariff don't hit any two men the same. What suits you don't feel so good to me. You want everything you buy to come in tariff free, you want everything you sell to be protected by having a tariff on any of that same stuff coming in. Now unfortunately everybody in the country is not in exactly the same business.

"The tariff is an instrument invented for the benefit of those who make to be used against those who buy. As there is more buys than there is makes, it is a document of the minority."

(see TRADE)

TAXES

If you want lower taxes, Will Rogers said, "the only thing I would advise you to do, is not to have anything they can tax away from you.

"Taxation is about all there is to government. People don't want their taxes lowered near as much as the politician tries to make you believe. People want *just* taxes, more than they want lower taxes. They want to know that every man is paying his proportionate share according to his wealth.

"All taxes should be on income, and where there is no income either personally, or on your property, why you shouldn't pay anything. You should pay on things that you buy outside of bare necessities.

"For a man to give up three million out of four is tough; but on the other hand, 90 percent of the people would be willing to give up 99 percent of a million if allowed to make one.

"You can't legitimately kick on taxes when the money

has been made; it's taxes on farms, ranches, and business property that has lost money for years. Those folks have the holler coming. Now excuse me while I hide before some of my good friends shoot me."

It ain't taxes that is hurting this country; it's interest.

—*Weekly Articles:* January 6, 1924

There is only one fundamental thing that must be the backbone of every bill, and that is a tax.

—*Weekly Articles:* March 13, 1934
(see INCOME TAX, NATIONAL DEBT, NATIONAL SALES TAX, TAX ON MURDERS)

TAX ON AUTOMOBILES

The automobile industry was lobbying for tax exemptions in 1927. "They claimed that it was the government tax on automobiles that was holding back such struggling firms as General Motors," commented Will. "Those that wasn't selling cars never thought that it might be the quality of their cars that might be holding back sales."

TAX ON MURDERS

"There is only one scheme that they could possibly come forward with that would raise more money," Will Rogers proposed, "but I don't think they dare put it forward. That would be the putting of a tax on murders, robberies, and liquors, and all its subsidiaries. But I don't think they dare do that. You can't, in politics, go against your constituency."

(see CRIME AND PUNISHMENT, ROBBERY)

TAXPAYERS

There just don't seem to be any volunteer taxpayers. I see now what makes a congressman so unpopular. He just will not fix it so that tax falls on nobody.

—*Daily Telegrams:* August 4, 1933

TAX RELIEF

"Taxes will be relieved," Will Rogers prophesied, "but not until after your death.

"When a party can't think of anything else they always fall back on lower taxes. It has a magic sound to a voter, just like fairyland is spoken of and dreamed of by all children. But no child has ever seen it; neither has any voter ever lived to see the day when his taxes were lowered.

"Presidents have been promising lower taxes since Washington crossed the Delaware by hand in a row boat. But our taxes have gotten bigger and their boats have gotten larger until now the president crosses the Delaware in his private yacht."

(see ELECTIONS, PROMISES, POLITICIANS)

TEACHING

If you send somebody to teach somebody, be sure that the system you are teaching is better than the system they are practicing.

—*Weekly Articles:* April 23, 1933
(see EDUCATION, SCHOOLS)

TECHNOCRACY

Technocracy wants to do everything by machinery. Machinery is just doing fine. If it can't kill you, it will put you out of work.

—*Daily Telegram:* December 27, 1932
(see HIGHER EDUCATION, UNEMPLOYMENT)

TEETH

It wasn't until the twentieth century that Americans learned the importance of good dental care.

"There are two things that seem like got started wrong in life," said Will Rogers. "One was the Constitution of the United States. The men that laid that out didn't seem to know what we needed, and so these modern smarter men have been all these years trying to improve it and get it fixed up properly. And the other thing was teeth. It seems the Lord when He laid out our original teeth didn't know much about teeth, so He just put those we have in temporarily till the doctors could come along and get 'em out or get 'em remodeled so they amounted to something."

(see CONSTITUTION, NOSE)

TESTIMONY

"Most of our public men spend over half their time testifying on the stand, especially the Republicans."

Will Rogers proposed to establish a school to train public officials in giving testimony. This way they would be better prepared to testify and wouldn't look so much like they were lying.

"I am going to start the school of public testimony laid out like a court. Instead of teachers we will have 'em made up as sheriffs, bailiffs, jurymen, and judges.

"The minute a person is elected to office like a senator or congressman, we will have him come and spend a few weeks and when he goes on to his public office, he will be all set for investigations.

"We will teach 'em not to be nervous, not to let the other fellow get 'em rattled and have 'em all trained to tell where they got every dollar they used in their campaign and how much they paid for each vote.

"It will persuade our big men to turn honest after elections and trust to the mercy of the jury. And we will coach 'em to tell everything the first time. That will save having to spend your life on the stand.

"Of course when some of my early pupils first start testifying they won't be believed. It will be such a radical change from the usual testimony.

"I think I will open the school at Claremore, Oklahoma. That's about the hub of everything. Remember it opens next year: Will Rogers School of Public Testifying, at Claremore, Oklahoma. After one term in my school you will welcome testifying instead of fearing it."

(see INVESTIGATIONS, SENATE HEARINGS)

TEXAS

If you think Texas ain't some size you just try to drive from one part of it to another.

—Daily Telegrams: January 27, 1931

THEORIES

Theories are great, they sound great, but the minute you are asked to prove one in actual life, why the thing blows up. So professors back to the classroom, idealists back to the drawing room, communists back to the soap box (and use some of it).

—Daily Telegrams: August 28, 1933
(see COMMUNISM, IDEAS)

THIRD SOLUTION

When the Farm Board proposed burning every third row of cotton to help relieve the poverty of farmers, Will Rogers recognized the nub of a great idea—the third solution.

The third solution is to eliminate one third of the problem.

"What would give more relief than extinguishing every third senator," Will proposed, "every third congressman, every third committee, every third stockbroker, every third law. Make a third of the vice presidents of concerns go back to work. Turn the cows back into every third golf course. Convict every third gangster arrested. One-third of all millionaires that issue optimistic reports from aboard yachts. Too many banks, bump off a third. Stop up every third oil well and every third political speaker.

"The matter with the whole world is there is too many people. Shoot every third one. The whole plan is inexpensive and a surefire scheme back to prosperity."

(see MUSSOLINI)

THIRD WORLD

If you are going to do anything at all for 'em, feed 'em, even if they don't become Christians.

—*More Letters:* April 30, 1932
(see LITTLE NATIONS)

TIME

Every invention during our lifetime has been just to save time, and time is the only commodity that every American, both rich and poor, has plenty of. Half our life is spent trying to find something to do with the time we have rushed through life trying to save.

—*Daily Telegrams:* April 28, 1930
(see PROGRESS, SPEED)

TOKYO

In his visit to Tokyo Will was struck by all the bicycles on the streets, at least by several of them. There were bicycles everywhere. "Millions of 'em. Did you ever see a kimona on a bicycle? And carry stuff? Say they will move your grand piano any day and do it on a bicycle. They have always got a billiard table, or a stove or bed, or a couple of mattresses on the wheel."

(see JAPANESE)

TOURISM

I had visited some strange places in the world, but it was always so full of tourists by the time I got to it that the tourists were stranger than the place.

—*Weekly Articles:* April 14, 1929

TOURIST MATING SEASON

Winter is coming and tourists will soon be looking for a place to mate.

—*Daily Telegrams:* October 27, 1932
(see HUMAN MATING)

TOURISTS

"I told you how bad it's getting with the tourists over here. Some of them are getting almost what they deserve," Will Rogers wrote to President Coolidge from Europe in 1926.

"We, unfortunately, don't make a good impression collectively. You see a bunch of Americans at anything abroad and they generally make more noise and have more to say than anybody, and generally create a worse impression than if they had stayed at home.

"There should be a law prohibiting over three Americans going anywhere abroad together."

(see AMERICANS, EUROPE, INTERNATIONAL RELATIONS)

TRADE

All this open-door stuff is a lot of hooey. Any door is only open to those that have the best product at the cheapest money.

—*More Letters:* April 30, 1932
(see TARIFF)

TRADITION

"What is tradition?" asked Will Rogers. "It's the thing we laugh at the English for having, and we beat them practicing it.

"While we can't trace our ancestors back any further than you can trust a congressman, why we naturally think we are saturated with tradition when as a matter of fact it's only payments on objects that we are immersed in.

"The minute you teach a man he is backed up by tradition, why, you spoil him for real work the rest of his life."

(see ANCESTORS, PARTY HISTORY)

TRAFFIC

The only way to solve the traffic problem of this country is to pass a law that only paid-for cars are allowed to use the highways. That would make traffic so scarce that we could use our boulevards for children's playgrounds.

—*Weekly Articles:* January 6, 1924

TRANSPORTATION

Trouble with American transportation is that you can get somewhere quicker than you can think of a reason for going there. What we need is a new excuse to go somewhere.

—*Daily Telegrams:* March 12, 1934

TREATIES

Trouble with all these treaties is that the guys that make 'em are generally kicked out by the time they get home, and the new bunch say, "That's not our signature."

—*Daily Telegrams:* April 15, 1935
(see CONFERENCES, INTERNATIONAL RELATIONS, PEACE)

TRICKLE DOWN

Trickle-down economics, associated with the Reagan White House, is nothing new. President Herbert Hoover practiced it during his administration. That's why he lost his bid for re-election in 1932, according to Will Rogers.

"The money was all appropriated for the top in the hopes that it would trickle down to the needy.

"Mr. Hoover didn't know that money trickled *up.* Give it to the people at the bottom and the people at the top will have it before night anyhow. But it will at least have passed through the poor fellow's hands."

(see DEBT, POOR PEOPLE, UNEQUAL DIVISION)

TRUTH

The truth eventually comes out, no matter how much it is covered up. To illustrate this Will Rogers told a story about a lady with a broken corset string.

"The fear of every fleshy lady is the broken corset string. I sat next to a catastrophe of this nature once. We didn't know it at first, the deluge seemed so gradual, till finally the gentleman on the opposite side of her and myself were gradually pushed off our chairs.

"To show you what a wonderful thing this corsetting is, that lady had come to the dinner before the broken string episode in a small roadster. She was delivered home in a bus."

It proves, Will concluded, "The truth will gradually come out."

(see CORSETS, COVERUP)

TRUTH HURTS

"A remark generally hurts in proportion to its truth," observed Will Rogers.

TRUTH SERUM

Will Rogers talked about truth serum during a 1933 radio broadcast for unemployment relief: "Say, we have a discoverer out here in California, a Dr. House of Texas, who has invented a serum called Scopolamin, a thing that when injected will make you tell the truth, at least for a while, anyway. Now, I don't know that the stuff is any good, but he certainly come to the right state to get material to try it on. If he can make us fellows in California tell the truth his experiment will be a total success. He don't have to look for subjects—just jab his needle into the first guy out here and await results.

"They tried it on a male movie star in Hollywood and he told his right salary and his press agent quit him. They then tried it on a female movie staress and she recalled things back as far as her first husband's name, and remembered her real maiden name.

"Their only failure to date has been a Los Angeles real estate agent. They broke three needles trying to administer the stuff to him and it turned black the minute it touched him, so they had to give him up. He sold Dr. House three lots before he got out of the operating room.

"It really is a wonderful thing, and if it could be brought into general use it would no doubt be a big aid to humanity. But it will never be, for already the politicians are up in arms against it. It would ruin the very foundation on which our political government is run.

"If you ever injected truth into politics you have no politics."

(see HUMOR, POLITICS)

TULSA

Tulsa is the nearest large city to Will Rogers' hometown of Claremore. "Tulsa," explained the Claremore native, is "a residential suburb of Claremore, where we park our millionaires to keep them from getting under our feet."

U

UNEMPLOYMENT

"The unemployed here ain't eating regular, but we will get round to them soon as we get everybody else fixed up okay."

The solution to the unemployment problem, said Will Rogers, is work. "Now everybody had got a scheme to relieve unemployment—there is just one way to do it and that's for everybody to go to work. *Where?* Why right where you are; look around, you will see a lot of things to do, weeds to cut, fences to be fixed, lawns to be mowed, filling stations to be robbed, gangsters to be catered to. There is a million little odds and ends right under your eye that an idle man can turn his hand to every day. Course he won't get paid for it, but he won't get paid for not doing it. My theory is that it will keep him in practice in case something does show, you can keep practicing so work won't be a novelty when it does come."

Unemployment is terrible, but employment is worse.

—*Daily Telegrams:* October 26, 1930
(see WORK)

UNEQUAL DIVISION

There is just as much of everything as there ever was. What's the matter with us is the unequal division of it. Our rich is getting richer, and our poor is getting poorer all the time. That's the thing that these great minds ought to work on.

—*Weekly Articles:* December 14, 1930
(see AMERICA, DISTRIBUTION OF WEALTH, INCOME TAX)

UNITED STATES OF NORTH AMERICA

Will Rogers advised American diplomats abroad to say they are from the United States of North America instead of America.

"Mexico kinder figures that she is in America, too; and they have some legitimate claim to the fact. Then there is all the Central and South American countries. When we call ours America, they also feel that they are America too."

He recommended it to Americans traveling abroad. "You are liable to make a lot of friends by following this advice."

(see AMERICANS, TOURISTS)

UNIVERSITY LIFE

Columbia University illustrates the challenges of university life at a big city campus. "It is remarkable to have thirty-two hundred courses there," remarked Will Rogers. "You spend the first two years in deciding what courses to take, the next two years in finding the building that these are given in, and the rest of your life in wishing you had taken another course."

(see COLLEGE, HIGHER EDUCATION)

UNOFFICIAL PRESIDENT

Will Rogers was declared the unofficial President of the United States by *Life Magazine* on the eve of the 1932 election.

He resigned, fulfilling his only campaign pledge. "The country hasn't sunk so low," he said, "that it wants a comedian intentionally for the presidency."

(see NOMINATION, RESIGNATION)

URUGUAY

Down here the people vote on whether they will hold a football game or a revolution, both equal in casualties.

—*Daily Telegrams:* October 22, 1932

(see FOOTBALL, LATIN AMERICAN REVOLUTIONS)

USED CARS

"I see by today's statistics that a big item is secondhand cars," noted Will Rogers. "I am sorry to hear it. We haven't got twenty men in America that are rich enough to support one."

(see AUTOMOBILE AGE, CAR ACCESSORIES)

V

VENICE

"I must tell you about Venice," Will said after returning from a trip to Italy. "I stepped out on the wrong side of a Venice taxicab—and they were three minutes fishing me out."

VENUS DE MILO

During a European tour, Will Rogers sent a picture post-card of the Venus de Milo—the sensuous statue sans arms—to his young niece. On the back of the card he wrote this stern admonition: "See what will happen to you if you don't stop biting your fingernails!"

VETERANS

"I think the best insurance in the world against another war is to take care of the boys who fought in the last one," said Will Rogers. "You may want to use them again."

(see ARMED FORCES, MILITARY DEFENSE)

VICE PRESIDENT

Will Rogers usually refrained from making jokes about the helpless and the powerless. However, he made an exception in the case of the vice president.

"There is nothing that a vice president can do but be a vice president. You take that title away from him and he can't hand you a card."

Always sympathetic to the underdog, Will felt compassion for vice presidents and urged us not to judge them too harshly. We don't have enough information on which to form a judgment, he said, because no vice president had ever done anything yet.

"How can you tell when a vice president makes good and when he don't?" Will asked. "They have never given one anything to do yet to find out."

VIOLENCE

What foolishness makes human beings believe they are entitled to use violence, Will Rogers wondered. We all think we're right, we all think we've been wronged. "We all know a lot of things that would be good for our country," Will wrote to President Coolidge in *Letters of a Self-Made Diplomat*, "but we wouldn't want to go as far as to propose that everybody start shooting each other till we got them. A fellow shouldn't have to kill somebody to prove they are right."

(see MARINES)

VIOLIN

Will Rogers had many talents, but playing a musical instrument was not one of them. He loved music and spent hours playing the violin, although not well.

Once in Omaha, Nebraska, Will was on the bill with Madame Kalich, whose dressing room was located directly below his. One afternoon as he was hacking away on his violin, a maid appeared with a message from below. Please stop playing! The noise was annoying Madame Kalich.

"Madame doesn't like that tune!" Will said with a wink. "Will you tell madame to pick her own tune. I can play anything she wants."

(see MARX, GROUCHO)

VIRGINIA

"I am down in Old Virginia, the mother of presidents when we thought presidents had to be aristocrats," wrote Will from a state which has produced the most presidents. "Since we got wise to the limitations of aristocrats, Virginia has featured their ham over their presidential timber."

(see JEFFERSON, WASHINGTON)

VIRTUES

With all our virtues in America we have two boobs to every virtue.

—*Weekly Articles:* October 31, 1926

VODKA

Vodka was Russia's leading export. Returning from a trip to Russia, Will Rogers revealed one of the great secrets of the Russian state: the actual ingredients of Russian vodka.

"It's made from fermented Russian wheat, corn, oats, barley, alfalfa, or jimsonweed, just which ever one of these they happen to have handy. Then they start adding the ingredients.

"Potato peelings is one of 'em, then Russian boot tops. You just take the tops of as many Russian boots as you

255

can get when the men are asleep, you harvest 'em just above the ankle.

"The next ingredient (the Russians always deny this to me, but I have always believed it's true) is the whiskers. They say that they don't put 'em in vodka, that they are only used in that soup called borsch.

"Finally it's fermented and the Russian vodka is ready to drink.

"When you do your eyes begin expanding, and your ears begin to flopping like a mule's. It's the only drink where you drink and try to grit your teeth at the same time. It gives the most immediate results of any libation ever concocted, you don't have to wait for it to act. By the time it reaches the Adams apple it has acted. A man stepping on a red-hot poker could show no more immediate animation. It's the only drink where you can hit the man that handed it to you before he can possibly get away.

"It's a timesaver. It should especially appeal to Americans, there is nothing so dull in American life as that period when a drinker is at that annoying stage. He is a pest to everybody, but vodka eliminates that, you are never at the pest period."

(see BEER, PROHIBITION, WINE)

VOTE

Anything important is never left to the vote of the people. We only get to vote on some man; we never get to vote on what he is to do.

—*More Letters:* April 30, 1932
(see DEMOCRACY, FREEDOM)

VOTERS

"Every guy just looks in his pockets and then votes," Will Rogers observed. "And the funny part of it is it's the last year that is the one that counts.

"A voter don't expect much. If you give him one good year he is satisfied.

"The short memories of American voters is what keeps our politicians in office."

It's up to the voter to believe one man's promise or another man's alibis.

—Weekly Articles: October 23, 1932

In this country people don't vote for; they vote against.

—Radio Broadcasts, June 9, 1935

The way most people feel, they would like to vote against all of 'em, if it was possible.

—Daily Telegrams: April 27, 1932
(see CANDIDATES, ELECTIONS, PROMISES)

W

WALL STREET

"This stock market thing was a great game," said Will Rogers, "but, after all, everybody just can't live on gambling. Somebody has to do some work."

Even experts don't know what the weather will do. Even millionaires don't know what Wall Street will do.

—*Daily Telegrams:* September 6, 1933

I tell 'em this country is bigger than Wall Street, and if they don't believe me, I show 'em the map.

—*Weekly Articles:* December 1, 1929
(SEE WORK)

WAR

"I have a scheme for stopping war. It's this—no nation is allowed to enter a war till they have paid for the last one."

The rising cost of war was forcing nations to plan their

wars further ahead. "You can't go out and git a war like you used to could," said Will Rogers, "just on a moment's notice, you know. Wars is gittin' kind of hard to arrange. You got to bill them way ahead.

"Nowadays we have diplomats work on wars for years before arranging them. That's so when it's over, nobody will know what they were fighting for. We lost thousands and spent billions, and you could hand a sheet of paper to one million different people, and tell 'em to write down what the last war was for, and the only answer that will be alike, will be 'd____ if I know!'

"Why don't some of them offer a prize for a definition of what the last war started over? That would be the biggest bit of news of our generation.

"Diplomats are just as essential to starting a war as soldiers are for finishing it. You take diplomacy out of war and the thing would fall flat in a week."

The ones who arrange the wars are not the ones who have to fight the wars or pay for them, of course.

"They think the future generations should pay for the war, and the present generation should keep them in office."

Will Rogers warned against impoverishing future generations to pay for war. "Fighting wars on credit can put you in the ash can, just like buying everything on credit has put us there.

"There is no industry under the sun you can get credit for as quick as you can war."

I tell you wars will never be a success until you do have a referee, and until they announce before they start just what it's for.

—*Weekly Articles:* January 21, 1923

There is only one way in the world to prevent war, and this is, *for every nation to tend to its own business.* Trace any war that ever was and you will find some nation was

259

trying to tell some other nation how to run their business.

—*Weekly Articles:* June 28, 1925

Moral: Stay out of the war unless it is on home grounds.

—*Weekly Articles:* August 22, 1926

You know you can be killed just as dead in an unjustified war, as you can in one protecting your own home.

—*Weekly Articles:* May 26, 1929

When you get into trouble 5,000 miles away from home, you've got to have been looking for it.

—*Daily Telegrams:* February 9, 1932
(see CONFERENCES, DIPLOMATS, PEACE, WOMEN)

WAR PROFITS

Take the profits out of war, and you won't have any war.

—*Daily Telegrams:* December 14, 1934

WARS

At one point in 1927 the United States was contemplating involvement in three different wars at once. Will Rogers protested against involvement in too many wars at once, saying it prevented full appreciation of any of them. "The American people nowadays can't keep their mind on three wars at once. We got to have fewer and bigger wars or they will mean nothing to the public."

(see NEWS SHORTAGE)

WASHINGTON, D.C.

"I came to the county seat of Cuckooland yesterday," wrote Will Rogers after arriving in the capital and visiting Congress, "and spent the day prowling around the old 'fun factory,' watching the hired help trying to fool the boss and make him think they were doing something."

Will was impressed by the architecture of the Capitol, especially the underground passages. "Washington, D.C., has an underground tunnel running from the government offices to the Capitol. That's so when the senators and congressmen receive their checks every month, they can get to their homes without someone arresting them for robbery."

(see CONGRESS, CRIMINALS, ROBBERY, SENATE)

WASHINGTON, GEORGE

We romanticize our Revolutionary heroes, especially Washington. "There wasn't any Republicans in Washington's day. No Republicans, no boll weevil, no income tax, no cover charge, no disarmament conferences, no luncheon clubs, no stop lights, no static, no headwinds. Liquor was a companion, not a problem; no margins, no ticket speculators, no golf pants or Scotch jokes. My Lord, living in those times, who wouldn't be great?"

Admittedly, George Washington was an extraordinary man. "He was a politician and a gentleman—that is a rare combination."

Washington was also a surveyor. "He took the exact measure of the British and surveyed himself out about the most valuable piece of land in America at the time, Mount Vernon. George could not only tell the truth but land values."

(see REAL ESTATE)

WEALTH

"Ten men in our country could buy the world, and ten million can't buy enough to eat," remarked Will Rogers in a radio broadcast the last year of his life. Although he often called attention to unequal distribution of wealth, he was skeptical of fantastic schemes such as Huey Long's Share-the-Wealth program to redistribute income.

"I know a lot of tremendously rich people that should share their wealth with me," said Will, "but they just don't see it my way."

To just be rich in this country is no longer any novelty. It's not the wealth they had that we remember, it's what they did with it.

—*Weekly Articles:* July 20, 1930
(see AMERICAN WEALTH, DISTRIBUTION, UNEQUAL DIVISION)

WEATHER

Weather? The weather in Washington has been ... yes and no.

—*Weekly Articles:* November 12, 1933
(see WASHINGTON, D.C.)

WELFARE

Nobody can kick on honest deserving relief, and nobody can be blamed for kicking on relieving somebody when they won't work. The governments and towns have got to find some way of telling them apart.

—*Daily Telegrams:* February 1, 1935
(see UNEMPLOYMENT, WORK)

WIFE

The governor of New York, Al Smith, created a stir one night in 1924 when he came to see Will Rogers and the Follies *with his wife.*

This was such a notable event that Will Rogers mentioned it:

"Well, he was at our opera house the other night and I want to say this for him, he brought his own wife which is considered enough of a novelty to attract attention, even if he were not governor."

(see GUEST)

WILLS

Modern history has proven that there has never yet been a will left that was carried out exactly as the maker of the money intended. So if you are thinking of dying and have money, I would advise you to leave the following will: "Count up the lawyers in the state and divide it among them. If there should by any miracle be any left, let my relatives, all of them, God bless 'em, fight over it."

—Weekly Articles: May 31, 1925
(see INHERITANCE TAX, LAWYERS)

WILSON, WOODROW

The greatest thrill of his career as a performer, Will Rogers confessed, was making a president of the United States laugh—at himself. The fondest memory of all was the first time it happened with Woodrow Wilson.

"It just seemed by an odd chance for me every time I played before President Wilson that on that particular day there had been something of great importance that he had just been dealing with. For you must remember that each day was a day of great stress with him. He had no easy days. So when I could go into a theater and get laughs out of our president by poking fun at some turn in our national affairs, I don't mind telling you it was the happiest moment of my entire career on the stage.

"The first time I shall never forget, it was the most impressive and for me the most nervous one of them all. We were billed for Baltimore but not for Washington. President Wilson came over from Washington to see the performance. It was the first time in theatrical history that the president of the United States came over to Baltimore just to see a comedy.

"It was just at the time we were having our little set-to, and when we were at the height of our note-exchanging career with Germany and Austria. The house was packed with the elite of Baltimore.

"I was the least known member of the entire aggregation, doing my little specialty with a rope and telling jokes on national affairs, just a very ordinary little vaudeville act by chance sandwiched in among this great array.

"Well, I am not kidding you when I tell you that I was scared to death, I am always nervous. I never saw an audience that I ever faced with any confidence. For no man can ever tell how a given audience will ever take anything.

"But here I was, nothing but a very ordinary Oklahoma cowpuncher who had learned to read the daily papers a little, going out before the aristocracy of Baltimore, and the president of the United States, and kid about some of the policies with which he was shaping the destinies of nations.

"How was I to know but what the audience would rise up in mass and resent it? I had never heard, and I don't think anyone else has ever heard of a president being joked personally in a public theater about the policies of his administration.

"Now, by a stroke of what I call good fortune (for I will keep them always) I have a copy of the entire acts that I did for President Wilson on the five times I worked for him. My first remark in Baltimore was, 'I am kinder nervous here tonight.'

"Now that is not an especially bright remark, and I don't hope to go down in history on the strength of it, but it was so apparent to the audience that I was speaking the truth that they laughed heartily at it. After all, we all love honesty.

"Then I said, 'I shouldn't be nervous, for this is really my second presidential appearance. The first time was when Bryan [William Jennings Bryan] spoke in our town once, and I was to follow his speech and do my little rop-ing act.' Well, I heard them laughing, so I took a sly glance at the president's box and sure enough he was laughing just as big as any one.

"So I went on, 'As I say, I was to follow him, but he spoke so long that it was dark when he finished, they couldn't see my roping.'

"That went over great, so I said, 'I wonder what ever become of him.' That was all right, it got over, but still I made no direct reference to the president.

"Now Pershing was in Mexico at the time, and there was a lot in the papers for and against the invasion. I said, 'I see where they have captured Villa. Yes, they got him in the morning editions and the afternoon ones let him get away.'

"Now everybody in the house before they would laugh looked at the president, to see how he was going to take it. Well, he started laughing and they all followed suit.

" 'Villa raided Columbus, New Mexico. We had a man on guard that night at the post. But to show you how crooked this Villa is, he sneaked up on the opposite side.'

" 'We chased him over the line five miles, but run into a lot of government red tape and had to come back.'

" 'There is some talk of getting a machine gun if we can borrow one. The ones we have now they are using to train our army with in Plattsburg. If we go to war we will just have to go to the trouble of getting another gun.'

"Now, mind you, he was being criticized on all sides for lack of preparedness, yet he sat there and led that en-tire audience in laughing at the ones on himself.

"At that time there was talk of forming an army of two hundred thousand men. 'Mr. Ford makes three hundred thousand cars every year. I think, Mr. President, we ought to at least have a man to every car.'

" 'See where they got Villa hemmed in between the Atlantic and Pacific. Now all we got to do is to stop up both ends.'

" 'Pershing located him at a town called Los Quas Ka Jasbo. Now all we have to do is to locate Los Quas Ka Jasbo.'

" 'I see by a headline that Villa escapes net and fleas. We will never catch him then. Any Mexican that can escape fleas is beyond catching.'

" 'But we are doing better toward preparedness now, as one of my senators from Oklahoma has sent home a double portion of garden seed.'

"After various other ones on Mexico I started in on European affairs which at that time was long before we entered the war. 'We are facing another crisis tonight, but our president here has had so many of them lately that he can just lay right down and sleep beside one of those things.'

"Then I first pulled the one which I am proud to say he afterward repeated to various friends as the best one told on him during the war. I said, 'President Wilson is getting along fine now to what he was a few months ago. Do you realize, people, that at one time in our negotiations with Germany that he was five notes behind?'

"How he did laugh at that! Well, due to him being a good fellow and setting a real example, I had the proudest and most successful night I ever had on the stage."

WINE

"The wine had such ill effects on Noah's health that it was all he could do to live 950 years. Just nineteen years short of Methusaleh," mused Will. "Show me a total abstainer that ever lived that long!"

(see BEER, VODKA)

266

WISHES

"Every time you wish for something for your own personal gain, you are wishing somebody else bad luck," said Will, "so maybe that's why so few of our wishes come to anything."

(see MONEY)

WITHDRAWAL

Will Rogers' name was repeatedly entered into nomination for various offices without his consent. "If you see or hear of anybody proposing my name either humorously or semiseriously for any political office, will you maim said party and send me the bill?" he wrote on June 28, 1931.

Will Rogers withdrew his name from nomination and urged other candidates to do the same: "I hereby and hereon want to go on record as being the first presidential, vice-presidential, senator, or justice-of-the-peace candidate to withdraw.

"I hope in doing this that I have started something that will have far-reaching effect. Who will be the next to do the public a favor and withdraw?"

(see NOMINATION, RESIGNATION, UNOFFICIAL PRESIDENT)

WOMEN

Will Rogers didn't believe in the equality of women—he believed in the superiority of women. But the progress of civilization would make the sexes equal, he predicted. "I'll bet you the time ain't far off when a woman won't know any more than a man."

Women are the world's second greatest mystery, said Will. "Money and women are the most sought after and the least known about of any two things we have.

"The whole thing about the women is, they just love to be misunderstood. They always want you to have the wrong impression about what's in their minds and not the right one. There has never been anything invented yet, including war, that a man would enter into that a woman wouldn't too."

Women had the power to prevent war, Will claimed. "As a matter of fact six or eight women could prevent any war. The wives of the prime ministers, diplomats, and presidents would only have to say, 'If you allow war to come to this country I will leave you so help me.' But history records no record of one having left for that reason though they left for everything else.

"All the wars in the world, even if you won 'em, can't repay one mother for the loss of one son. But even at that when she says to you, 'That's my oldest boy's picture. He was lost in the war,' there is behind that mist in her eye, a shine of pride."

Will Rogers recommended that men not fight but surrender in the battle of the sexes. His advice to men in dealing with women was to let them have their way. "If you let them have their way," he said, "you will generally get even with them in the end."

(see MONEY, WAR)

It won't be no time till some woman will become so desperate politically and just lose all prospectus of right and wrong and maybe go from bad to worse and finally wind up in the senate.

—*Weekly Articles:* March 31, 1929
(see MONEY, WAR)

WOMEN MURDERERS

The automatic pistol was a boon to women murderers. "Look at the women murderers that in the day of the six-shooter was afraid to take a chance on missing their husbands," Will Rogers marveled. "But with this cute little automatic, which just fits into their handbag—'why you just can't miss him.' In the old days a woman had to go out and practice shooting for weeks, perhaps months, before she would dare open up on the 'better half.' But with this marvelous invention, the automatic, the more hysterical she gets and the more he dodges about the more direct hits will be scored. Then comes the pictures in the paper and a wonderful trial and the acquittal, with her parting remark to the newspapers, 'The dear men on the jury were just lovely to me.' If she had been compelled to use the old-time weapon the crime would never have happened, because the present-day woman don't wear enough clothes to conceal a real six-gun. Women used to be the alleged 'weaker sex' but the automatic and the sentimental jury have been the equalizer. Why divorce him when you can shoot him easier and cheaper?"

(see AUTOMATIC PISTOL, DIVORCE, HUSBAND KILLERS)

WOMEN'S BRAVERY

You can't pass a park without seeing a statue of some old codger on a horse. It must be his bravery, you can tell it's not his horsemanship. Anyhow, women are twice as brave as men, yet they never seem to have reached the statue stage, but one is due.

—*Daily Telegrams:* April 2, 1934

WOMEN'S ENDURANCE

"You know, women always could endure more than men," testified Will Rogers. "Not only physically, but mentally—did you ever get a peek at some of the husbands?"

"I hate to say it, but the women that spoke were all ter-rible," Will Rogers reported from the 1928 Republican convention. "They were pretty nearly as bad as the men. That will give you an idea how bad they were."

WORK

When the senate approved a thirty-six hour work week Will Rogers disapproved. "A week's work is to consist of thirty-six hours! I doubt very much if the people working now will agree to an increase in time of work like that. We stick to the old American principle of only working when the boss is looking."

Will Rogers said the solution to all our problems was work, and avoidance of work was the cause of many of those problems. "The world ain't going to be saved by nobody's scheme. It's fellows with schemes that got us into this mess. Plans get you into things, but you got to work your way out."

The government should provide work to those who cannot get work, he said. "If you live under a govern-ment and it don't provide some means of you getting work when you really want it and will do it, why then there is something wrong."

On the other hand, he said, there was also something wrong with giving people money for not working. "We shouldn't be giving people money, and them not doing anything for it. No matter what you had to hand out for necessities, the receiver should do some kind of work in return."

Many Americans were being rewarded more for not working than for working and were getting out of the habit of working. "The trouble with us in America is we are just muscle-bound from holding a steering wheel," said Will Rogers. "The only place we are calloused from work is the bottom of our driving toe."

We're living in a peculiar time. You get more for not working than you will for working, and more for not raising a hog than raising it.

—*Radio Broadcasts*, January 14, 1934

Never did things look brighter for the working man, but none of us want to work.

—*Weekly Articles:* December 22, 1929
(see NATURAL RESOURCES, PROSPERITY, UNEMPLOYMENT)

WORKING PEOPLE

Even at the height of his stardom, Will Rogers' sympathies lay with working people. "The illiterate ones will all work, and you will have no trouble with them," Rogers wrote to President Roosevelt during the Depression.

"But watch the ones that are smart, for they have been taught in school they are to live off the others. In fact, this is about all that is the matter with our country."

(see EDUCATION, ROBBERY)

WORLD

Ever wondered what the world would be like without you?

"I don't want to appear rude," said Will Rogers, "but I actually believe it could get along great without any of us."

We hear a lot now about the world becoming little, but I tell you it's plenty big yet. It will be a long time before we know much more about each other than we do now.

—*Weekly Articles:* July 19, 1931

WORLD SAVERS

My motto is, "Save America first."

—*Weekly Articles:* April 23, 1933

It's all right to fix the world, but you better get your own smokehouse full of meat first.

—*Daily Telegrams:* January 16, 1935
(see INTERNATIONAL AFFAIRS)

WORRY

When the government released statistics to show that people were living cheaper, Will Rogers was not surprised. After all, there was a Depression going on. Prices were low.

"You might live that much cheaper, but that don't figure in the worry," he said. "If worry is worth anything, we never was living as expensive."

(see CONFUSION, LIVING TOGETHER, PRICE)

WRITING ARTICLES

Will Rogers earned a good portion of his income writing articles for the press, but he refused to read the articles he had written. He said he wasn't paid well enough for that.

"For when I write 'em I am through with 'em. I am not being paid reading wages. You can always see too many things you wish you hadn't said, and not enough that you ought to."

WRITING JOKES

Will Rogers prided himself on writing all of his own material. On one occasion a well-known Hollywood gag writer offered to write jokes for him at a salary of a thousand dollars a week. Rogers shook his head and said, "For a thousand dollars a week, I'll write jokes for *you*."

(see HUMOR, SOFT JOB)

WRITING UP

Will Rogers was one of the most popular writers of his time. His newspaper column was read by millions daily. He claimed his success as a writer was due to the fact that he wrote *up* to his readers instead of down to them. "I never was in any shape to tell you anything you didn't know. In other words I always had to write UP to my Readers and not down."

WRONG

It don't take much to see that something is wrong, but it does take some eyesight to see what will put it right again.

—*Weekly Articles:* July 28, 1935

YOUNG FOLKS

"Young folks," said Will Rogers, "they are no better or worse than the rest of us.

"We are always drilling into them, 'When I was a boy we didn't do that.' But we forgot that we are not doing those same old things today. We changed with the times, so we can't blame the children for just joining the times, without even having to change.

"We are always telling 'em what we used to not do. We didn't do it because we didn't think of it. We did everything we could think of."

YOUNG WOMEN

Your mother gets mighty shocked at you girls nowadays, but in her day her mother was just on the verge of sending her to a reformatory, so we just got to live and let live and laugh the whole thing off.

—*Weekly Articles:* August 24, 1930

ZIEGFELD'S FOLLIES

"We have a hard time keeping our girls together," said Will of the Ziegfeld Follies on tour. "Every time we get to a new town some of them marry millionaires, but in a few weeks they catch up with the show again."

I am to go into Ziegfeld's new Follies, and I have no act. So I thought I will run down to Washington and get some material. Most people and actors appearing on the stage have some writer to write their material—but Congress is good enough for me. They have been writing my material for years.

—Weekly Articles: June 8, 1924

WILL ROGERS:
A BRIEF BIOGRAPHY

~1879~

Will Rogers is born on his father's ranch near Oolagah, Indian Territory, Oklahoma. The eighth child (fifth surviving) of Clem and Mary America Rogers, he is named William Penn Adair after a prominent Cherokee leader.

I am the only child in history who claims to November 4 as my birthday, that is election day. That's why I've always had it in for politicians.

~1887~

Young Will attends school at Drumgoul.

Drumgoul was a little one-room log cabin built of post-oak logs, four miles east of Chelsea. The school stayed with such books as *Ray's Arithmetic* and *McGuffey's First* and *Second Readers.* We had a geography around there, but we just used it for the pictures of cattle grazing in the Argentine and the wolves attacking the sleighs in Russia.

It was all Indian kids that went there, and I, being part Cherokee, had just enough white in me to make my honesty questionable.

~ 1890 ~

His mother, Mary America Rogers, to whom Will is very close, dies when he is ten years old.

My mother's name was Mary, and if your mother's name was Mary and she was an old-fashioned woman, you don't have to say much for her. Everybody knows already.

~ 1892–96 ~

Will attends Willie Halsell College, Vinita, in Indian Territory, and various other schools at the behest of his father.

He sent me to about every school in that part of the country. In some of them I would last three or four months. I got just as far as *McGuffey's Fourth Reader*, when the teacher wouldn't seem to be running the school right, and rather than have the school stop, I would generally leave.

Will is not a disciplined student, for his attention wanders, but he excells in speaking exercises. He is popular among the students but not the teachers.

~ 1897–98 ~

He attends Scarritt College Institute in Neosho, Missouri, and finally Kemper Military School in Boonville, Missouri.

I spent two years there, one in the fourth grade, and one year in the guardhouse. One was as bad as the other. I spent ten years in the fourth grade and knew more about *McGuffey's Fourth Reader* than McGuffey did.

After leaving Kemper, Will never returns to school again.

~1898~

Will works as a cowboy on the Ewing Ranch in Higgins, Texas, then returns to Claremore to manage his father's ranch.

~1899~

On July 4, 1899, he enters a steer-roping contest at Claremore and garners first prize.

> It was the first one I ever was in, the very first thing I ever did in the way of appearing before an audience in my life. Well, as I look back on it that had quite an influence on my little career, for I kinder got to running to 'em, and the first thing I knew I was just plum 'honery' and fit for nothing but show business. Once you are a showman you are plum ruined for manual labor again.

At the age of twenty-one he meets Betty Blake of Rogers, Arkansas, who is visiting her sister in Oolagah. He falls in love with her immediately, but eight years will pass before she agrees to marry him.

~1900~

Will writes his first love letter to Betty.

> My Dear Betty:
> Now for me to attempt to express my delight for your sweet letter would be utterly impossible so will just put it mild and say I was *very very much* pleased. I was also surprised for I thought you had forgotten your Cowboy (for I am yours as far as I am concerned).
> I know you had a fine time when your Sweetheart was down to see you. Oh! how I envy him for I would give all I possess if I only knew that you cared something for me, for Betty you may not believe it or care anything about it

but you do not know that you have made life miserable for one poor boy out in I.T. [Indian Territory] But you did for I think of you all the time and just wish that you might always have a remembrance of me for I know that I cant expect to be your sweetheart for I am not "smoothe" like the boys you have for sweethearts. But I know you have no one that will think any more of you than I do although I know they may profess to. Now Betty I know you will think me a Big Fool (which I am) but please consider that you are the one that has done it. But I know you dident mean to and I ought not to have got so broken up over you. But I could not help it so if you do not see fit to answer this please do not say a word about it to anyone for the sake of a brokenhearted Cherokee Cowboy.

Now Betty if you should stoop so low as to answer this please tell me the plain truth for that is what you should do and not flirt with me for I would not be smoothe enough to detect it.

Well Betty please burn this for my sake. Hoping you will consider what I have told you in my undignified way and if not to please never say anything about it and burn this up.

I am yours with love,
Will Rogers

Betty, more conventional than Will, is somewhat shocked by this letter and does not reply. Discouraged, Will leaves town to join Colonel Mulhall's rodeo show and tours the Midwest.

~1901–2~

Overcome by wanderlust, Will Rogers journeys to England, South America, and South Africa. He does not write to Betty for two years.

~1903~

In South Africa Will joins Texas Jack's Wild West Show, billed as the Cherokee Kid. He tours Australia and New Zealand with a circus.

> There are four of us who ride bucking horses, but I do all the roping and am called the Cherokee Kid on the programs. I have learned quite a bit about fancy roping and it takes fine over here where they know nothing whatsoever about roping.

~1904~

Will appears at a Wild West Show at the St. Louis World's Fair. He obtains a few vaudeville bookings in Chicago and begins incorporating a few quips into his act.

> I tried about everything to make a living, outside of work. All kinds of writing and playacting, and trying to appear foolish and trying to appear smart.

~1905–7~

Will Rogers' first vaudeville appearance in New York leads to a ten-year career. He discovers that audiences are more enthralled by what he has to say than by his rope tricks. He expands his act to include original jokes and comments on current events.

~1908~

At last Will persuades Betty Blake to marry him, by promising to give up vaudeville at the end of the current season.

Along about that time Betty Blake down in Rogers, Ark., had a mental relapse and said "yes" after several solid years of "no's." She threw her lot with "Buck" and I, and the pony "Teddy." From cheap hotels to dark stage door entrances, she trudged her way.

Will Rogers marries Betty Blake on November 25 at Rogers, Arkansas, and joins him in his life as a touring vaudeville performer, along with his assistant Buck and his horse Teddy.

I was married too in 1908. And sometimes the salary wasn't any too big to ship Buck and his wife and Teddy, and my wife and self, to the next town. In fact I think Buck rode some of the short jumps. It was great fun, not a worry. I regret the loss of vaudeville more than any part of it. It was the greatest form of entertainment ever conceived. Nothing in the world ever gives the satisfaction of a good vaudeville show.

Will's success as a performer prevents him from keeping his promise to retire from show business, for he keeps receiving more and more lucrative offers.

~ 1911 ~

Will's father Clem Van Rogers dies and his first son, Will Rogers, Jr., is born in New York City.

~ 1913 ~

A daughter, Mary Amelia Rogers, is born in Rogers, Arkansas.

~ 1915 ~

Will takes his first airplane flight in Atlantic City. A second son, James Blake, is born on Long Island, New York.

~ 1916 ~

Will Rogers joins the Ziegfeld Follies as a comedian and emcee. He later calls this his "literary apprenticeship."

> We spent our literary apprenticeship in the same school of knocks, Mr. Ziegfeld's Follies. We eked out a bare existence among nothing but bare backs. There was diamond necklaces to the right of us and Rolls Royces to the left of us, and costumes of powder completely surrounding us.... Those were hardship days, but great training for our journalistic future.

He gives his first presidential performance before Woodrow Wilson in Baltimore.

~ 1918 ~

Will makes his first motion picture in New Jersey while still working at the Follies. A third son, Fred Stone Rogers, is born.

> The first movie I ever made was in '18, an Alaskan story by Rex [Beach] called *Laughing Bill Hyde*. I played by request of Mrs. Rex Beach in one of his stories. The part was rather that of a crook, who received money under false pretenses. Mrs. Beach had seen my little act in the Follies, so she decided that I was the one to do naturally ... this crook who obtained money under false pretenses.

~1919~

Will Rogers moves the family to California to start a two-year contract with Goldwyn Studio to make silent films.

> It's the grandest show business I know anything about, and the only place where an actor can act and at the same time sit down in front and clap for himself.

Before leaving New York his literary career is launched with the successful publication of two books of his collected Follies comments, *The Cowboy Philosopher on the Peace Conference* and *The Cowboy Philosopher on Prohibition*.

~1920~

Fred Stone Rogers dies during a diphtheria epidemic at age twenty months. Will mourns the death the rest of his life but never speaks of it publicly.

~1921–22~

Will Rogers produces and stars in three of his own motion pictures, *Fruits of Faith, The Roping Fool,* and *One Day in 365*. Plunged into debt, he returns to New York and rejoins the Follies. He enters the after-dinner lecture circuit, often speaking at two or three banquets a week. He starts a series of weekly syndicated articles, which will continue until his death. He also makes his debut on the infant medium of radio in Pittsburgh.

> I was nervous as I ever was on a first night. Radio is a tough thing, especially for a comedian. It's made to order for a singer and a person making a straightforward speech or explaining something. To try to get some laughs, it's the toughest test. That little microphone is not going to laugh.

~1923~

Will's weekly articles, appearing at first in the *New York Times*, are so well-received that they are soon syndicated by the McNaught Syndicate and become a regular Sunday feature nationwide.

~1924~

The weekly articles create demand for another book. Will publishes *Illiterate Digest*, a collection of weekly articles.

~1925~

Will travels all over the United States on a lecture tour, flying whenever possible.

> Would stay all night in the town I had just played, get a good night's rest, then take my time about getting out in the morning, and leave just whenever I wanted to. Fly over the beautiful mountain tops, and in two or three hours catch up with the train that had left the night before. Then when we get to the next town and the committee would come and want to take me for a drive to see their town, I could tell them all about it. Fly over a town and you get more of an idea of it than you could get in a week from driving around.

He lectures 151 nights in eight months. After the close of Ziegfeld's Follies, Will returns to California again.

~1926~

Will Rogers travels to London and writes *Letters of a Self-Made Diplomat to His President*.

I felt that the president needed a foreign diplomat that could really go in and dip, and he didn't even have to ask me to do it; that same intimate understanding that had told me he needed someone, had told me that I was the one he needed. And that's all there has ever been between us.

He and his family traveled over much of Europe after a request from the *Saturday Evening Post* to do a series of articles. He also begins a series of *Daily Telegrams*. Returning home from a lecture tour he finds he's been elected honorary mayor of Beverly Hills in his absence.

~ 1927 ~

Will publishes *There's Not a Bathing Suit in Russia* and is made "congressman-at-large" by the National Press Club in Washington. His *Daily Telegrams* are syndicated in over 400 newspapers.

The great trouble in writing for the papers is that you are so apt to hit on some subject that does not appeal to a certain class of people. For instance, if I write a learned article on chewing gum, I find that I lose my clientele of readers who are toothless. Then when I write on just strictly politics, I find that the honest people are not interested. Then, if I write on some presidential candidate, I find that there are so many of them that few know the one I am writing about.

He suffers severe stomach pains and undergoes an emergency gallstone operation on June 19. After his recovery he makes his final silent film, *The Texas Steer*.

~ 1928 ~

Will fills in for his injured friend Fred Stone in a Broadway musical comedy *Three Cheers*.

~ 1929 ~

Will makes his first sound film for Fox Film Corporation, *They Had to See Paris*. He leaves town to avoid the premier.

> As it was to appear with a sort of Ballyhoo opening, charging those poor people $5, I just couldn't be a party to such brigandage. First night audiences pay their money to look at each other. If they get stuck they can't blame me—it will be because they don't look good to each other. So I figured I better kinder take to the woods until the effects blew over.

He publishes *Ether and Me*, a humorous account of his gallstone operation.

~ 1931 ~

Will journeys to London to observe the disarmament conference, and also visits Nicaragua and the Orient.

> Early in the autumn, Mrs. Rogers and I sent two sons away supposedly to schools. (We got tired of trying to get 'em up in the morning.) One went north, here in this state; another to New Mexico. Since then we have received no word or letter. We have looked in every football team all over the country. Guess they couldn't make the teams, knew their education was a failure and kept right on going.

Will makes *A Connecticut Yankee*, one of his best and most durable films.

~ 1932 ~

Will tours Central and South America. He addresses the Democratic national convention. When Roosevelt comes to Los Angeles and the Republican mayor refuses to welcome him, Will Rogers performs the honors at Olympic Stadium. Later he is criticized for saying that both candidates take themselves too seriously.

Now that the election is over and people can't write in and complain about my "remarks," why I figure that this department of the paper will be withdrawn. One day when I thought I had written a good article (by accident, I suppose, it certainly wasn't through habit), well, it seems that this one sensible article that I wrote was such a change from the usual bunk I had been dishing out that even the *Times* themselves rose up in protest.

The one thing that I am proud of is the fact that there is not a man in public life today that I don't like, most of them are my good friends, but that's not going to keep me from taking a dig at him when he does something or says something foolish.

And when I said that they both were taking themselves too serious, that the United States was bigger than any two men or any two parties, why that's the way I feel about it.

~1933~

Will Rogers attains the status of the highest-paid film star in Hollywood.

Out in Hollywood, they say you're not a success unless you owe fifty thousand dollars to somebody, have five cars, can develop temperament without notice or reason at all, and have been mixed up in four divorce cases and two breach-of-promise cases. As a success in Hollywood, I'm a rank failure and I guess I am too old to be taught new tricks. Besides, I'm pretty well off domestically speaking and ain't yearning for a change. I hold only two distinctions in the movie business: ugliest fellow in 'em and I still have the same wife I started out with.

On November 25 Will and Betty celebrate their silver anniversary.

> Yesterday was my wife's and my twenty-fifth wedding anniversary. I got her an awful pretty silver thimble, you know, it was our silver anniversary. She had the old one just about worn out. I also contributed quite a few silver hairs to the occasion. But you know, my wife hasn't got a single gray hair—she ain't got a one. You see, I've never worried her!

~ 1934 ~

Will does a world tour. He reaches the status of the number-one box-office star in the United States. There are rumors that he is being considered for a gubernatorial nomination.

> I am not a candidate for anything. I'd rather be a poor actor than a poor governor. After rawhiding these fellows for so many years, I'm satisfied to remain fancy free, to go where I please, when I please.

He stars in Eugene O'Neill's stage play *Ah! Wilderness.*

~ 1935 ~

He makes his last picture, *Steamboat Round the Bend.* Shortly before his death Will is approached by a biographer, but he insists he is not ready for a biography.

> Besides, I am a young man (get that) yet, and I haven't even started living. I am going to cut loose here someday and try and get some life into my life and even then it won't be fit to tell about. The first part will be uninteresting and the last part will be too scandalous.

Will Rogers dies August 15 in a plane crash with aviator Wiley Post near Point Barrow, Alaska. He is buried in Claremore, Oklahoma, location of the Will Rogers Memorial.

ADDITIONAL SUBJECT
REFERENCES

Actors, Weekly Articles: November 4, 1928; *Advertising*, Radio broadcast, June 1, 1930; *Advising*, Weekly Articles: January 15, 1928; *Advisors*, Weekly Articles: August 21, 1932; *America*, Daily Telegrams: February 5, 1934; Daily Telegrams: December 3, 1930; Weekly Articles: June 1, 1930; Daily Telegrams: November 26, 1930; *Americans*, Weekly Articles: July 17, 1935; *American Wealth*, Radio Broadcasts (for unemployment relief), 1931; *Ancestors*, Weekly Articles: November 30, 1924; *Arguments*, Daily Telegrams: April 14, 1930; Daily Telegrams: February 13, 1930; *Arkansas*, Daily Telegrams: July 30, 1935; *Armed Forces*, Daily Telegrams: May 30, 1934; *Arms Trading*, Daily Telegrams: February 28, 1933; *Athletics*, Daily Telegrams: September 27, 1929; *Automatic*, Daily Telegrams: June 7, 1931; *Automobile*, Radio Broadcasts, October 18, 1931; *Automobile Age*, "The Grand Champion," *American* magazine, December 1929; *Bankers*, Daily Telegrams: October 11, 1929; Daily Telegrams: March 2, 1933; *Banking Crisis*, Daily Telegrams: March 10, 1932; *Beans*, Weekly Articles: February 25, 1934; *Beliefs*, Weekly Articles: July 5, 1931; Weekly Articles: January 20, 1924; *Beverly Hills*, Weekly Articles: August 28, 1927; *Bible*: Daily Telegrams: March 18, 1934; *Bootlegger*, Convention Articles: p. 27; *Business*, Daily Telegrams: September 24, 1930; Daily Telegrams: April 2, 1929; *Cal-*

ifornia, Daily Telegrams: September 9, 1932; Weekly Articles: April 30, 1933; Weekly Articles: September 16, 1933; *Canada,* More Letters: November 20, 1931; Daily Telegrams; November 6, 1934; *Chaplin,* Daily Telegrams: February 26, 1935; *Cherokees,* Weekly Articles: May 4, 1930; More Letters: January 8, 1927; *Chewing Gum,* Prospectus for "The Remodeled Chewing Gum Corporation," Illiterate Digest; *Children's Vote,* Daily Telegrams: August 25, 1930; *Chili,* Weekly Articles: June 24, 1923; *Chinese Myths,* Daily Telegrams: August 22, 1934; Daily Telegrams: January 1, 1932; *Cigarettes,* More Letters: p. 81; *Civilization,* Weekly Articles: July 5, 1931; Weekly Articles: January 20, 1935; *College Degrees,* Weekly Articles: September 11, 1932; *Communism,* Weekly Articles: November 6, 1927; Weekly Articles: October 3, 1926; Weekly Articles: January 11, 1931; *Conference;* Radio broadcast, April 6, 1930; Daily Telegrams: July 5, 1933; Daily Telegrams: December 13, 1934; Daily Telegrams: January 22, 1930; Weekly Articles: July 30, 1933; Weekly Articles: September 26, 1926; Daily Telegrams: July 21, 1930; *Confidence,* Daily Telegrams: November 19, 1929; Daily Telegrams: November 20, 1929; Daily Telegrams: September 19, 1933; Daily Telegrams: December 1, 1929; *Contact Man,* Daily Telegrams, April 10, 1929; *Coolidge,* Weekly Articles: March 24, 1929; Weekly Articles: January 27, 1924; Weekly Articles: March 9, 1930; Weekly Articles: November 16, 1924; More Letters: January 8, 1927; *Congress,* Weekly Articles: March 22, 1925; *Conservative,* Weekly Articles: April 2, 1933; *Constitution,* Daily Telegrams: October 23, 1933; *Corsets,* Weekly Articles: March 4, 1923; *Country Boy,* Weekly Articles: August 31, 1924; *Cowboy,* Daily Telegrams: July 10, 1931; *Coverup,* Weekly Articles: October 4, 1925; *Credit,* Daily Telegrams: September 6, 1928; Daily Telegrams: September 6, 1928; *Crime,* Self-Made Diplomat, pp. 195–6; Daily Telegrams: March 20, 1931; *Crime and Punishment,* Weekly Articles: February 26, 1928; *Criminals,* Daily Telegrams: February 2, 1934; Weekly Articles: June 7, 1931; Daily Telegrams, December 18, 1930; Daily Telegrams, June 10, 1935; Daily Telegrams, December 1, 1930; Daily Telegrams: December 18, 1930; *Dark Horse,* Daily Telegrams: July 6, 1924; *Death,* Daily Telegrams: January 30, 1926; Weekly Articles: June 30, 1935; Weekly Articles: May 24, 1925; *Democracy,* Weekly Articles: April 12, 1925; *Democrat,* Daily Telegrams: July 29, 1932; Radio broadcast, April 27, 1930; Weekly Articles: June 24, 1928; Daily Telegrams: July 11, 1930;

Convention Articles: June 29, 1928; *Depression,* Daily Telegrams: December 20, 1929; Weekly Articles: October 25, 1931; Daily Telegrams: February 15, 1933; *Detroit,* Weekly Articles: January 30, 1926; *Diplomacy,* Weekly Articles: June 30, 1929; Daily Telegrams: July 3, 1933; Daily Telegrams: November 17, 1931; Daily Telegrams: July 18, 1929; April 17, 1932; *Diplomats,* Daily Telegrams: November 17, 1931; Daily Telegrams: July 18, 1929; *Disarmament,* Daily Telegrams: January 28, 1930; *Distribution,* Weekly Articles: June 1, 1930; Weekly Articles: April 17, 1932; *Dollar,* Weekly Articles: June 30, 1933; *Dopey,* Weekly Articles: December 16, 1934; *Drought,* Daily Telegrams: January 3, 1930; *Eclipse,* Weekly Articles: September 23, 1923; *Economic Jargon,* Radio Broadcasts, May 7, 1933; *Economist,* Radio Broadcasts, May 26, 1935; Daily Telegrams: December 10, 1934; Daily Telegrams: October 30, 1933; *Education,* Weekly Articles: December 4, 1930; Weekly Articles: July 31, 1932; Weekly Articles: January 6, 1928; *Elections,* Weekly Articles: September 14, 1930; Weekly Articles: May 10, 1925; Weekly Articles: January 30, 1927; *English Gentleman,* Weekly Articles: September 8, 1928; *Equality,* Weekly Articles: May 8, 1927; *Europe,* Daily Telegrams: August 10, 1926; Radio Broadcasts, March 31, 1935; Weekly Articles: June 27, 1926; Self-Made Diplomat, p. 251; Daily Telegrams: February 12, 1933; *Explanations,* Weekly Articles: January 28, 1934; Convention Articles: June 29, 1924; *Exports,* Daily Telegrams: January 9, 1933; *Fame,* Weekly Articles: June 3, 1923; *Family Tree,* Weekly Articles: April 29, 1928; *Farmers,* Daily Telegrams: June 4, 1934; *Fashions,* Weekly Articles: April 20, 1930; *Father's Day,* Daily Telegrams: May 11, 1930; *Filibuster,* Radio Broadcasts (for unemployment relief), 1931; *Fishing,* Weekly Articles: March 11, 1928; *Flying,* "How to Be Funny," January 28, 1928; Weekly Articles: August 18, 1935; Daily Telegrams: October 30, 1929; *Food,* February 25, 1934; *Football,* Daily Telegrams: January 5, 1931; Weekly Articles: November 29, 1925; *Ford,* Daily Telegrams: July 30, 1929; Radio Broadcasts, June 1, 1930; *Foreign Affairs,* Weekly Articles: January 7, 1934; *France,* Weekly Articles: August 8, 1926; Daily Telegrams: August 2, 1926; *Friends,* Self-Made Diplomat, p. 250; *Gambling,* Self-Made Diplomat, p. 197; *Golf,* Daily Telegrams, August 5, 1930; Weekly Articles: January 21, 1923; Weekly Articles: September 7, 1924; Weekly Articles: January 24, 1926; *Good Intentions,* Self-Made Diplomat, p. 252; Weekly Articles: August 20, 1933; *Government,*

Weekly Articles: June 8, 1924; Weekly Articles: November 11, 1928; Daily Telegrams: July 28, 1930; Daily Telegrams: March 27, 1931; *Governmentese,* Daily Telegrams: January 28, 1930; *Government Overthrow,* Daily Telegrams: July 26, 1929; *Government Spending,* Weekly Articles: March 27, 1932; Daily Telegrams: February 28, 1935; Daily Telegrams: November 7, 1933; Daily Telegrams: December 20, 1932; *Graft,* Weekly Articles: November 25, 1934; *Greatness,* Daily Telegrams: February 28, 1930; *Gunboat Diplomacy,* Daily Telegrams: August 3, 1930; *Hamilton,* Weekly Articles: May 19, 1929; *Healing Waters,* Weekly Articles: June 24, 1923; *Heroes,* Weekly Articles: July 17, 1928; *Higher Education,* Weekly Articles: July 31, 1932; *High Society,* Weekly Articles: February 25, 1923; *High Standard,* More Letters: June 2, 1928; *History Makers,* Weekly Articles: June 29, 1928; *Holding Company,* Daily Telegrams: March 13, 1935; *Hollywood,* Weekly Articles: June 21, 1931; Radio Broadcasts, May 12, 1935; Weekly Articles: May 1, 1932; Weekly Articles: June 24, 1923; *Home,* Daily Telegrams: October 26, 1926; Weekly Articles: May 24, 1925; Weekly Articles: November 15, 1925; *Home Run,* Weekly Articles: October 26, 1930; *Hooey,* Weekly Articles: July 31, 1932; Weekly Articles: July 10, 1932; Daily Telegrams: October 8, 1933; *Humanitarian,* Daily Telegrams: February 28, 1933; *Human Mating,* Weekly Articles: August 4, 1929; *Human Nature,* Radio Broadcasts, June 1, 1930; Daily Telegrams: December 9, 1930; *Humor,* Weekly Articles: December 18, 1932; Weekly Articles: June 29, 1930; Weekly Articles: August 19, 1923; *Hunger,* Daily Telegrams: January 7, 1931; *Husband Killing,* Weekly Articles: May 1, 1927; *Ideas,* Daily Telegrams: October 25, 1933; *Ignorance,* Weekly Articles: August 31, 1924; Daily Telegrams: August 11, 1929; *Income Taxes,* Weekly Articles: April 8, 1923; Weekly Articles: January 18, 1931; Daily Telegrams: December 8, 1929; Daily Telegrams: March 31, 1935; *Indians,* Weekly Articles: June 10, 1934; Weekly Articles: February 5, 1928; Radio Broadcasts, April 14, 1935; *Inheritance Tax,* Daily Telegrams: March 23, 1931; Weekly Articles: February 28, 1926; Daily Telegrams: February 24, 1929; *International Relations,* Self-Made Diplomat, August 26, 1926; *Investigations,* Radio Broadcasts, April 30, 1933; Daily Telegrams: December 28, 1934; *Investigative Committees,* Weekly Articles: April 27, 1924; *Invitations:* This story cannot be substantiated, according to Pat Lowe, Librarian of Will Rogers Memorial; *Ireland,* Convention Articles: July 2, 1920; Daily

Telegrams: September 8, 1926; Daily Telegrams: August 1, 1926; *Jackson*, Weekly Articles: February 5, 1928; *Japanese*, Weekly Articles: May 4, 1924; More Letters: March 12, 1932; Weekly Articles: February 6, 1927; Weekly Articles: January 17, 1932; *Jeffersonian*, Weekly Articles: December 2, 1928; Weekly Articles: October 28, 1928; *Jobs*, Weekly Articles: June 7, 1931; *Jockey*, Weekly Articles: August 17, 1924; *Killers*, Weekly Articles: June 7, 1931; *Knees*, Weekly Articles: April 20, 1930; *Knowledge*, Daily Telegrams: September 19, 1933; Weekly Articles: May 11, 1930; *Labor*, Weekly Articles: November 12, 1933; *Lawyers*, Daily Telegrams: December 30, 1934; Daily Telegrams: February 14, 1935; Weekly Articles: July 28, 1935; Weekly Articles: May 31, 1925; Weekly Articles: January 14, 1923; *Legislature*, Weekly Articles: March 6, 1927; *Liberty*, Daily Telegrams: September 30, 1934; *Lincoln*, Weekly Articles: February 22, 1925; Daily Telegrams: February 12, 1934; *Living Together:* Weekly Articles: April 12, 1925: *Long, Huey*, Weekly Articles: March 4, 1934; Weekly Articles: January 29, 1934; *Long Skirts*, Weekly Articles: April 20, 1930; *Los Angeles*, Weekly Articles: June 7, 1931; *Lunatics*, Daily Telegrams: June 5, 1930; *Man*, Weekly Articles: April 17, 1932; *Marines*, Weekly Articles: July 5, 1925; *Marriage Prediction*, Weekly Articles: July 2, 1933; *Marx, Groucho*, Daily Telegrams: December 31, 1933; *Mass Production*, Weekly Articles: March 27, 1932; *Mayors*, Weekly Articles: September 4, 1927; *Mergers*, Weekly Articles: March 23, 1930; Weekly Articles: November 27, 1932; Daily Telegrams: August 8, 1929; Weekly Articles: November 27, 1932; *Mexico*, Daily Telegrams: March 16, 1930; More Letters: May 19, 1928; More Letters: May 19, 1928; Convention Articles: July 3, 1920; *Military Defense*, Weekly Articles: December 9, 1928; *Momentous Times*, Weekly Articles: July 8, 1928; *Money*, Daily Telegrams: March 22, 1935; Weekly Articles: January 3, 1926; Daily Telegrams: February 17, 1931; Weekly Articles: December 6, 1925; Weekly Articles: July 22, 1923; Weekly Articles: October 2, 1932; Daily Telegrams: December 15, 1933; Weekly Articles: December 28, 1930; Daily Telegrams: February 17, 1931; *Morning*, More Letters: February 27, 1932; *Moses*, Weekly Articles: March 17, 1935; *Mosquitoes*, Weekly Articles: February 24, 1929; *Mothers*, Radio Broadcasts, May 11, 1930; Daily Telegrams: May 10, 1932; *Movies*, Weekly Articles: August 22, 1926; *Movie Ads*, Weekly Articles: May 17, 1931; *Movie Audiences*, Weekly Articles: April 17, 1932; *Movie Busi-*

ness, Weekly Articles: October 2, 1932; *Movie Opening,* Weekly Articles: October 6, 1929; *Movie Reviews,* Weekly Articles: November 11, 1934; *Movie Stars,* Weekly Articles: February 24, 1935; *Movie Technology,* Daily Telegrams: March 20, 1930; *Movie Titles,* Weekly Articles, May 17, 1931; Weekly Articles: October 13, 1929; *Movie Violence,* Weekly Articles: May 17, 1931; *Murders,* Weekly Articles: June 30, 1929; Weekly Articles: September 20, 1925; *Murderers,* Weekly Articles: November 8, 1931; *Murder Suicides,* Weekly Articles: November 23, 1930; *Mussolini,* Weekly Articles: April 18, 1926; *Nations,* Weekly Articles: April 9, 1933; Daily Telegrams: March 7, 1929; *Nation,* Weekly Articles: April 9, 1933; Daily Telegrams: March 7, 1929; *National Affairs,* Daily Telegrams: February 14, 1934; *National Debt:* Weekly Articles: January 10, 1926; Weekly Articles: November 25, 1934; Daily Telegrams: May 7, 1934; *National Health Care,* Weekly Articles: July 13, 1930; Weekly Articles: May 11, 1924; *Native Americans,* Weekly Articles: September 9, 1928; Daily Telegrams: April 22, 1935; *Natural Resources,* More Letters: June 2, 1928; *Nevada,* Daily Telegrams: August 31, 1930; Daily Telegrams: March 20, 1931; *Nevada Divorce,* Daily Telegrams: March 10, 1931; *New Cars,* Weekly Articles: January 22, 1928; *Newspapers,* Weekly Articles: August 2, 1925; Daily Telegrams: July 19, 1934; *News Shortage:* Weekly Articles: August 30, 1931; *New York:* Weekly Articles: May 31, 1925; More Letters: November 20, 1931; *Nicaragua,* Weekly Articles: November 27, 1927; Weekly Articles: December 5, 1926; Weekly Articles: February 19, 1928; Daily Telegrams: November 28, 1928; *Nomination,* Daily Telegrams: July 1, 1930; *Nose Jobs,* Weekly Articles: September 7, 1924; *Nude,* Daily Telegrams: July 27, 1930; *Oklahoma,* Weekly Articles: January 27, 1924; *Packer, Alfred,* Weekly Articles: November 2, 1930; *Pageant,* Weekly Articles: September 24, 1933; *Pall Bearer,* Weekly Articles: May 1, 1932; *Parades,* Daily Telegrams: September 1, 1933; Daily Telegrams; March 17, 1929; Weekly Articles: September 24, 1933; *Party,* Weekly Articles: November 11, 1928; Weekly Articles: December 11, 1922; November 9, 1924; *Party Founders,* Daily Telegrams: February 26, 1933; *Party Platform,* Daily Telegrams: June 29, 1928; *Party Politics,* Weekly Articles: March 29, 1925: Weekly Articles: July 1, 1928; *Patriotism,* More Letters: April 30, 1932; Weekly Articles: July 15, 1928; *Peace,* Weekly Articles: October 20, 1929; Daily Telegrams: November 3, 1929; Weekly Articles: February 9, 1930; Daily Telegrams: November 12, 1930; Daily Telegrams: May 31, 1929; Weekly Articles: August 20, 1933; Daily Telegrams: August 9, 1933; *Pessimists,* Daily Telegrams: August 20, 1929; *Places,* Daily Telegrams: March 12, 1933; *Plans,* Radio Broadcasts, April 21, 1935; *Police,* Weekly Articles: May 31, 1925; *Politicians,* Weekly Articles: January 13, 1924; Weekly Articles: March 25, 1923; Weekly Articles: August 17, 1930; Weekly Articles: September 4, 1932; Weekly Articles: October 14, 1928; *Politics,* Weekly Articles: December 18, 1932; Weekly Articles: September 16, 1928; Weekly Articles: December 18, 1932; Weekly Articles: July 6, 1930; Daily Telegrams: June 28, 1931; Weekly Articles: July 8, 1928; More Letters: June 2, 1928; Daily Telegrams: November 1, 1932; Weekly Articles: November 4, 1928; Weekly Articles: January 6, 1924; Weekly Articles: June 17, 1934; *Polo Spills,* Weekly Articles: April 20, 1924; *Presidents,* Weekly Articles: November 20, 1932, Weekly Articles: September 12, 1926; Weekly Articles: July 18, 1928; Weekly Articles: May 5, 1923; Weekly Articles: September 22, 1929; *Presidential Campaign,* Daily Telegrams: November 1, 1932; Daily Telegrams: October 30, 1932; *Prince of Wales,* Weekly Articles: September 7, 1924; *Prison,* Daily Telegrams: August 7, 1929; Daily Telegrams: December 12, 1929; *Prosperity,* Weekly Articles: October 10, 1926; Weekly Articles: September 30, 1928; Daily Telegrams: May 9, 1930; Daily Telegrams: April 2, 1933; Daily Telegrams: August 19, 1931; *Public Office,* Weekly Articles: March 22, 1925; *Queen,* Weekly Articles: November 28, 1926; *Ranches,* Weekly Articles: June 19, 1932; Daily Telegrams: August 30, 1932; *Reading,* Weekly Articles: April 14, 1935; Weekly Articles: March 18, 1934; *Real Estate Agents,* Weekly Articles: July 1, 1923; *Religion,* Weekly Articles: January 8, 1933; Weekly Articles: March 11, 1923; Weekly Articles: July 19, 1925, Weekly Articles: July 19, 1925; Weekly Articles: March 11, 1923; *Republicans,* Weekly Articles: September 20, 1931; Daily Telegrams: September 26, 1932; Weekly Articles: February 10, 1929; Weekly Articles: April 29, 1928; Daily Telegrams: February 27, 1931; Weekly Articles: July 1, 1928; *Republican Convention,* Convention Articles, June, 1920; *Riding High,* Daily Telegrams: April 24, 1930; Weekly Articles: June 1, 1930; *Robbery,* Weekly Articles: April 25, 1926; Weekly Articles: September 11, 1932; *Rogers, Betty,* Weekly Articles: January 8, 1933; *Rogers, Will,* Weekly Articles: June 29, 1930; *Rogers Hotel,* Daily Telegrams: February 16, 1930; *Rome,* Self-Made Diplomat, June

5, 1926; *Russians*, More Letters: March 19, 1932; *Sales Tax*, Daily Telegrams: March 17, 1932; Daily Telegrams: September 7, 1931; *Saving*, Daily Telegrams: November 24, 1930; Daily Telegrams: July 9, 1930; *Schools*, Weekly Articles: July 31, 1932; *Scientists*, Weekly Articles: January 13, 1929; Weekly Articles: February 1, 1925; *Seasickness*, Self-Made Diplomat, April 30, 1926; *Senate*, Daily Telegrams: November 1, 1929; Weekly Articles: May 11, 1930; Weekly Articles: March 31, 1935; Weekly Articles: October 16, 1932; *Senate Investigations*, Weekly Articles: February 10, 1924; Daily Telegrams: June 12, 1930; *Senators*, Weekly Articles: August 4, 1929; Convention Articles: June 8, 1920; *Seriousness*, Daily Telegrams: June 11, 1924; *Sermon*, Daily Telegrams: January 8, 1933; *Shaw, Bernard*, Daily Telegrams, January 10, 1933; *Sister*, Weekly Articles: August 31, 1930; *Skill*, Weekly Articles: January 24, 1926; *Small Town*, Daily Telegrams: April 16, 1930; Weekly Articles: January 3, 1926; *Society*, Weekly Articles: August 10, 1930; More Letters: January 8, 1927; *Soft Job*, Daily Telegrams: August 21, 1930; *Speaker Reform*, Convention Articles: June 28, 1924; *Speeches*, Weekly Articles: April 28, 1933; Weekly Articles: March 27, 1927; *St. Paul*, Weekly Articles: November 8, 1925; *Stalin Era*, Daily Telegrams: November 25, 1930; *Statesman*, Weekly Articles: March 12, 1933; Daily Telegrams: July 5, 1934; Daily Telegrams: November 4, 1930; *Statistics*, Weekly Articles: February 24, 1929; Daily Telegrams: May 16, 1930; *Stock Market*, Weekly Articles: March 23, 1930; *Success*, Weekly Articles: July 29, 1928; *Talking*, Weekly Articles: August 24, 1924; Weekly Articles: June 24, 1923; Daily Telegrams: September 10, 1934; Daily Telegrams: June 4, 1929; *Talking Pictures*, Weekly Articles: June 16, 1929; Weekly Articles: June 10, 1928; Daily Telegrams: June 4, 1929; *Tariff*, Daily Telegrams: April 6, 1930; Weekly Articles; August 25, 1929; Daily Telegrams: June 28, 1929; *Taxes*, Weekly Articles: March 13, 1934; Weekly Articles: November 2, 1924; Weekly Articles: March 27, 1932; Daily Telegrams: August 3, 1933; *Tax on Automobiles:* Weekly Articles: December 4, 1927; *Tax on Murder*, Self-Made Diplomat, p. 195; *Tax Relief*, Weekly Articles: October 19, 1924; *Teeth*, Weekly Articles: June 6, 1926; *Testimony*, Weekly Articles: March 25, 1928; *Third Solution*, Daily Telegrams: August 16, 1931; *Tourists*, Self-Made Diplomat, August 11, 1926; Self-Made Diplomat, August 26, 1926; Weekly Articles: August 17, 1930; *Tradition*, More Letters: May 26, 1928; More Letters: April 2, 1932; *Trickle Down*,

Weekly Articles: November 27, 1932; *Truth Serum,* Radio Broadcasts (for unemployment relief), 1933; *Unemployment,* Radio Broadcasts, November 18, 1931; *United States of North America,* More Letters: p. 104; *Veterans,* Weekly Articles: December 30, 1923; Weekly Articles: December 30, 1923; *Vodka,* Weekly Articles: December 3, 1933; *Voters,* Weekly Articles: October 23, 1932; Daily Telegrams: August 8, 1930; Daily Telegrams: April 7, 1930; Radio Broadcasts: June 9, 1935; Daily Telegrams: April 27, 1932; Weekly Articles: September 12, 1926; *Wall Street,* Weekly Articles: November 24, 1929; Daily Telegrams: September 6, 1933; *War,* Weekly Articles: January 20, 1935; Daily Telegrams: January 1, 1928; Daily Telegrams: September 29, 1930; More Letters: April 30, 1932; Daily Telegrams: June 24, 1934; Daily Telegrams: July 17, 1929; *Wars,* Weekly Articles: May 1, 1927; Weekly Articles: January 20, 1935; More Letters: June 9, 1928; Daily Telegrams: September 29, 1930; Daily Telegrams: June 24, 1934; More Letters: April 30, 1932; *Wars,* Daily Telegrams: July 17, 1929; *Washington, George,* Radio Broadcasts, June 1, 1930; *Wealth,* Radio Broadcasts, April 21, 1935; *Wife,* Weekly Articles: August 10, 1924; *Wills,* Weekly Articles: May 31, 1925; *Wilson, Woodrow:* Weekly Articles: February 17, 1924; *Wishes,* Weekly Articles: October 2, 1932; *Withdrawal,* Daily Telegrams, June 28, 1931; *Women,* Weekly Articles: December 17, 1933; Weekly Articles: March 31, 1929; *Women Murderers,* Weekly Articles: September 20, 1925; *Work,* Weekly Articles: January 18, 1931; Daily Telegrams: June 24, 1931; Weekly Articles: January 18, 1933; Radio Broadcasts, October 23, 1931; *World,* Daily Telegrams: October 7, 1934; *World Savers,* Weekly Articles: October 2, 1932; *Worry,* Daily Telegrams: July 28, 1932; *Writing Articles,* Weekly Articles: September 1, 1929; *Writing Up,* Weekly Articles: December 20, 1931; *Young Folks,* Weekly Articles: January 19, 1930; Weekly Articles: June 30, 1929; *Young Women,* Weekly Articles: August 24, 1930.

BIBLIOGRAPHY

Alworth, E. Paul. *Will Rogers*. Twayne, 1974.

Brown, William Richard. *Imagemaker: Will Rogers and the American Dream*. University of Missouri Press, 1970.

Carter, Joseph H. *Never Met a Man I Didn't Like: the Life and Writings of Will Rogers*. Avon, 1991.

Collins, Reba Neighbors (editor in cooperation with Will Rogers Memorial Staff). *Will Rogers Says*. Will Rogers Heritage Press, 1988.

Croy, Homer. *Our Will Rogers*. Duell, Sloan and Pearce; 1953.

Day, Donald, ed. *The Autobiography of Will Rogers*. Houghton Mifflin, 1949.

Day, Donald. *Will Rogers*. McKay, 1962.

Garst, Shannon. *Will Rogers, Immortal Cowboy* (illus. by C. Gabriel). Messner, 1950.

Kaho, Noel. *The Will Rogers Country*. University of Oklahoma Press, 1941.

Ketchum, Richard M. (in cooperation with the Will Rogers' Memorial Commission and staff of the Will Rogers Memorial). American Heritage, 1973.

Love, Paula McSpadden, ed. *The Will Rogers Book*. Bobbs, 1961; Texian Press, 1972.

Mathews, Wendell, ed. *Will Rogers: The Man and His Humor.* Glenheath, 1991.

Milsten, David Randolph. *Will Rogers: The Cherokee Kid.* Glenheath, 1987.

O'Brien, Patrick Joseph. *Will Rogers: Ambassador of Good Will, Prince of Wit and Wisdom.* Winston, 1935.

Payne, William Howard. *Folks Say of Will Rogers.* Putnam, 1936.

Rogers, Betty Blake. *Will Rogers: His Wife's Story.* Bobbs, 1941.

Rogers, Will. *Convention Articles of Will Rogers.* Oklahoma State University Press, 1976.

Rogers, Will. *The Cowboy Philosopher on Prohibition.* Oklahoma State University, 1975.

Rogers, Will. *The Cowboy Philosopher on the Peace Conference.* Oklahoma State University Press, 1975.

Rogers, Will. *Daily Telegrams: Volume I, Coolidge Years, 1926–1929.* Oklahoma State University Press, 1978.

Rogers, Will. *Daily Telegrams: Volume II, Hoover Years, 1929–1931.* Oklahoma State University Press, 1978.

Rogers, Will. *Daily Telegrams: Volume III, Hoover Years, 1931–1933.* Oklahoma State University Press, 1979.

Rogers, Will. *Daily Telegrams: Volume IV, Roosevelt Years, 1933–1935.* Oklahoma State University Press, 1979.

Rogers, Will. *Ether and Me, or "Just Relax."* Oklahoma State University Press, 1973.

Rogers, Will. *"He Chews to Run": Will Rogers' Life Magazine Articles, 1928.* Oklahoma State University Press, 1982.

Rogers, Will. *"How to Be Funny" and Other Writings of Will Rogers.* Oklahoma State University Press, 1983.

Rogers, Will. *The Illiterate Digest.* Oklahoma State University Press, 1974.

Rogers, Will. *Letters of a Self-Made Diplomat to His President.* Albert and Charles Boni, 1926; Oklahoma State University Press, 1977.

Rogers, Will. *More Letters of a Self-Made Diplomat.* Oklahoma State University Press, 1982.

Rogers, Will. *Radio Broadcasts of Will Rogers.* Oklahoma State University Press, 1983.

Rogers, Will. *There's Not a Bathing Suit in Russia and Other Bare Facts.* Oklahoma State University Press, 1973.

Rogers, Will. *Weekly Articles: Volume I, Harding/Coolidge Years, 1922–1925.* Oklahoma State University Press, 1980.

Rogers, Will. *Weekly Articles: Volume II, Coolidge Years, 1925–1927.* Oklahoma State University Press, 1980.

Rogers, Will. *Weekly Articles: Volume III, Coolidge Years, 1927–1929.* Oklahoma State University Press, 1981.

Rogers, Will. *Weekly Articles: Volume IV, Hoover Years, 1929–1931.* Oklahoma State University Press, 1981.

Rogers, Will. *Weekly Articles: Volume V, Hoover Years, 1931–1933.* Oklahoma State University Press, 1982.

Rogers, Will. *Weekly Articles: Volume VI, Roosevelt Years, 1933–1935.* Oklahoma State University Press, 1982.

Sterling, Bryan B. *The Best of Will Rogers.* Crown, 1979.

Sterling, Bryan B. and Sterling, Frances N., eds. *Will Rogers in Hollywood.* Crown, 1984.

Sterling, Bryan B., ed. *The Will Rogers Scrapbook.* Gosset and Dunlap, 1976.

Sterling, Bryan B. and Sterling, Frances N., eds. *Will Rogers' World: America's foremost political humorist comments on the twenties and thirties—and eighties and nineties.* M. Evans, 1989.

Sterling, Bryan B. and Sterling, Frances N., eds. *A Will Rogers Treasury.* Bonanza, 1982.

Trent, Spi M. *My Cousin Will Rogers.* Putnam, 1938.